Out of Quisqueya

Out of Quisqueya
From Trials to Triumphs in America

MILLIARDAIRE SYVERAIN, M.D.

Archway Publishing books may be ordered through booksellers or by contacting:

Archway Publishing
1663 Liberty Drive
Bloomington, IN 47403
www.archwaypublishing.com
844-669-3957

ISBN: 978-1-6657-1509-6 (sc)
ISBN: 978-1-6657-1508-9 (hc)
ISBN: 978-1-6657-1510-2 (e)

Library of Congress Control Number: 2021923184

Print information available on the last page.

Archway Publishing rev. date: 1/12/2022

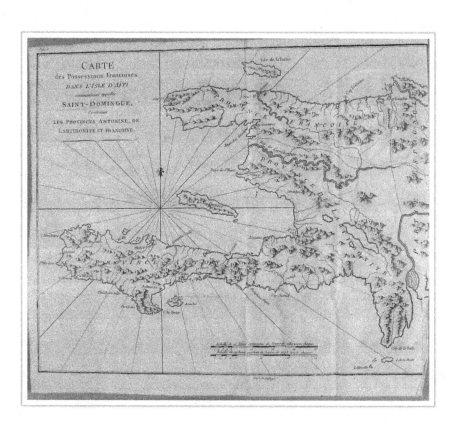

This book is dedicated to my parents and grandparents, for their resilience, courage, strength of character, and steadfastness.
It is dedicated to all my siblings in Haiti and the diaspora.
and
It is dedicated to my wife, Yves-Renée (Youlamou), my best friend on earth-and my son, Milliardaire Yves Rashid Kwame Syverain III. Thank you for your patience and your faith. I love you.

Aut viam inveniam aut faciam.

Author's Note

The accounts in this book are all based on real people, places, and events. A few names have been changed to protect the identity of those individuals.

He has showed you, O man, what is good.
*And what does the L*ORD *require of you?*
To act justly
and to love mercy
and to walk humbly with your God.
MICAH 6:8

Contents

1
CHAPTER

Cry of Agony

"For I know the plans I have for you," declares the Lord, "plans to prosper you and not to harm you, plans to give you hope and a future."

—JEREMIAH 29:11

"Y̶ou lazy slacker! You useless son of your pitiful father! Go clean up the yard!" Rosa Castor growled, trampling the floor so hard she made the windows rattle. "Even if I kill you, your dad wouldn't care," she said.

My heart pounded as she lurched toward me. I raced for the doorway, but I wasn't fast enough. She grabbed my right hand in her vise grip and dragged me back into the room. She grumbled again, then sneered, her puffy red gums showing. "You've defied my orders again. You must pay for this with your hide," said Mrs. Castor, the mother of my stepmother, Yvette.

From the waist of her pleated skirt, she pulled the four-strip cowhide whip, a *martinet* as it was called in Haiti. I knew all too well what came next. A knot of fear churned in my belly. She hesitated for a few seconds, holding the whip over my head to taunt me. Her lips curled into a smirk as she raised the whip higher and held it for another painful moment. Then came the whacks—one, two, and three times.

I let out a long, yowling *"Ammwwey!"*

I could instantly feel the welts rising where the lashes had pelted my bare back, leg, and arm. In seconds, the burning sensation had spread through my body. My eyes watered; my knees buckled.

I knew she would take a moment to gloat and relish in the effects of the whacks, so while she admired her cruel handiwork, I shook loose from her grip and dashed out the door.

"Come back!" she roared, chasing after me.

As I scrambled to escape, my bare foot hit a rock and I tripped and landed on my knee, sprawling onto the leaves she had ordered me to clean up earlier. In seconds, she was hovering over me and waving her finger in my face.

"Get to work!" she bellowed, shattering the early-morning silence of the neighborhood. She lowered her chin and flared her nostrils. I stared up at the whip, fearing the worst. She raised it again. Somehow I regained my strength, got to my feet, walked thirty feet away from her, and began to clean the yard before she could wallop me again.

I looked back to see her waving the whip at me. We stared at each other for a moment. Then she turned, her skirt billowing, and went back inside the house. We both knew I would come back home. I had nowhere else to go.

I hated that woman. I knew from my catechism that one of the commandments—I forget which one—said I had to honor my parents. But she was not even my direct family. She was the mother of my stepmother. Even at nine, I had figured out that she wasn't a family member. It gave me small comfort to know the commandment didn't apply, but Mrs. Castor lived with us like family, so what could I do?

I trudged back into the yard and started to pick up the leaves. She leaned against the door frame and held the whip in her right hand, slapping the handle against the palm of her left—a warning of pain to come. She was gloating again. I piled the leaves into a heap to burn later that night.

I looked up to see that the hot sun had a bright-orange crown. It hovered over the horizon behind the Quisqueya Mountain Range on the west side of our house. Beyond the mountain range, gray clouds had begun to creep into the sky, and I could hear the croaking of frogs in the ponds not far away. For visitors to our island, this would be a romantic scene they would share with family and friends back home. To me, it was another nightmare in paradise.

With the leaves piled up, I had nothing to do but return to the house, where Lucifer awaited. I called her Lucifer, but only to myself. As a boy in Catechism, I'd learned that Lucifer, once an angel of light, had fallen in disgrace for defying the supremacy of the Lord. As a result, the Lord had banished this fallen angel.

I knew a worse whipping awaited as soon as I stepped into the house. As I approached the open door, Lucifer roared, "Ti Milliardaire!" I froze.

My father had named me Milliardaire Jr. after himself. In Creole and French, *milliardaire* means "billion." I learned that my father hoped I would become a millionaire at least. How I wish my father's dream could have come true, but I guess God had other ideas. Instead, he inflicted me with the dreaded Lucifer.

"I am coming. I am coming," I said.

Before I could cross the yard, she barked, "I waited for you to clean up the yard two hours ago, and you are still goofing off."

I stiffened. Earlier that day, she had beaten me several times for failing to wake up early. I could see another goring coming, where she would savagely bloody my skin with the whip. She would continue her cruelty. I knew then I ought to escape, but to where? *Why doesn't God kill that shrew?* I thought.

She reached out for me. *Whack, whack, whack* went the handle of the cowhide whip, hitting my left temple and jaw. The neighbor's dog barked at me during the whipping.

I let out another wailing *ammweyyyyyyy* in agony. I could taste blood. My neck twisted, and my body swayed. Welts larger than my middle finger had formed on my face. They ran across my skin like skid marks on a dirt road. It felt as if she had hurled kerosene onto my cheeks, struck a match, and lit me on fire.

"Didn't your father teach you anything? I have no time to waste!" she hollered. "Diablo!" Midway through her lecture, she landed more whacks on my skinny legs and back. The thumps were hard. I thought she wanted to kill me.

"I didn't mean to do that." It was all I could manage to say. But what I wanted to say was *"Merde!"* and "Get *manman-ou!*"

At last, her need to inflict pain came to an end. I hovered in a corner as she left the room. In this moment of peace, as dusk crept up, I saw the sunlight fading over our backyard.

A day of darkness and gloom, of clouds and blackness, had come. My head pounded, and every inch of my body cried out in pain. With Lucifer's whipping finished, I turned my thoughts elsewhere in the hope of lessening my torment.

I heard a truck drive by, raising dust, and the house cat meowed. A gentle rain fell and cleared the smoke from the burning leaves Lucifer had set on fire hours earlier and sharpened the aroma of the plants in the backyard.

I went into my bedroom and sat on the bed I shared with my three brothers (Jean-Etienne, nicknamed Jean; Pierre-Rock, nicknamed Rock; and Dufresne, nicknamed Marco), looking for a cotton pillow on which to lay my bruised head. I wondered, *What's next?* I thought about the apartment my mom shared with Jean-Wilfrid (Wilfrid), my parents' second child. The boy had been eight years old when he left home one evening to look for Mom in Port-au-Prince. He'd searched until he found her because he couldn't bear to see Mom living alone. But I couldn't go there since my mom already struggled to support herself and Wilfrid.

Through the open door, I could see Lucifer pacing a few feet away, her hands on her waist. At last, she began scratching her elbows like a dog with ticks. I breathed a sigh of relief when she turned and withdrew to her bedroom for the night.

The jasmine tree in the front yard filled the room with its fresh fragrance. I knelt to pray before I lay down on the bed, and then, exhausted, I closed my eyes and tried to forget everything that had unfolded that day. Eventually, I fell into a deep sleep.

Another day had gone.

2
CHAPTER

Lucifer in Paradise

May inspire in all of the children of the Black race around the world the love of progress, justice, and liberty. In dedicating this book to Haiti, I bear them all in mind, both the downtrodden of today and the giants of tomorrow.

—ANTENOR FIRMIN,
The Equality of the Human Races

tepmothers and stepchildren frequently endure relationships fraught with conflict and antagonism. But not in my case. I could always vouch for Yvette. Her mother, Mrs. Castor, Lucifer, was a different story. She was cruel and possessed every bad quality a human being could possess. She was worse than a witch. We have a Haitian proverb that says, "Dèyè morne gin morne." It means, "Behind every mountain, there is another mountain." It always made me think of her because for every evil in her character, there lurked a worse evil.

She was in her fifties when she joined our family in Carrefour (a suburb of Port-au-Prince) in the fall of 1970, invading our three-bedroom, unpainted brick house on a dead-end country road. I'd met her once, before she moved to Carrefour, in an open marketplace in the city of Port-au-Prince. For some reason, she disliked me immediately. She was the wrong person to live with my brothers and me, but nobody had asked me.

One morning in the summer of 1970, my stepmother found me relaxing under the mango tree in the yard outside our house. A breeze whistled; the air smelled fresh after a light rain. She asked me, "Ti Milliardaire, I am going to the city today to meet my mother. Would you come along?" Before I could agree, she said, "Get ready!"

Each time she asked me something, I knew good things awaited, for she was a woman with a proper disposition. I don't recall when Yvette came to live with us; I was perhaps three or four years old when Dad and Mom got separated. Soon after, Yvette had moved in. By the time I reached my fifth birthday, I'd recognized that she wasn't my actual mother. But she came close. Back then, I felt closer to her than to my true mother, Marie Madeleine Thibaud. I spent most of my formative years with Yvette, and she was a good influence on me. Unlike Lucifer, my stepmother treated me with kindness and respect.

"Yes, Miss," I said, referring to her by the Haitian name they used for nurses. "I am going to change my clothes now."

"I have something important to talk to her about," she said. "And it would be good that you are there."

"Oui." I nodded.

She treated me like the son she hadn't borne.

The morning air was crisp under a cloudless sky as we took the short walk down our street to catch a tap-tap, a small minibus, on the main road.

The tap-tap took us through a shantytown within Port-au-Prince called Marché-Fort-Sinclair. We then crossed a ditch toward a dirty, dusty road. In the distance, I saw a mass of tough, proud individuals, sweating and toiling under the inferno of the sun as they gleaned the scraps of life for daily survival. These were vendors of food staples. Though impoverished, their integrity, humility, and self-respect remained intact. I recalled what my mother had once said to me: "The poor have strong moral fibers which are borne out of their hardships and simplicity."

We got off the tap-tap, and Yvette pointed to someone hunched over a chair a short distance ahead. "My mother works over there," she said. "She wakes up before dawn every day and comes here earlier than most folks. She needs to get that same spot each time to make a living selling her wares." Yvette scratched her scalp. "Many people hate selling food, forgetting that they must eat every day." In Haiti, selling food staples on the streets is considered beneath one's rank by some poor Haitians who act like snobs, preferring not to work instead of humbly doing the kind of work they are qualified to do.

I agreed with Yvette. I realized her work at the hospital a year earlier had made it possible for my siblings, my dad, and me to live decently. Dad was in hiding from the country's militia because he had fallen out of favor with the Duvalier's government, a brutal regime bent on killing all enemies, imaginary or real. Dad was a friend of the president's son-in-law, Max Dominique, who had been accused of being part of the twenty military officers plotting against the government. As a result, Dad had to hide to ensure his safety.

We stopped before a large blue tarpaulin beside the road. There, Yvette's mother, Lucifer, sat leaning to one side as she dozed in a chair, her wrinkled forehead buried beneath a cheap straw sombrero. Her hair had been tightened into a knot of gray and faded-black strands. Her cheeks looked drawn and ashen. She wore thin-soled black leather sandals that showed her toes, her nails as sharp as knives. Her old gray skirt had a sad, bleached look, and the yellow collar of her blouse was smooth and stained at the edges. I looked at her, and my heart sank.

Lucifer sold dry rice, beans, cornmeal, cooking oil, and other food staples. Most of the sellers were women. They hawked their wares to new customers, returning ones, and curious visitors. Lucifer had the look of an old Haitian warrior who was tired of fighting.

Yvette reached out and touched her mother's arm. "Mom," she said softly.

Her mother opened her eyes to slits. She seemed confused at first. She looked up at Yvette, then lowered her eyes and locked them on me. The fire in her stare made my neck stiffen. Yvette noted my nervousness and put her hand on my shoulder to comfort me. I took a small step back.

As the old woman continued glaring at me, an alarm went through my body, and I turned away. After a moment, I turned back to find her still gawking at me. What was she thinking?

"Yvette! Who is this boy with the lumpy nose?" she shouted in a raspy voice. My ears felt warm, and my heart skipped a few beats. It felt as if a vacuum cleaner had sucked all the air around me. I wanted to scream, "I can't breathe!"

"This is Ti Milliardaire, one of Milliardaire's sons," Yvette said, hoping to calm her mother. "Mom, is it a problem that I bring him along?"

"But why did you come here with him?" she demanded. "You should dress up his nose next time before going out with him." She said this sarcastically to embarrass me about my nose. She hooted. *Was that a joke?* She thought me too young to figure out her flippant talk. Her voice cracked, and she jerked her head and scrunched her lips in disgust. She had been unhappy with my dad for shacking up with her daughter and for fathering seven children out of wedlock with three other women plus another child from his first wife.

"Well, mother of mine, I asked him to come along so you could get acquainted with Milliardaire's children."

"Why should I care?" Yvette's mother barked.

"I need you to come live with us in Carrefour," Yvette said, taking a step closer to her mother as though she talking to her in confidence. "You know Milliardaire has gone to New York. I have no one to stay with the children when I work the night shift at the hospital."

"I, Mrs. Moleus Castor, am going to Carrefour?" She bent her head, grimaced, and slapped the right side of her butt. Then she laughed harshly.

Nearby, a pile of burning rubbish glowed bright red; thick black smoke rose upward. The wind blew the foul-smelling smoke into our faces. I gasped. Yvette's mother yawned; she must have been used to the smoke. Yvette pulled a handkerchief from her purse and covered her nostrils for a second.

"You know something, Yvette," her mother said. "I am not sure I want to do that." She made a scratchy sound in her throat while fanning the fumes. Then she paused, coughed, and said, "I like my work here." She sneezed, wiped her nose with her palm, and sniffled.

Desperate to convince her mother to come to Carrefour, Yvette said, "True. I know how much you like to work here, but your last child, Zagalo, still suffers from asthma spells because of the time he spent here as an infant. Here, it is bad for him. Carrefour would be better for his health."

Yvette's voice grew desperate. "You must know that this place is not good for your health either. To be in the heat, the dust, the noise, and the hardship; returning here day after day cannot be good for you. Once I get paid as a full-time nurse, I could help you a bit." Little did I know that Yvette already had her papers to go to America, where her mother's fortune would change for good because Yvette would be able to send her money.

Without turning my head, I moved my eyes back and forth between Yvette and her mother as the women argued. Yvette raised her eyebrows and gazed at her mother, then nodded. She acted like a supplicant hoping her mother would agree. She dabbed the sweat off her face with the handkerchief she pulled from her purse. A gray Volkswagen drove past. It sputtered and blew more dust off the ground with its black diesel smoke.

I looked at Yvette, who now fanned herself with her handkerchief. She took one deep breath, opened her worn brown purse, and placed the soaked cloth, rolled up like a ball, inside.

"What am I going to do if I stop doing this?" Yvette's mother queried, revealing her toothless grimace for the first time. She glanced at her daughter, then down at her ankles. "I don't want to think about it. I know it is getting harder and harder to bring something home every night … and at my age, it is rough standing here all day. Yet …"

"Mom, think about it." A big bead of sweat dripped down my stepmother's face. "I will come back Friday when we can talk about it."

Her mother croaked, "You know where to find me." I could see anger and anguish flash through her eyes as she squinted at me. She likely felt that her options were shrinking when it came to doing the hard work of selling food in the streets at her age, and moving to Carrefour could turn out to be a huge mistake if Dad ever asked that she return to her house in Martissant. At times, Dad was a bit unpredictable; it would only take a phone call from Boston to overturn Lucifer's life.

"I know, Mom. I know." Yvette sighed. "You are right." She patted her mother's arms and hugged her, then said to me, "Let's go." She grabbed my wrist as though I were planning to escape. I could feel the heat of Lucifer's eyes on me. They stung when I glanced at her.

The old woman's calloused fingers swept the sweat from her brow as she yawned again. I felt awkward. I adjusted my posture and tried not to stare at the stern-looking middle-aged lady.

"Yvette, you alone could deal with these things," her mother said.

"What do you mean, Mother? I am concerned about your well-being here."

"Who wants complications now?" Yvette's mother asked. "Remember what I went through when your father spent a year in prison."

"It was terrible," my stepmother agreed.

Yvette's mother gave her daughter a scornful look and then turned to look at me. I looked sideways to distract myself from her piercing stare, fearing she would scold and embarrass me again.

At last, we left Yvette's mother to her misery. We took a tap-tap home and sat tightly between other passengers. As the car coasted downhill, the driver turned off the engine to save fuel. It got quiet inside the minivan. I said nothing to Yvette about my unpleasant feelings toward her mother.

But the memory of her mother's eyes disturbed me when I went to bed that night.

Yvette had planned to leave Haiti since Dad's departure, but she couldn't tell us for fear the word would fall on the wrong ears and the government would stop her. In those days, medical professionals couldn't leave the country without the regime's sanction.

That first meeting with her mother took place two months before Yvette left Haiti to join my dad sometime in September of 1970. A day after Yvette had left for America, Lucifer arrived in paradise to live with my brothers and me as the wicked caretaker she was. And it was hell.

3
CHAPTER

Scary Dream

Therefore do not worry about tomorrow, for
tomorrow will worry about itself.
Each day has enough trouble of its own.

—MATTHEW 6:34

A few weeks after Lucifer moved in, I woke up in a crowded bed after a muggy night only to realize our lives were changing fast. Yvette's godfather had died only two weeks before she had gone to America. He'd tripped on the gravel floor inside the house and hit his head. Three hours later, he was gone. Parrain Vivi, as we called him, had been a loving octogenarian with very little meat under his clothes. Every morning, it was my job to cook meals for him made from leftover legumes; uncooked, dry rice; and cornmeal.

It pained me when he died because I had enjoyed his presence in the house. Besides, I felt useful in getting him breakfast. He'd impressed me with his stories of being a sugarcane worker in Cuba in early 1900. He had remained single all his life, never had children, and was quite happy for having lived as a bachelor. Father liked the old man for his life of self-denial.

I sat in the armchair across the empty dining room table, my feet dangling and my toes reaching across the floor, longing for sunshine. My back was turned toward the door; my father's one-shelf, three-book library stood to my right. I held in my hands a copy of Martin Luther King's book, *I Have a Dream*. Father's second book was *Mémoires d'un Leader du Tiers Monde*, written by President Francois Duvalier. Its binding was made of a red hard cover. I couldn't remember the title of the third. I was at peace then. Because I knew a black man would always be a god.

Soon I heard the shuffling of people in the yard. I caught a glimpse of a familiar face, and a sinking feeling grabbed me by the throat. Our nightmare had begun.

None of my brothers or I knew that Lucifer had made up her mind to move to Carrefour, but she'd come to stay with us after the short visit Yvette and I had paid her. She had seen heaven on a platter and seized the moment. Dad always said, "Be careful with people you've helped. Soon they will want to hurt you." Otherwise, why was she angry at me? Since she didn't know me, it was likely because she disliked anything that had to do with or reminded her of my dad.

I wasn't the only one who was shocked by her arrival. We all stopped in our tracks when we heard the not-so-familiar voice in the yard. My younger sibling, Marco, was playing with his marbles under the mango tree. A mangled branch lay on the ground, the result of a recent tropical storm. Rock, an older sibling, knelt in the shade, designing a truck for the next neighborhood car competition. My oldest brother, Jean-Etienne, was talking to some high school friends in front of the house. They were each stunned into silence as they watched Lucifer go inside the house.

As if awoken from a scary dream, I winced at the sound of her oppressive nasal voice. Her last two children, Julienne and Zagalo, both older than I was, followed her into the house. She took another step inside, and her menacing eyes fixed on me, forcing me to rise and pay her homage. All the hair on my scalp stood up. I raced toward her, then kissed her on her tense and wrinkled cheek. She had a face that screamed of authority, intimidation, and bluster. Her sudden arrival horrified me. We were all frightened and fascinated by her forcefulness.

She became our guardian after our stepmother, Yvette, left Haiti. I shrugged my shoulders and wondered, *Should a dog go roaming through the nighttime streets when his master's gone, or must he stay much closer, hoping for his master's return?*

The sun shone into the room as Lucifer began to inspect our corner of paradise. Confident Rock winked at Marco and told him, "Don't worry. Everybody is going to be fine."

Marco replied in the voice of a seven-year-old who hadn't seen or understood the bizarre behaviors of adults yet, like when Lucifer scowled at us, pursed her lips, and sneered to show her disapproval of finding the yard untidy. Marco pointed toward her and begged Rock, "Are you sure of that troublemaker? How would I ever know?"

"You got nothing to fear, Ti Marco," Rock said.

"Did you see her face?" He groaned.

The boys didn't know who she was, so I told them since I had met her before. "Sure, I did."

"When will Dad come back?"

"Ti Marco, I told you not to worry about her. She won't be here for long. I promise." Rock flashed his white teeth and raised his palm. Rock had a slender frame and stood as straight as a soldier. He beamed his Sidney Poitier smile at us and said, "Dad is alive and will come here any minute." I agreed but dared not say it out loud.

"Well, I don't like that lady here," Marco whispered. "She looks too mean to live with us."

Upon Lucifer's triumphant arrival, everything began to fall apart. It was beatings for breakfast, thumpings for lunch, and canings for dinner. Though she never hit her own children, to my knowledge. Heaven had turned its back on me. *A while ago, I met Lucifer in the marketplace. Today she came to live with us,* I thought as I inspected Lucifer's demeanor. She looked tall and had gray, cornrowed hair; high cheekbones; and piercing, menacing hazel eyes. Her mouth made her look like a fish. She was fat in the middle but had muscular thighs and thick calves. She was a beautiful black woman of a dark-brown complexion that breathed strength, luster, and resolve—and trouble.

When she walked, she strode with the conviction of a staff sergeant, the ground seeming to shake beneath her. She had the energy of a child playing with a new toy. She shouted when she called us. In spite of her menacing looks, she struck me as a misfit and a joker. Or so I thought at first. I shook my head and turned away when I saw her talking to the walls of the house. I went outside and mumbled, "She is as crazy as a white bear on Mont-Blanc in summer."

It was a mid-October morning in 1970, and the sun shone on everything below it. I looked at the breadfruit tree and the petals of the blooming flowers in our backyard. I listened to the long, soft murmurings of a symphony of hundreds of doves singing in the background. A few of the doves scuttled off as if they sensed Lucifer was about to display every diabolical weapon in her arsenal. She began to show her two-faced nature each day until we knew there was danger every time she was home. She would be a gentle person one minute, then flip to her other self the next. We never knew which side of her we were going to deal with.

Before Lucifer arrived, our house had been a humble, peaceful abode located in a quiet part of town, its shade trees helping protect it from the hot sun. But the day she descended upon the house, we knew that nature had conspired against us. Lucifer held the secret to our undoing.

It was strange—before she arrived, I'd never noticed how our brick house had a rectangular shape. Outside, the exterior concrete walls looked like they had sharpened stone edges. The gray cement kept everything together. Inside, the house looked like the whitewashed wall of a craggy cemetery.

I watched a pigeon settle on the breadfruit tree. Others joined it, clucking once they perched. Lucifer hated the birds and tried to stop them from cooing as she felt they were mocking her. A few times, their droppings splashed on her face like lukewarm water, making her want to puke. I loved the birds for making me giggle at her expense. They became my favorite allies. Father and Yvette had brought the flock to Carrefour from Rue Montparnasse.

Who had Lucifer been before she came to our home? Her husband, Mr. Castor, had lost all his wealth in the 1950s at the hands of the Haitian government after the election of Dr. Francois Duvalier (Papa Doc). Mr. Castor had suffered political retribution for supporting vanquished presidential candidate Louis Dejoie and had gone to prison for more than a year for confusing freedom of speech with freedom of thought. Crime was almost nonexistent during the Duvaliers' regime.

Lucifer had taken up her lot with a gusto that confused even her detractors. Since she had six children, she became a street merchant to support the family overnight. She was a strange sort of country girl when she came to Port-au-Prince. She wore her hair pulled up on top of her head and tied with a ragged band, giving her a stern look. She would bark a solitary laugh that frightened children and grown-ups alike and make shocking and caustic comments, like the time she heard a small child had been hit by a car. "I thought that he was dead," she'd said mockingly.

With Yvette headed to America, we had no choice but to take her in, and she degraded us when it suited her. She even drove away Tante Orica, who had lived with us up to that time, and forced her to return to Jacmel. One day, I hurried over to sit in a chair in the dining room. I was hovering around because I had seen Mrs. Castor place a plate of grits with cooked beef liver on the countertop. When she noticed my presence, she smirked. I was content to be there, just imagining the savory taste of that sizzling meat exploding in my mouth. However, Lucifer simply steered the house dog, Tang, outside to give him a bath. I watched her walk to the back of the house near the water fountain, stoop down, pull out a basin, and pour soap into the tepid water. She began scrubbing the dog. Meanwhile, steam was coming off the food, and its smell put me in a jovial mood. I smiled as the sweet aroma made my mouth water. After she had washed and dried Tang, she came back inside, took the meal, and placed it in a bowl—for the dog. I sat there, horrified. Then she went inside the kitchen to retrieve a small bowl with grits and herring. As she did so, she called my brothers. She shoved the bowl before us to share. As we wolfed down the scraps, she stood laughing and lectured us, saying, "You act like pigs."

Since her arrival, I was hungry most of the time. My brothers and I always looked pale. The havoc she wreaked in our lives bordered on lunacy. Years later, many people asked us how we survived such an ordeal in our father's absence for so long. But no one knew how much we endured living with her.

She was suspicious of almost everything. People, pets, the shaking of a tree, shadows, and fast clouds made her wary. She saw danger lurking everywhere. She would go sniffing about like a bloodhound, looking for a reason for whatever happened.

In her previous house, the people had known her as a lady who hid behind doors. She listened to people's conversations. She would peep from behind brick walls to see what her neighbors had cooked for dinner. She would stop her entire workday if she hit her big toe against an object, thinking it portended terrible luck.

Now, in our town of Carrefour, her senseless behavior continued. She disliked small talk, even with the lady next door. She forbade us to go outside to play and refused to let our playmates enter the house for fear that someone would come in and poison her coffee. She made up names for every one of our neighbors. Madame Mombrun Nelson was a pest. Madame Semelfort was an old lady. Madame Serge Moneau was a bagatelle. Madame Orel was a werewolf. Annette was a crazy cockroach. Monsieur Dumont was a crank, and Monsieur Desirat was an eccentric, grumpy old man.

And so it was that I took a carefree delight in naming Mrs. Rosa Castor, Lucifer. She too had muttered a name for Father, but I never caught what it was. She got angry each time his name would come up in a conversation where someone would call him a generous, good fellow.

Years later, my father told me that before I was born, he and my mother had lived in a slum called La Cour Desrosiers—a place of tiny houses on crooked wooden frames. That small encampment in the city had no electricity and running water. At night, rodents crisscrossed the rusted sheet-metal roofs of these houses. They drummed their dances and nibbled on folks' toes in the dark. Nobody seemed to enjoy their midnight melodies.

There, Mother and Father were Lucifer's neighbors. They did her small favors. The days grew darker for her to get money to feed her family. Lucifer's older boys took it hard. At times, they got so desperate for food they went scavenging. Dad gained her children's admission into the city's public schools. He drew breath for them. Because of this, Lucifer had chosen him to be the godfather of her last child, Zagalo, a petulant but very bright boy, but they were never on good terms once Dad ran away with her daughter.

One day in late October 1970, in my tenth year, Lucifer's piercing voice came thundering through the house. "I want to see everybody before me now!" she shrieked. "Don't let me find you still in bed, you people!" Marco patted a wrinkle on the bedsheet and grinned, showing his missing front teeth.

Like most days in the Caribbean islands, it was a lovely sunny day. The roses had bloomed overnight. The sweet fragrance of the jasmine tree at the gate permeated the front yard. The sun rising over the Quisqueya Mountain Range edged out of the deep blue sky on the horizon.

In the afternoon, the sky became overcast. The sun was covered by clouds streaks that left the zigzag trace of colors so often seen in the tropics in the afternoon. A branch from the breadfruit snapped in the gentle breeze. The noise startled me. The doves that had perched there were scared, the din having made them scatter.

For me, these small events meant nothing. They held no significance in the broader context of what lay ahead. I had felt worried since the day Lucifer arrived. After all, this was Carrefour. This corner of the country felt surreal. It reminded me of a place of retreat and healing. A small creek watered the trees and crisscrossed through our little garden. Who could disturb our paradise?

The following day, as Lucifer walked past me on her way to the back of the house, she sniffed the air as if searching for rotten cheese. The smell came from the pair of dirty socks hanging from my pants pockets. I walked over to the water fountain and filled a small washbowl. Next, I picked up a tiny bag of detergent from the kitchen and poured it into the bowl, then began scrubbing the socks in the washtub.

"Good morning. Is Rose there, little boy?" someone shouted from outside the bathroom window. I stood up and searched for the face, but it disappeared and showed up again in front of the house. I didn't know Lucifer's first name was Rose.

The sun had already climbed high over the Quisqueya Mountain Range. The sky was clear and cobalt blue. A bird skittered over the leaves of the breadfruit.

"You want to talk to Madame Castor?" I asked. "In a minute, I will go looking for her." Meanwhile, I went back to scrubbing my socks and let the lady wait. I grabbed another handful of detergent and added it to the suds in the bowl, then scurried into the makeshift family room and poured the soapy water onto the ceramic floor, hoping to make her fall. It spread quickly.

"She will be right with you," I said to the lady. That was when I noticed her long, scraggly fingers with baby pink nails at the base. She frightened me, so I dashed about like a mad dog, looking for Lucifer. After all the misery she had put my brothers and me through, I wanted to see her rush in, slip on the wet floor, fall down, and break a bone or two or hit her head. If she could fall into the wrought-iron front porch, so much the better. If she could snap her neck or crack her skull on the brickwork, that would be delightful.

As Lucifer approached, I snuck into the living room and hid behind the large sofa. The next few years of my life depended on what happened next. A sense of vindication overpowered me. Revenge was not always a sin. A warm feeling enveloped me, and an enormous weight lifted off my shoulders as I saw justice in the making. I smiled to myself as I waited for the sound of the strangled gasp that signified I was free of her once and for all.

That was not my destiny. My heart grieved when all I heard was the visiting lady holler, "Madame Castor, so good to see you!"

CHAPTER

Rue Montparnasse

*Do not depend on the promises of those
whose interest it is to deceive you.*

—AESOP

It was one afternoon around Christmas 1965 when Rock and Jean-Etienne got excited to go watch a movie. The theater was next to our second-floor apartment. From our balcony, they jumped onto the roof of the theater, where they crept along like lizards until they found a slit in the roof where they could watch a western movie playing.

"Could I come with you?" I asked them.

Rock shook his head. He frowned. "It's too dangerous for you to cross. You're too small. But you can help. You can be our lookout, and as soon as you see Dad's truck, clap your hands. We'll be in big trouble if he catches us. He expects us to be studying."

As they watched the movie, I looked out our window and watched down the road where I would see Dad returning from work. I never got bored with my brothers' antics. It made me feel grownup to watch them take risks.

It took Dad only a short time to get wise to them, and he figured out they weren't spending their time off from school studying the way he'd ordered them to. As soon as he would leave for work in the morning, they'd start playing. Yet, when he came home later, they were in the same place at the dining table, pretending to study. They both failed the first quarter. Dad wanted to make sure they would get better grades in the next quarter, so he told them to study in his absence.

Determined to catch them at their game, Dad stopped his truck several blocks from our building. I didn't see him walking through the corridor downstairs until it was too late. He'd appeared at the door to our apartment before I could warn my brothers.

For me not to appear as an accomplice to their *Bonanza* cabal, I slipped into my bedroom, where Dad wouldn't see me. I covered my ears with my hands, not wanting to hear the commotion I knew was coming.

Dad walked up the stairs and went to a bedroom window. He looked out and saw my brothers on the roof next door. They were so engrossed in the movie they did not suspect anything. I waited, expecting the worst as the seconds turned to minutes.

My silence alerted Jean-Etienne to the problem. I would normally have been asking them what they were watching. He made a slow turn to look back at me only to see Dad's six-foot, five-inch frame silhouetted in the window.

In a moment of panic, Jean-Etienne turned to Rock and uttered something inaudible. They froze as Dad shouted, "Come on over! Come on over! I guess you were studying on that roof, huh?"

That afternoon, they got a gargantuan whipping that stood as the alpha and omega of all floggings from Dad. When you consider Dad's upbringing, it was easy to understand his obsession with education for my brothers and me.

As a child, Dad had only gone as far as the third grade. He resented it when my grandfather pulled him out of school to work in the fields or tend the herds. Dad completed the ninth grade in his mid-thirties. Later, he attended a vocational school to become a mechanic. At the same time, his future wife, Yvette, my stepmother, was attending nursing school.

Dad's life in Haiti in the sixties was difficult. He was a complex person. Though an affable and cooperative individual, he had little patience for nonsense. He didn't like to see abuse, and he couldn't tolerate anyone who tried to bully him. In those days, it was hard for people to stand up to their abusers. He worked as a truck driver hauling construction materials. One day he went to work at the gravel mine. Usually, the trucks queued in the order of their arrival. That day, he confronted a group of men who had bypassed his vehicle. Five journeymen soon came toward him. "Milliardaire, we are not going to fill your truck today," said one of them. "And we want you to move it out of the way before we make this your last day." Dad was puzzled at what to make of this.

"Shut him down!" one of the journeymen shouted.

"Shut me down for what?" Dad retorted.

"Grab him! Grab him!"

Three other journeymen came up from behind him. They forced Dad's arms behind his back, preventing his escape. Surprised and shocked, Dad could barely speak. Sweat rolled down his face and dripped down his neck as he fought to get free, but he couldn't untangle himself.

"Hold him tight," the leader of the group said.

"Hurry up. We are holding the rascal tight!" screamed another.

Dad shifted to break away, but they put him in a chokehold, and he was having trouble breathing. Out of the corner of his eye, he saw one of the stronger journeymen race toward him with a large, jagged rock. He aimed it at Dad's face and sneered, "You talk too much. I will shut your dirty mouth once and for all!" Many of these guys were jealous of my dad's popularity with the ladies who lived in town. Others picked up shovels and approached Dad with the intent of maiming—or even killing—him.

What none of them realized was that Dad had worked as a fisherman in his youth and was a keen oarsman who'd often survived stormy waters and learned to keep his composure in dangerous situations. Dad pretended to close his eyes as though he were afraid and resigned to his fate. He waited until the man with the rock was about five feet away, then sprang into action.

He leaned on the men behind him for support and threw both feet forward, his heavy shoes pounding into the man's chest. Surprised and in pain, the man fell to the ground, hitting his head on the rock he'd intended to use to hit Dad.

Pandemonium reigned as the attacker began to bleed from a deep gash in his head. The other attackers panicked, released Dad, and took flight, frightened by the sight of one of their colleagues lying on the floor.

From that day on, Dad had their respect. They nicknamed him the "giant of Madame Gano," the gravel pit where they all gathered to do their work.

Only a few months earlier, Dad had shown his courage and fierce loyalty to our family. A security guard was chasing Jean-Etienne with a whip at the Stadium Sylvio Cator because he had been playing with other boys on the grass before a soccer game. By chance, Dad had come upon the scene and found Jean-Etienne in danger. He pulled out his.38 and pointed it at the armed security guard, then barked a warning for the guard not to touch his revolver. When the guard saw Dad was serious, he backed away and let Jean-Etienne run toward Dad.

Working long hours each day at the mine pit was a treacherous affair for my father. Because of the dirt and dust, he was at times forced to take to his bed. He labored in the mine every weekday and on some weekends to support our family, and he had no penchant for anyone who was lazy or irresponsible. "Idleness is the killer of the spirit," he would say.

One evening after a difficult day at the mine, he told us he never wanted to see any of his children doing this type of work. Every day, he reminded us he wanted to see us succeed in school and encouraged us with his love of reading. His crowning achievement came in June of 1983 when Jean-Etienne obtained his medical doctor's degree from the State University of Haiti.

Dad's desire to help others went beyond our immediate family. He used our home to receive many from the countryside who sought the opportunity for a better life. There were future doctors, agronomists, engineers, and others among them—as well as a few unscrupulous troublemakers.

One of the worst was a man who moved into our home from Jacmel, Dad's place of birth. His name was Ti Lamisère. At first, he seemed pleasant enough, but that didn't last long. He wasted no time in telling the grown-ups far-fetched tales of the countryside. As a twenty-year-old man, he was already dishonest. Dad was not in the mood to hear his outrageous stories, but he still tolerated him.

One evening, I became frightened by this young man's presence in the house. I heard him tell my folks he could improve their finances if they gambled with their children and that he planned to use their children in a scheme to get rich by communicating with the stars from a child's point of view. He said to Dad, "Père Milliardaire, life in this city is hard for you and Miss Yvette." He stroked his chin with the back of his hands in a show of arrogance as he quipped, "Things could get better if you let me help you."

Dad was not impressed by Ti Lamisère's boasting. "You lived in the country all your life, and you had a hard time making things better for yourself," he said, then asked him, "You have been here for a while. Has anything changed for you yet?"

Ti Lamisère grinned while playing with his whiskers. "Père Milliardaire, I learned a lot from the country folks." He looked over the balcony and pointed at the sky. "If you allow me to communicate with the stars, things could get much better for the family."

"Your father told me you needed a stepping stone in the city, and I gave you one," Dad said. "So far, what I see in you does not look encouraging." Dad walked away, closing the back door behind him and leaving the young man outside the apartment.

But Ti Lamisère persisted. He tried to impress my family any way he could. I heard him hold many eerie conversations with Yvette. He hinted at the guarantee of a fortune-teller. I eavesdropped on one conversation he had with her and couldn't believe what he was saying. He claimed he could do a séance, communicate with the stars, and use numerology to get the next lottery numbers. He guaranteed the end of our family's financial difficulties. His wild predictions bewitched me—until I learned what the cost would be. He said if he communicated with the stars, they would need him to invoke the name of a child in the household. "If by some misfortune the stars don't return to their proper orbit after the séance," he warned, "it would be the end for that boy or girl."

Since no young girls lived in the house, my younger brother Marco and I were the only choices. It would be hard for Dad to live without his last-born child back then. In my young mind, I reasoned the child would be me.

With his forceful personality and deceit, Ti Lamisère managed to convince Yvette to draw lots to decide between Marco and me. To my horror, the "prize" fell to me.

Ti Lamisère had worked his magic spell on Yvette because he knew my father's work was fraught with danger, and Yvette believed my father had a chance of surviving his ordeals using the luck Ti Lamisère offered. For me, it was a different story. Who would get me out of this predicament? I guessed there was no one. Dad saw Ti Lamisère as a fake—a charlatan and an opportunist—and yet Yvette had become fascinated by the young man's bombastic talk.

As a five-year-old, I was terrified by his claims. I thought every word he spoke was real. Many nights, I tried to stay awake, fearing I would die if I fell asleep.

In the end, Ti Lamisère finally accepted that no one believed his wild boasting and cheating schemes and shortly thereafter left the house. "Good riddance," I said to myself. Dad often reminded me that one man with knowledge was always more valuable to a village than a thousand missionaries who dissembled.

Aside from terrifying events like the ones brought on by Ti Lamisère, our two-bedroom apartment became the place where, at the age of four, I first began to make sense of the people and things around me. I cherish those memories. Yet, at times, for Marco and me, the house also held unexpected dangers. The only entrance leading to the stairs opened outward. Marco and I were very small for our age and often played on the stairs in the corridor leading to the street. If, by accident, someone opened the door as we came up the stairs, the door would hit us and we would fall down the stairs. It happened several times. To avoid such accidents, most landlords didn't rent their properties to large families.

It was during these moments that I realized the softer sides of my stepmother and Dad. We got bruised, scraped, and cuts our scalps in these accidents with the door. We never broke our noses or our limbs or our spines, but we came close. My parents would pull the bottle of Lwil Maskriti (black castor oil), our Haitian panacea, from the cupboard and pour it on our bodies and scalps. They would massage our weak limbs while we lay still on a bedsheet, then roll us back and forth, trying to soothe the pain.

It was sometime in late February of 1966 when, one evening, Dad gave Jean-Etienne some coins to buy us ice cream at Mardi-Gras. He and Yvette stayed home. The rest of our family went near the Sylvio Cator stadium, which sat only a block from where we lived, to celebrate the holiday. Jean-Etienne had just bought us the ice cream cones when out of nowhere I heard *Boom! Boom!* The loud bangs echoed through the crowd.

"Did you hear that firecracker nearby?" asked Rock.

"Yes, I did," Jean-Etienne answered.

In less than a minute, a volley of gunfire began to crack in the direction of the tree above us. What had started out as an annual festival in the streets had turned into dangerous chaos as people began stampeding. Jean-Etienne braced himself by tightening his grip on Marco's wrist on one side and mine on the other. My heart pounded.

"Let's run away from here," Marco said. "We need to get back home quick." Then he added, "Stay away from the rushing crowd."

Before he finished his sentence, the panicked mob was headed straight for us. The sounds of the guns and rifles and Thompsons (American rifles that looked like the AK-47s that were made in the '50s and '60s) felt like thunder raining over us. Our dash through the crowd worried me a great deal since I couldn't see everything. In previous years, Dad would pack us in his truck and drive along one of the parade routes, and we all would stand inside and enjoy ourselves as we watched the parade and Mardi Gras floats from the safety of the vehicle. And Dad's height and strength offered a sense of security.

Poor Jean-Etienne, not yet a full teenager, had to care for himself and the three of us at this moment of crisis. In the commotion, I panicked, but Jean-Etienne sensed my fear and squeezed my hand tighter. An agitated lady tried to break through his grasp but failed. Jean-Etienne asked Rock to move ahead of us to make way for us to follow, and we began sprinting. *Where were we going?* I didn't know. Somehow Rock knew how to direct our path. He followed one of those truck floats into an alley and away from the huge, panicked crowd.

People began screaming and racing in every direction, pushing others down and trampling those who fell to the ground. All along, I kept thinking about the four ice cream cones. Only a few seconds earlier, Jean-Etienne had thrown them down. There was no time for ice cream now. People were running for their lives.

Children who had lost their parents cried harder every time they heard a volley of gunshots. One young boy about my age fell and got trampled. I avoided stepping on him. I don't know if he survived.

All around us was mayhem. People cried and shouted for their children and loved ones. Children clung to their parents and sprinted away from the streets. My heart was in my throat as my older brother ushered us away. I screamed each time I saw the flash of gunfire in the trees near the stadium. Some of the gunfire hit innocent people, who fell to the ground. From what I could see, many looked dead.

One had to ask who was responsible for the destruction. When we got home, Dad said it was the communists causing this trouble and that they wanted to destabilize the country at all costs.

Two months after the Mardi-Gras fiasco, we moved to Carrefour. Dad had already built his house there without me knowing. Our truck picked up more speed as I looked back and saw a plume of smoke rising over Port-au-Prince. After eleven years of living in its cramped corners, Dad was anxious to leave the city. He hoped to find a safer place for our family.

5

Carrefour

Negro peddler of rebellion, you know all the routes of rebellion,
since you were sold in Guinea.

– JACQUES ROUMAIN

The sun had seemed brighter than usual that morning. We felt the excitement as we began clearing the grown-ups' twin-sized mattress by pulling the sheet off. We brought down the dinette, our wooden bed frame, our toys, Jean's small plastic speedboat, and the rest of our belongings and crammed them into the truck. The day before, in honor of the occasion, Dad told my brothers and me to give his GMC a good scrub.

With the truck loaded, Dad said, "Okay, everybody, get in. We're leaving. Even though the new house still stands unfinished, it's good enough to live in."

I had to take one final look at the bedroom I had shared with my brothers, though I knew I wouldn't miss the pale colors of the wall, the cracked floor, or the cramped space. I waved goodbye as I ran down the stairs to find everyone waiting for me. I climbed into the back of the truck with my brothers, where we wedged ourselves in between the bed, the mattresses, the chairs, and the dining room table. We didn't mind. It was a new adventure.

Dad sat down in the driver's seat, and Yvette slid in next to him, all smiles and impatient to leave. Dad gunned the engine, slammed it into gear, and off we went toward our new destination—Carrefour.

The ride to Carrefour took about a half hour. The bustling historical city of Port-au-Prince, Haiti's capital, and Rue Montparnasse faded behind us as we motored toward the main road and Dad steered the truck into open land. When I turned back to look at the city, all I could see was a mass of bodies hustling about, bodies that became black dots the farther away our truck drove.

The wind blew against my face as I stuck my head out above the window guard of the truck, eager to see the open landscape with its rolling hills and the bay off to the north. It's a sight I remember to this day. No skyscrapers of any sort existed in that part of Haiti. As we approached the vast expanse of open country, we left behind the sprawling, noisy city of a quarter-million people.

Except for the rattling sound of the truck, the silence of the countryside seemed queer. I had never felt so peaceful as when the sound of the wind whooshed by our speeding truck. The air was crisp and clear and fresh. The farther we trekked, the greener the horizon grew. My brothers stared forward as I did, watching the truck cut her way into paradise.

From time to time, the truck jerked, hitting a pothole, the rocking motion making us laugh. As we left Port-au-Prince behind, I could count the few people I saw on our way. It wasn't like the crowds in the city. Soon I saw fewer tap-taps on the main road. I grew mesmerized by the sound of the road, which seemed like distant waves on a sandy shore without breakers. At last, we turned onto a gray dirt road—an unnamed street in the part of Carrefour called Waney.

Dad drove on for a few minutes, then stopped the truck in front of a Haitian type of brick house called a bloc. Wooden sticks protruded from the recently cemented roof. We jumped out of the truck and ran into the house. The main entrance had a white gravel floor made from the stone found in the mines of Haiti and used for construction. As my brothers and I explored, found three tiny bedrooms, one bathroom, a living room, a dining room, and a kitchen. It seemed like a palace.

I noticed a hint of personal satisfaction in Dad's smile as he strolled inside and stopped in the middle of the living room, his head almost touching the ceiling. He had such a great smile. It looked like he was laughing at himself.

Yvette turned toward him as though seeing him for the first time and asked, "How do you feel now?"

"How do I feel?" he asked. "What do you think?"

"You have a smug grin."

"Wouldn't you if you were me? I spent the last decade searching for a place to stay with the children. I argued with landlords, getting rejection after rejection once they noticed my flock. Today I feel worthy of my name. I am a Milliardaire."

Yvette gave him a pat on the back and said, "I am glad you could take pleasure or even a vacation from your hard work. While we lived in Montparnasse, I worried. What if something bad happened to you? What would I do with these four boys?"

Once we had settled in, Yvette set the table with dishes and spoons. Then Dad began to pour a hefty amount of the gumbo that had been prepared earlier that day. Earlier in the truck, I had sat across from the bouillon, which was in a large bowl inside a box. I spent the whole ride inhaling its sweet fragrance. The food distracted me on our way out of Montparnasse and helped me pass the time until we reached Carrefour. Food was scarce. A few months earlier, I had gotten whipped for eating Yvette's leftovers. My teenage cousin Blanc, who'd been more famished than I was, had lied and used me for a cover since he had eaten most of the leftovers and handed me the scraps.

When we arrived at our new home, I counted four houses on the street corner. I learned that the most families in these houses had also moved into the neighborhood a short time ago. One of the neighbors told me this section had once been a small forest that belonged to a wealthy landlady who'd developed it into several parcels so she could sell them.

One house caught my attention. It was the only one in the area that was painted and had electricity and running water. A thirty-something woman named Madame Serge owned it. The rumor was that her husband Serge had recently been taken away. A notorious, powerful henchman named Ti Bobo, meaning a brute without emotion, who worked for President Francois Duvalier had been responsible. Her husband was a woodworker who had done work for Ti Bobo. When Serge asked for payment for his work, he was told to wait a week. One evening, the henchman came to his house to pick him up under the pretense that he would receive payment for his work on their way. It was the last time Serge's family saw him. For fear of personal injury and reprisal, no one dared ask Ti Bobo about Serge's whereabouts. At last, word came that Ti Bobo had been gunned down by a military soldier.

Serge had left behind a wife, two boys, and two girls, and everything that could go wrong went wrong for Madame Serge. The children were always in poor health. They suffered from allergies, eczema, many other childhood diseases, poor nutrition, and all died young.

It was painful to see the tragedies these children endured. Couldn't the other families have helped them? An old African proverb that has since become famous around the world says "It takes a village to raise a child." Where was Madame Serge's village?

In 1966, when my family moved to Carrefour, we called it a "lost paradise." It was a clear departure from the social whirl and commotion of the capital. Even though we lived away from the noise, pollution, and sprawl of city life, Carrefour teemed with hardship, isolation, and fear. And yet, our house, though unfinished, was good enough. It had the charm and appeal of a comfortable dwelling and was nestled in a peaceful woodland area. To me, it seemed like an enchanted Garden of Eden. I wanted nothing else.

The small creek that crossed through our yard watered our plants. We had a breadfruit tree, a mango tree, and other tropical fruits in the yard. The tranquility of this pastoral area seemed matchless. We raised chickens in our backyard, modest as it was, which meant we could have fresh eggs for breakfast. Sometimes I would find the neighbors' chickens laying eggs in our backyard, which was a boon for me.

Dad also had an assortment of doves. Every morning they would surround him before he went to work. These birds would leave the house after feeding and not return till evening.

The bareness of Waney appealed to my dad's stoic nature. I liked it for its slow pace and quiet environs. Living that Arcadian lifestyle was fun, but it had its drawbacks. Not having electricity was the hardest thing. Every night, we made do with candlelight or our kerosene lamp for illuminating the house. The light they produced also warded off creeping critters, like spiders, scorpions, and millipedes.

One evening, I became the unfortunate target of one of these horrid pests. As I slept on my makeshift sleeping mat, a millipede crept inside my right ear canal and caused such pain I couldn't sleep. At last, my Dad figured out what happened and was able to remove it.

The night we moved into the house, we enjoyed calm as never before. It was totally different than the nights we'd spent in Port-au-Prince, which swarmed with constant activity. There, we experienced unrelenting noise from cars, trucks, vans, buses, and raucous pedestrians. Militiamen and women in blue khaki uniforms patrolled the streets, their Thompsons slung across their shoulders. They would clamor, "Vive Duvalier!" throughout the night. Here in Carrefour, no one shouted "Duvalier for life!"

Carrefour would have been even quieter had it not been for the dogs barking in the distance, the frogs croaking in the nearby ponds, and the crickets chirping from every corner. The darkness scared me a bit, but I loved it. The adults told us children to always stay tight-lipped because they believed evil spirits and dangerous animals lurked about. All nocturnal animals came with a foreboding warning.

On moonlit nights, I felt less concerned. I'd hear children outside playing *cache-cache-libin*, our Haitian tag game, or singing, or doing something else fun.

When morning came, I would breathe a sigh of relief because I was still alive. I'd go into the backyard to pick up some small tropical berries before going to school. They tasted delicious. At last, I met some of my neighbors. Madame Serge was a brunette with an eagle nose and small lips. She talked and walked back and forth, making me feel nervous whenever I saw her. Her calling out to her children rattled me. She piqued my curiosity every time she boomed out their names in her jarring voice. It bothered me every time she spoke. Most of the time, she screamed in a harsh voice, but some days she would stand there quietly staring, as if trapped in her thoughts.

I feared her. As a child, I imagined she wanted to wake up her lost husband from wherever he was in case he was tone-deaf. The sound of her voice jabbed at me and straightened the hairs on the back of my neck.

She had a swimming pool in the middle of her yard. Though it never had any water in it, it still posed a danger to small children, yet it was strange that no one ever got hurt in it. I made sure I never went near it. One of Madame Serge's children told me she had stopped filling the pool with water when her husband vanished. She vowed to refill it once he returned, and so, for now, it remained empty. A few years later, she tore it down altogether.

There were many rumors about sightings of her husband, each a painful reminder for the family. As long as the sightings continued, everyone could be optimistic and they would wait. Some said they'd seen him walking with a hunched back at Fort-Dimanche, a notorious penitentiary for political prisoners. Others said they saw him in a nearby town and that he looked old, ragged, and lost. Some went further and said Serge was no different than the henchman involved in his criminal behavior. Serge's whereabouts became legendary.

One thing was sure: this was a tragedy for the family. Madame Serge had to care for her four young children alone. At one point before her husband's disappearance, she'd had a small store in her front yard from which she sold household goods. By the time we moved to Carrefour, she had closed it. She likely didn't have enough money to run it. She survived by renting space in her house.

A year after our arrival in Carrefour, Dad learned that Madame Serge planned to put her store up for rent. He excitedly spoke to my stepmother about its potential. He thought he could earn a profit running it.

"We could rent it and furnish it with the goods that are necessary. We could compete with Raphaël's storehouse," Dad said. Raphaël owned the only grocery store in the neighborhood. Dad was anxious to rent the space. "You know that driving the truck is a risky way of making a living," Dad told Yvette. "Besides, I almost died three times already at the hands of bandits. Business is very slow these days, and who knows how long it will be profitable."

Dad wasn't interested in seeing the two sides of running a business. Whether his argument was logical or practical mattered little to him. He became convinced this was his "eureka moment." Who could argue in the face of such certainty?

Within a month, the shelves of the little storehouse were filled with goods of all sorts. Planning was Dad's strength. Yet running a mini mart soon became an impossibility. He woke up early to open the store by six each morning. After serving a few customers, he would leave it in the hands of one of Yvette's brothers so he could go drive the truck. Yvette worked the graveyard shift in the Pediatrics Pavilion as a nursing student at the General Hospital, the country's main hospital, yet she did her best to help with the store on her days off.

Raphaël, the owner of the nearby grocery, intended to run his store better than he had in the past. With competition from Dad's store, Raphaël knew he could no longer take his customers for granted. He began cutting prices to a point where, I suspected, his store was barely profitable.

It mattered little to Raphaël, however, who knew what he was doing. He had operated the business for a very long time and was well liked and savvy in the art of pleasing his customers. Within six months, Dad had to close the store and became unemployed. It was my first lesson in Economics 101: "Don't compete with a bigger business than yours unless you plan for the long haul." By then, Dad had lost all his savings, and Raphaël had gained our respect and admiration.

One evening, Dad came to me and asked if I had finished my homework. I told him I was having difficulty memorizing Ms. Léone's assignment. I was six or seven years old at the time. Ms. Léone was a tall, lanky lady with soft, maroon skin; smart, bright eyes; prominent eyebrows, and curly coils of black hair that fell above her ears. She was a loving second-grade teacher with a contagious smile. She embodied beauty and captivated me with her vitality and zest for teaching. I felt her commanding presence and wanted to pay her all the respect I could.

She had a gentle voice, like a brook in a desert. She would queue us before her class and teach us math in a song. Her soft and steady voice with its staccato rhythm directed us in learning our addition tables. "Students, I want you to learn this for tomorrow: What does the word article in grammar mean by tomorrow?" She'd said this day before I left her class.

When I got home that afternoon, I wondered, *How am I going to remember it by tomorrow?* Dad got his way by making me stay up late to study. After dinner, I sat by the kerosene lamp, trying to memorize the grammar lesson. It was already nine in the evening, and I had yet to recall any of what I had learned that day. As soon as I'd begin to read, I'd fall asleep. Dad would come over and give me a slight jolt to wake me up. He'd remind me I could only go to bed when I recited the whole lesson. I felt queasy from the smell of the kerosene, and the glow of the lamplight seemed so faint. I closed my eyes and fell asleep again. Dad approached me and said, "Go take a cold shower and return to study once more." It was almost midnight when he realized his approach to motivating me wasn't working. He knew I needed to go to bed.

Despite my need for sleep, in the middle of the night, the bed my siblings and I shared seemed to come alive. I figured out that our mattress had become infested with bedbugs. Their feasting on our sweet blood made sleep almost impossible. Scratching, shifting, and swatting, we somehow managed to get some rest. School and the forgotten lesson awaited me in the morning.

6
CHAPTER

Mom's Discovery

In spite of its poverty, its political upheavals, its lack of resources,
Haiti is not a peripheral place. Its history has made it a center.

—YANICK LAHENS

he political situation in Haiti began to deteriorate in 1968, political intrigue de rigueur. Although I was much too young to understand all the events taking place, I sensed the danger in the way people spoke in whispers and the many military soldiers on patrol near our home, and I heard the rumors of an impending rebellion against President Francois Duvalier's regime. President Duvalier ruled the country with dictatorial power.

In February of the previous year, the enemies of Duvalier attempted to overthrow him. Rumors spread that the neighboring Dominican Republic had plotted with Haitian mercenaries known as Kamoquins as part of the conspiracy. Later, on June 8, Duvalier had twenty military officers he suspected of conspiring against him arrested, nineteen of them executed the same day at Fort-Dimanche, a prison notorious for its use of torture and the murder of political enemies. Among the accused was Duvalier's son-in-law, the twentieth army officer, Max Dominique. In a desperate plea for mercy, Dominique's wife had asked her father to send them both into exile in France. I recall my grandmother, Bernadette Boncoeur Syverain (nicknamed Magrann) saying, "People drag the truth like a broken old donkey but will teleport a lie faster than light." After all, everything Duvalier's regime had accused the officers of was a lie, and they had died for naught.

I learned of these events because Dad and Dominique had a strong friendship, and since they were friends, Dominique had intervened for Yvette, helping her get accepted into the national nursing school. Few applicants got accepted into the state school on merit alone. They had to be among the top 5 percent of students who applied. And one needed the recommendations of influential people in the country—military officers, government ministers, and friends of the president.

This phenomenon of recommendation by prominent people was not unique to Haiti. In March 2019, the Federal Bureau of Investigation, in an operation code-named Operation Varsity Blues, uncovered a multimillion-dollar college-admissions scam that helped the children of more than eight hundred wealthy families cheat their way into admission to elite colleges, such as Stanford, Yale, USC, Georgetown, UCLA, and many others. In Haiti in those days, there were no private institutions of higher learning, just the lone State University of Haiti.

Duvalier soon declared a vicious purge in Port-au-Prince to find all the friends and family members of the twenty military officers arrested in the coup.

One morning in late 1968, a pair of plainclothes Tonton Macoutes, the murderous military unit of Duvalier, rapped on our front door. Jean-Etienne opened it, and the men peered inside, asking to speak to a grown-up. Jean-Etienne called for my stepmother, who came to meet the men.

"Do you know where a certain Milliardaire Syverain lives?" asked one of the men.

Knowing the danger if she answered yes, she pretended to be sleepy after working long hours at the hospital the night before. She told them she had just come home from work and didn't understand their question. She asked them permission to go back to sleep. For some reason, the men took Yvette at her word and walked away.

With Duvalier's reign of terror spreading throughout Haiti, the neighbors adopted a code of silence to protect one another. They all knew about the sudden disappearance of Serge Moneau and had learned that the only reason Duvalier had spared his son-in-law Max Dominique's life was because of the pleading of the president's daughter.

Life in Haiti became untenable. Danger lurked everywhere. Everyone feared they were in danger of disappearing in the middle of the night if someone exposed them as a communist sympathizer or, worse, an anti-Duvalierist.

Dad was fortunate the day the Tonton Macoutes came to the door because all the neighbors knew him by Joseph, his middle name. When the men asked for Milliardaire, the neighbors thought they were joking. No one believed a person would have a name like Milliardaire. Besides, the Tonton Macoutes seemed hesitant in their inquiry. After they left the last house on the block with no luck, they never returned.

While we had escaped danger for the moment, the encounter with the Tonton Macoutes had shaken the security of our paradise. We had not only left Montparnasse and taken refuge in a country home in Carrefour away from the hubbub and dirt of the city but also away from tormentors and unscrupulous landlords. But that day, Dad's peace in paradise was shattered. He had no good use for politicians. He believed a man should rely on his capacity to create his future and to think for himself and not rely on others for the development of his full potential. That afternoon, a bell rang in his brain, and he realized that if he hoped to remain alive, he would have to leave Haiti.

At first, Dad thought he would move to the family house in the beach-front village of Ti Mouillage on the Caribbean Sea. But he and Yvette rejected the idea because they realized he might not be safe there either. Instead, they decided he would remain in Carrefour. While Yvette would continue to work at the hospital, Dad accepted he would have to go into hiding. Otherwise he might make a foolish mistake and get caught by the feared Tonton Macoutes. To avoid the possibility of such a fatal error, during the day, he hid in a recently excavated hole intended for a septic tank. It measured fifteen feet deep by four feet wide. He used a ladder to descend into the hole at dawn. Yvette would camouflage it with a screened tarpaulin covered by green tree branches. At night, he slept on the roof of the house. Dad performed this routine, sleeping on the roof at night and going in and out of the muddy hole for almost a year.

With the sole breadwinner in hiding, the grown-ups became increasingly anxious about how the family would survive. Yvette had one more year before she would become a graduate nurse, and her government stipend was insufficient to feed all of us. Dad dared not return to his old job driving the dump truck for fear one of his enemies would expose him. He became desperate. He knew he had to make some arrangements to provide for Yvette and the rest of the family. As much as he did not like the idea, he decided he would contact my mother. Dad wanted her to take responsibility for raising me and my brothers for now. Because of the danger and uncertainty caused by the threat of discovery by the Tonton Macoutes, he knew he could not hide any longer. He contacted my mom since, without employment, he couldn't financially care for us four siblings.

Since his separation from Mom had been painful, it was difficult for him to appeal to her motherly conscience, but he had run out of options, and he hoped she would overlook the troubles that had caused them to part. When they lived together, Dad, a jealous man, had slapped Mom many times and on several occasions used a cot frame to beat her. One night, after another beating, he'd kicked her out of their apartment for good. She had no money and no friends in the city. The only skill she had was raising us.

It would not be easy to find her since he had to stay in hiding most of the time. At last, he asked Jean-Etienne if he knew which school Jean-Wilfrid attended. Once Dad knew the school, he could find a way to reach Mom.

With Jean-Etienne's resourcefulness, it took Dad only a short time to find out that Wilfrid attended College Jean XXIII, a Catholic primary school in Port-au-Prince. Dad made the dangerous trip back to Port-au-Prince although he could encounter the feared Tonton Macoutes at any time. When he got to the school, he hid near the main gate, waiting for Wilfrid. He made that trip three days in a row, but Wilfrid never showed up. On the fourth day, Dad decided to wait for him at the back gate instead.

At last, Dad spotted Wilfrid leaving the school with two friends. Dad walked up to Wilfrid, who seemed shocked and surprised to see him. They hadn't had any contact for at least five years. Wilfrid could not imagine why Dad had shown up without warning.

"Hello, Wilfrid," Dad said. "I'm sure you didn't expect to see me here. May I speak to you alone for a moment?"

At first, Wilfrid hesitated, then he realized from Dad's intense look that he was serious. He stepped away from his friends and followed Dad to a quiet place.

I can only imagine the anguish Dad suffered when he had to confess to Wilfrid that his new family needed help. Worse, he was having to ask his former mistress for the support he could not provide. Although Wilfrid did not grasp all the problems Dad faced, my brother brought him to the house he shared with Mom.

I did not know all the reasons my parents lost the love they once had. Perhaps it happened once my dad began to have eyes for Yvette.

Lafleur Ducheine

When I was eight years old, all the pain we felt began to make some sense. I met Mom again, this time inside a courtroom.

In spite of their long-held dislike for each other, Mom and Dad knew the only way they could reconcile their differences was through a legal settlement, and so they arranged for a trial date with the local family court. The courthouse where my parents' case would be heard was a large, tall, ivory building with two Roman revival columns at the front corners. Concrete pillars supported the cement roof. Anxious people filled the corridor outside the courtroom as they waited for the court officials to call their case.

Soon Dad pointed a finger at a beautiful lady a few feet away. "This is your mother." He said.

I looked out and saw several people I didn't know. Among them was a young, good-looking teenager who made eye-contact with my mother; she smiled back at him. I wondered who he was. The young man was Wilfrid, whom I vaguely remembered as a toddler. When my parents got separated, Dad decided to keep us with him. Mom couldn't afford to take us with her. My mind flooded with questions. Did my mother live alone, or did she have a husband? Why did Dad leave her, or why did she separate from him? Why did she look so concerned? Why was Dad so nervous?

I looked back and forth between Mom to Dad and forced myself not to cry. The tension between them could not have been clearer. Mom made only a small acknowledgment of our presence. Everyone felt uncomfortable. I didn't want to stare at her to embarrass either of us, so I stole glances out of the corner of my eyes. However, years later I remembered vividly some specific moments I had with her.

She looked majestic. But I would guess she was five feet, four inches tall. She wore a long white dress that stood in stark contrast to her curly black hair. She had a stern look on her face, and her arched forehead and thick, furrowed eyebrows gave her a self-assured appearance. She had rosy cheeks, a pious nose, and was poised, petite, and feminine. She folded her arms tightly across her chest, her keen eyes staring off into the distance.

Dad paced up and down the corridor, one hand deep in his jacket pocket, the other grasping the gray fedora he'd removed before entering the court gate. Under his jacket, he wore the cleanest starchy-white shirt he could find. He had a white handkerchief around his neck to catch the sweat that poured down. I'm not sure if the sweat was as a result of the sweltering heat or his nerves.

We had to wait an agonizing hour before one of the court bailiffs approached Dad and said, "The judge will hear your case next. You come into the courtroom."

Not knowing what to expect, all seven of us—Mom, Dad, and the five boys—made our way into the courtroom as Dad held the door for us. Mom turned her head away as she passed him. As he followed us in, the closing door almost hit him in the head. He began to swear, but realizing where he was, pretended to cough, hiding his harsh words.

We all sat in the same row, as though we were attending Mass at church. Mom plunked herself at one end, and Dad sat at the other, the children between them.

After settling in, she raised her arms above her head and twirled her long hair into a bun. She then moved to sit between Marco and me.

For the first time in my life, I got a sense of what happened in a court-room. It all seemed very cold and strange as we waited in eerie silence for something to happen. At last, a man wearing beige shirt and black trousers with a khaki belt came out of a side room. I noticed his shirt had several wet spots around his arms and on his back. He wiped the sweat from his forehead with his hand.

Then he walked toward the bench and dropped a brown paper bag on the desk. I wondered what was in the bag. He then turned and shouted to a young man across the room, "Bring it here, Ti Gason!" He pointed to a stack of papers and added, "Judge Comeau will need those court papers." The men sounded like they were doing important work.

The young man hesitated, saying, "Last time I brought them, the judge forgot all about them." As he began walking, his right foot hit a pew and he stumbled. We all laughed.

The man in the sweat-stained beige shirt said, "Well, straighten yourself up. You never know what Judge Comeau may request. The best thing is to leave all the books on his desk. That way he won't harass our sore behinds." I stifled a laugh at the man's mention of his behind.

Jean-Etienne leaned over to me and whispered, "They are the court clerks. They keep track of the details of each case.

It seems strange that I should be so conscious of my surroundings. The details of the courtroom, the flag, the clerks, and all the people there remain with me. I remember those moments as if waking from a nightmare.

I wished this encounter were under more auspicious circumstances. It seemed clear my parents were still angry with each other. I sat with my hands crossed in my lap, both befuddled and mesmerized by all the trouble that had brought us there. A lot of unanswered questions remained in my head.

The large door behind the big bench opened, and the judge, wearing a white robe, strode into the courtroom.

"All rise," said the clerk. Everyone in the room stood and remained standing until the judge sat down and waved his hand, indicating for us to be seated. The judge was an old man with white hair and light eyes, and he spoke with a trembling voice. Sunlight streamed through the window across the judge's desk and fell upon his robe, which was thick and heavy. It made him sweat.

After he settled into his seat, he asked, "What is the next case?"

The clerk called my parents' names. They both approached the bench. Dad spoke first, his voice clear and confident. "Your Honor, I have cared for four of these boys all their lives while she only cared for one, Jean-Wilfrid. Lately, I have fallen on hard times. I cannot go back to my previous job as a truck driver because I am concerned for my safety." Dad said nothing of the fact that a few years earlier, he'd kicked Mom out of their rented room in the middle of the night. He also kept quiet about what had happened to his best friend, Max Dominique, who was now living in exile. The judge must have known the political climate in Haiti had become unsettling for many. Perhaps he knew it was dangerous for Dad. Luckily, he asked for no further clarification.

Judge Comeau's eyes tracked Dad as he stepped back from the bench and made way for Mom to come forward. Without looking at Dad, she spoke calmly. "Your Honor, I work at the Caressa Rawlings Industries, sewing eight dozen baseballs for less than ten gourdes a day. My meager salary isn't enough to sustain two people, let alone six. My income pays the rent, care for Wilfrid and myself, and provides for our necessities."

The judge made a few notes on his pad.

Mom continued. "It will be impossible to stretch my income any further. Otherwise, all of us will starve."

The judge looked at my mother and used the back of his hand to stop the sweat rolling off his face. He turned to Dad, who made a desperate gesture that told the judge there was no way he and Mom could salvage this situation. He was already married to Yvette.

After a quiet moment, the judge looked up at the ivory ceiling of the courtroom as if searching for some heavenly resolution. Not finding any, he scrunched his lips while tapping his pen on the desk. Then, looking down from behind the bench, he motioned to Mom and Dad. "Milliardaire and Marie Madeleine, I want you to take a thirty-minute break. Go outside. It's a beautiful day. It will inspire you to find some common ground and solve this on your own. Consider what would be the best solution for you and your children. Come back afterward. If you cannot come to an understanding, the court will resolve your case for you."

We all went outside, but no one said a word. I was both scared and jarred by the idea of taking sides but relieved that no one had asked me. Children can become very confused and scared when their parents argue. They are bewildered when their parents seem to hate each other. I was puzzled. What was happening to my parents? Finally, the clerk came outside and told us to come back into the court chamber.

After much deliberation, the judge asked my mother, "Would you rather see your children live with some strangers in an orphanage without the presence of their father amid all the perils, twists, junctions, and turns that await them? Or would you rather take a chance of caring for them yourself so they have the protection and care of their mother?"

We all looked at Mom as she considered her options. At last, in a quiet, determined voice, Mom said, "I agree to take responsibility for my children."

Dad tried to hide his sigh of relief. He nodded his approval at the judge.

The judge rapped his gavel and said, "Case dismissed."

Mom took Marco and me by the hand and pulled away from Dad while Jean, Wilfrid, and Rock walked behind us. Marie Madeleine Thibaud began chatting with us, almost as if nothing had happened. She had resigned herself to us living together. Mom brought us home that day.

It would be the first time we were out of Dad's sight. As we walked away, Dad stood on the courthouse steps and waved goodbye. I heard him call out in a loud voice, "One day I shall return." I guess he imagined himself like General Douglas McArthur, who told his troops he'd return as he left the Philippine Islands during the Korean War. Knowing Dad's determination, I believed he would pick us up when we could all live together again. We all waved back to him. No one cried.

Breaking the Ice

Mom did her best to figure out how she could live up to the judge's decision for her to take responsibility for us. At one point, I noticed how her steps became more confident as she realized she might as well make the best of it, even if at that moment she didn't know how.

A few years later, I learned that my mother had suffered terrible injustices when she lived with my father. She couldn't bear to see any harm come his way, though, because she knew his existence was intertwined with ours. She kept what happened between them private. It was only later in her life that I would hear a morsel or a snippet here or there about her ten-year ordeal and the dreadful reality that was her life when they lived together. In late years my older siblings seemed to have completely forgotten about Mom's tragic relationship with Dad until I began to ask them questions.

We passed many other neighborhoods on our way to Mom's apartment in Rue Lafleur Ducheine, a more sophisticated section of Port-au-Prince. It took us almost an hour. Large and beautiful mansions with balconies and well-painted walls adorned its paved streets. Carnations, roses, and jasmine were scattered all over the grounds.

Electric poles made of galvanized steel stood on its streets. Children often used them as targets, throwing pebbles or metallic objects at them, creating loud pinging sounds throughout the day. They even had a playground in the neighborhood. They called it Nan Bosquet. There was also a mini forest that provided a rare view of nature in its wild state in the middle of the city.

The clean streets and well-preserved residences gave me a glimpse of what Port-au-Prince used to be. It was a remarkable place—a "landing place for princes"—indeed.

But when we reached the one-room apartment Mom rented, it looked like a different neighborhood. The buildings had a weary look. They were wedged next to each other and had peeling paint.

The moment I walked into her apartment, I knew why she had resisted the idea of taking all of us in. How could she live in such a small room with five growing children?

The spotless but austere room was smaller than the average American kitchen. It would be a significant change for everyone. Like most Haitian families, my family had its share of sorrow, pain, and hardship, but we'd never sunk into self-pity. We came close that day.

My apprehension and concern changed after the first night when I noticed how clean and orderly Mom kept the apartment. She placed a green sheet on her bed, with no creases anywhere. It looked as crisp as a cold night. In the corner of the room, a broom stood like a soldier, ready at a moment's notice for Mom to sweep the floor in the event someone tracked in dirt.

At the bottom of her small table stood three clay pitchers filled with water to quench our thirst and soothe our throats. On one of the walls hung a black-and-white portrait of Mom; she wore a faint smile, and her black hair was arched over her eyebrows, giving her a youthful look. She wore a white, collarless blouse with short sleeves. A small gold chain with a cross hung from her neck, and beneath her hair on her left ear, a gold earring glinted in the sunlight.

Mom went right to work the day we arrived. She grabbed a large, empty cooking bowl from a small table, placed it on the ground, then picked up a water jug and poured its contents into the pot. She then stepped outside into the yard and grabbed her three-legged charcoal grill. She cleaned away the ash that had collected in the bottom and filled it with charcoal. Beneath the charcoal, she stuffed torn pages from Haiti's major newspaper, *Le Nouvelliste*, and held a lit match to the edge of the paper. Once the coals glowed white-hot, Mom poured dry black beans into a pot half filled with water and placed it on the grill, allowing to boil for two hours. The charcoal fire, aided by kerosene-laden amber and pieces of pine wood, raged.

She also prepared a bowl of grits to go with the black beans. We were hungry as we crammed around the small table to enjoy our first meal in Mom's apartment. I noticed a flash of delight in Mom's eyes as she watched us devour her food with gusto. It was a great comfort to discover she was an excellent cook.

It was well after dark when Mom finally sat down by the kerosene lamp, massaging her tired feet. She gave a smile of satisfaction because the first day had gone so well.

I squinted first at my four brothers, then at Mom. A flame of joy burned in me. This new arrangement with Mom would turn to our benefit. Soon we all settled down to sleep. Wilfrid shared his cot with Jean-Etienne. Rock, Marco, and I squeezed together on the bed with mother as she adjusted the little wick to a faint glow, saving the kerosene for another night. Outside, a gentle wind swayed the branches of a Haitian oak tree, lulling us to sleep. Through the claustra wall, an open partition of masonry, I could see stars sparkling against the dark sky. The fragrance of nearby plants filtered into our room and buried us in sleep. We paid little attention to the dog that barked through the night.

One of the first discoveries we made was how different Mom's style of parenting was from Dad's. Every morning before she left for work, she would prepare us breakfast and instruct Jean-Etienne to look after us on our way to school. As Mom's oldest child, Jean-Etienne accepted this responsibility.

Mom took our schooling very seriously. Two days after the four of us moved in with her, she requested a day off from work so she could visit our school and introduce herself to our teachers. If Dad was a hawk watching from a distance when it came to school matters, Mom gathered her brood under her protective wings and supervised every aspect of our learning both inside and outside the classroom.

The day she set foot in Lycée Toussaint L'Ouverture to meet our teachers was a memorable one for me. Our one-room apartment knew no fun because all five siblings had to study as soon as we got home from school. Mother believed that reading made a child emotionally stronger when it came to facing life's onslaught as an adult. While Dad would always meet our teachers at the beginning of each school year, Mom's continual involvement in our education took us by surprise.

She would visit the school and get feedback from our teachers every week. When it wasn't possible for Mom to drop by the school, my second-grade teacher, Miss Léone, would make the journey to our place to speak to Mom about what subjects I needed additional help with. We never knew when or why Mom would show up.

Along with the gained notoriety of Mom's visits to the school came the pressure to perform. Before, we had almost been invisible; no one took notice of us. Not anymore. Our teachers made it clear to us that there were certain expectations they had of Ms. Thibaud's children. They knew she wanted us to do our best in school. She valued education more than we did.

I learned in my twenties my mother's childhood aborted education haunted her. Her parents had stopped sending her to school at an age when most kids were only beginning to lay the foundation for lifelong learning. But they had run out of money and had no choice. Mom made it clear to all of us that she would not permit what happened to her to happen to us. "Haiti can't go forward without an educated and enlightened elite," both my parents used to say.

In addition to the demands we faced with our schooling, we had more problems with Mom's apartment. The ceiling, made of tin crisscrossed on wooden planks, was mounted on concrete masonry walls. Nails had been driven through this metallic cover and wooden frame so the tin sheet would not fly away when the wind picked up. At night, when the rain began to patter on the roof or when a light shower surprised us, water would go drip-drop, drip-drop through the nail holes into pots and pans we placed to catch the leaks. At other times, during significant downpours, the sound of the rain and thunder would echo into booms and crashes and keep us awake at night. When the lightning flashed, I would hide under the bed for fear of being struck dead. During these storms, Mom placed a bucket in the middle of the room to collect the water from the leaky roof. She only had one bucket she used for the leakiest hole. The pots and pans suffice for the rest.

Nighttime brought with it a unique form of misery, where we all got drenched with sweat and were unable to sleep. We endured constant heat waves where we barely moved and fanned ourselves in hopes of cooling down in the oppressive torpor. We couldn't bear to stay inside when the humidity became insufferable.

To escape the heat, we would often go into the yard to play with the other children in the neighborhood. That also had its risks. Many mango trees grew in the area where we played, and during their blooming season, we had to take precautions not to have one of the ripened fruits land on our heads. Mangos had a hard shell that caused significant bumps if you couldn't avoid getting hit.

To our delight, we discovered the mango trees also provided us with a delicious treat. They had a sweet taste I enjoyed. They also had another dangerous side. Once, I peeled a mango and took a bite only to find worms crawling inside. At the same time, a large rat came running through the tangled undergrowth near the tree trunk.

Although our living space was tight, it mattered little to me, for I felt secure in my mother's apartment. How different it was from Dad's house in that respect! In many ways, however, Mom's apartment and Dad's house were similar: There weren't enough beds in either, and we siblings had to share. Both places were kept neat and clean. But living with Mom gave me a sense of security. Dad's life was filled with tension and trauma, which caused each of us to become embroiled with his issues. They were two worlds to compare and contrast.

In Mom's apartment, I loved the sound of the wind blowing softly outside and the rustling of trees as they swayed back and forth in it. I missed the noisy crickets and the recurrent barking of lame and lonely dogs in Dad's home in Carrefour. I now lived in two different worlds: the reality of Mom's apartment in Port-au-Prince and the dream existence of my previous life in Carrefour. It seemed like Charles Dickens's *Tale of Two Cities*, although without the tragic ending. It took a while to adjust to my two worlds. While I imagined living in both homes, I knew that, all in all, things could never be as they used to be.

But in my mother's house, I was happy because I felt her love and affection and warmth. Adding to this good feeling, I found a happy ritual on the weekends. Every Sunday morning, I attended a special Mass for all students of the Lycée, the public school we attended, at Saint Anne, the Catholic church across from the school.

As soon as Father Kébreau, the parish priest, would finish the last blessing, the students would dash from the church grounds to the school, which sat across the street. No one wanted to be late—unless they'd had a failing report card that week. On Sunday mornings after Mass, students with passing reports could collect medals of honor and various ribbons. If your grades put you at the top of the class, you got a red ribbon along with your badges. A green ribbon meant you were in the second tier in the classroom, and a purple one meant you were in the third. Students also received awards for penmanship, neatness, and academic improvement. I was proud to be the winner of a few purple ribbons.

In addition to its cramped space and leaky roof, Mom's apartment had more significant concerns. On several occasions, when everyone seemed to be asleep, I heard a squeaking noise on the roof. At first I thought one of my brothers was grinding his teeth, but I soon realized the grating was coming from elsewhere. I knew that many of our neighbors had cats. The sound wasn't a meow or a howl, so I lay my head back on the pillow and tried to fall asleep. Before long, the high-pitched squeaking returned. Was it a rat or a cat? Could it be a loup-garou, a sort of Haitian werewolf?

As I lay there, unable to sleep with that puzzle in my head, I heard an old man next door shout, "If you are a vampire and think you are something, then put your head here so I can see you and teach you your last lesson!" I knew he had a machete because I had seen him use it to cut lumber to make amber for cooking. The noise stopped only to return when everything was quiet.

The next night I heard the sound again and discovered it was coming from rats running over the tin roof. The roof heaved and shook from their weight and movement. Then they found a way to slip into the space between the walls. We woke at dawn to find that Marco's right big toe had been gnawed in several places. Our next-door neighbor had warned Mom she had seen several rats coming out of a hole in our front wall a few days earlier. The situation seemed hopeless as we looked at the damage done to Marco's toe. Mom was shocked and decided it was time to move. She found an apartment several blocks away on Avenue Muller, and we left Lafleur Ducheine only two months after we had moved in with Mother.

7

CHAPTER

Plan your Escape

Shortly after we moved to Avenue Muller, Mom realized that, for many reasons, our new flat was an unpleasant place. The landlord complained there were too many of us. It was also a downgrade from our former living conditions, and the neighborhood was overcrowded. But at least we didn't have to deal with a team of rodents skittering across our chests as we had in Lafleur Ducheine, where they had jarred everyone awake from time to time.

My first night at Avenue Muller came as a shock because everything ger than the one in Lafleur Ducheine. In many ways, it was more sinister. It was so different. I did not sleep well. We moved there sometime in 1969, to a room a bit lard a front porch that got muddy when it rained, and the ground around the apartment had a dark-charcoal look, so we had a hard time keeping the floor clean.

The porch became our kitchen. The large room held my mother's bed and three cots for my two beloved uncles who arrived a few months earlier and Jean-Etienne and Wilfrid to share. Rock, Marco, and I were the youngest, so we slept on banana-leaf-straw mattresses called nattes. When we woke up in the morning, we'd roll up the nattes and place them in a corner, out of the way.

"Jean-Etienne, come quick! Help Uncle Bastien (Mom's younger sibling) with Rosanie (a visiting cousin of hers) to hide the rifle. Hurry up!" Mom spoke in such a harsh whisper it frightened me. She did not talk in her normal pleasant voice for fear a neighbor would hear her. She didn't want them to know we had the forbidden Winchester in the house.

"We need to bury that rifle in the latrine tonight before anyone outside our family knows about it. If word gets out," she paused, "the Tonton Macoutes will arrest us as coconspirators against President Duvalier."

Jean-Etienne glanced at Mom, then at Uncle Bastien. I could see the confusion in his eyes. He began to speak, but Mom stopped him. "Son, this is no time for talk. Hurry up. It has been three months since your Uncle Ramil vanished. He is dead." She lowered her eyes, and I could see she was about to cry. After a moment, she stood up straight. Her hands were clasped tightly, as if she were ready to fight anyone who threatened her family.

Mom had two siblings on her mother's side; my uncles Ramil and Bastien Jeudy were close in age to Jean-Etienne. Only a few months earlier, Ton Ramil had entered the Haitian Naval Corps.

We learned later that the day of the mutiny. The commandant of the navy, Colonel Cayard, had asked all the soldiers off duty to board the three ships—*La Crête-à-Pierrot*, the *Vertières*, and the *Jean-Jacques Dessalines*. He told them they were on their way to receive a new navy ship from the United States, but he had tricked them. Instead, he had the soldiers load the ships' cannons with ammunition, and by 10:00 a.m., they were shelling the National Palace. Ton Ramil served on one of Marine Haitienne's three ships during this event, which marked the beginning of the end of Papa Doc and the ascension of his son, Baby Doc (Jean-Claude Duvalier). Papa Doc had a heart attack that day and died within a year.

As an eighteen-year-old from the countryside, Ton Ramil knew nothing about politics. Because he was a good swimmer, the navy promised to send him to an upcoming competition in Panama. That pledge made him proud and boastful at times. Before that Friday afternoon of April 1970 ended, we thought he was dead, his absence causing Mom great pain. She struggled with how she would tell my grandmother, Grann Bébé (Abélide Alphonse Jeudy), as we called her. She would find the terrible news upsetting.

It was a dark time in the country in the early part of 1970, just as it had been the previous years. The rebellion of the country's naval forces led to the arrests and executions of many political prisoners.

The day of the event was hot and humid, the air thick and heavy during rush-hour traffic. Beads of sweat rolled down my face as I headed for school. For a moment, I wanted to stop to search for anything that would quench my thirst.

The streets bulged with activity. Women stood behind their stalls selling trinkets. Men sold frescos (cane syrup on ice) and peanuts, and old folks sat on their porches seeking a fresh gust of wind. It would be easy to get distracted and forget about school.

But I saw some school children hurrying to their homes, which reminded me to rush to class. I ran into the school, took my seat, and opened my sac.

The teacher said, "Students, open up your history book to page 57." Before he finished his sentence, two loud booms echoed throughout the schoolyard. Pupils and teachers began running in all directions, unaware of what had caused the noise. The headmaster signaled for everyone to leave the school grounds and hurry home. Jean-Etienne was in a nearby classroom for the high schoolers, so he rushed to pick me up.

As we ran home, the noise continued and caused chaos in the streets, which were packed with speeding cars and pedestrians racing about.

We heard rumors that enemies of the dictator, Dr. Francois Duvalier, had attempted another rebellion, but military forces loyal to the president had put the resistance down. We had no idea who the rebels were.

Days and weeks passed without us knowing about Ton Ramil's whereabouts. Mom knew she had to get rid of that Winchester. She didn't want the Tonton Macoutes to learn about it. They roamed the streets day and night and showed up at people's houses unannounced, like they had in Carrefour when they'd gone after Dad.

"If they find that rifle in our home, they will throw us in prison, and they will kill all as Kamoquins." Mom repeated, "We have all become subversives by our association with my brother Ramil. He had the misfortune of being a naval corps member on duty the day of the mutiny. He soon became an enemy of the government."

Night after night, Mom asked Jean-Etienne to bury the rifle in the latrine. But fear that they could be caught in the act had gripped all the grown-ups in the house. Finally, Jean-Etienne understood what he had to do. One night, aided by Ton Bastien and Rosanie, he took the rifle outside. The three wrapped it in some rags to camouflage it from onlookers, then Jean-Etienne carried it about twenty feet from our front porch toward the latrine. He inspected the area to make sure no one besides us had seen him. There, he jettisoned the rifle head up, burying it in the muck, I discovered later. For sometime while living there, I dreaded using the latrine for fear the rifle would discharge a bullet into my butt under crap pressure.

That act wasn't enough to console Mom. Her fears were grounded in the notion of her brother not coming home. She kept asking any friendly official she could find whether he had died during one of the explosions. The radio stations had gone mute by government edict.

Ton Ramil had left home on a Thursday morning. But military units loyal to President Duvalier had sent a plane to attack the ships and forced them out of Haitian waters. That night, the US Coast Guard had brought the mutineers to Guantanamo Bay, the US Naval base in Cuba.

Two agonizing weeks passed and without news of my uncle's whereabouts. "Did he die during the mutiny?" someone asked. "Was he thrown overboard?" Another neighbor wondered, "Did he escape by swimming back to shore and then got arrested?" My mother could not answer any of these questions.

It took us a year after President Francois Duvalier died to find out the whereabouts of Ton Ramil. He wrote us a letter under a great-granduncle's name, Durocher Dextra. We learned he had sought political asylum in America.

Superstitions and wild legends had much power over our lives in Haiti. Not long after we moved in, we heard rumors that infants and toddlers disappeared without a trace. Another frightening tale talked of loup-garous, or werewolves, with eyes like blazing fire. It said they landed on people's roofs at night. For some reason, Mom had a fear of hearing about flying witches in that part of town. Avenue Muller was populated with rickety rooms and flats made from scraps of wood and material found in dumps. The place stood as an eyesore for many working-class families, especially those moving in from the countryside.

One of the most nauseating parts of living in this area had to do with satisfying our natural functions. People living here had one common latrine with two seating areas divided by a thin plywood wall. It had a corrugated metal roof that overheated in the glaring sun. This two-seat latrine served at least fifty people living in that enclave and sometimes more. People had no choice but to relieve themselves amid the stench of human waste mingled with smoke from burning charcoal and kerosene-lamp fumes at night.

Even at my young age, I knew better than to have my keister meet those filthy seats. I didn't want some germ or unknown disease to bring on some catastrophic illness or shorten my life, so I never sat on them. Instead, I would crouch on the seat like a forklift hauling material above the ground. That was how most of us satisfied our need.

There could be a problem. If I shifted too quickly out of that excruciating position, I risked falling over, or worse, slipping into the fetid hole. The throbbing in my thin thighs, the agony in my nervous stomach, and the stench of stinking stool mingled with ammonia-scented urine sometimes made me dizzy. If by some unfortunate circumstance three or more people showed up at the same time, it became a very unpleasant and awkward affair. For the most part, people were considerate about letting children go first. For them, nature couldn't wait.

With its rancid outhouse, Avenue Muller was akin to the 1930s Limerick,

Ireland, neighborhood described by Frank McCourt in his Pulitzer Prize–winning book, *Angela's Ashes*. The city dwellers in Roden Lane had to carry buckets of poop from their apartments and deposit them in a common lavatory surrounded by flies. In the summertime, the flies would land on every inhabitant, every piece of bread, and every cup of tea, contaminating everything they touched.

In our case on Avenue Muller, we had an endless summer, so we had to endure cockroaches, swarming flies, and the infernal stench. A tragic rumor was spread about a small child having fallen into the hole and drowning before the firefighters could arrive.

In contrast, our former home in Carrefour seemed like a refuge. There, we could delight in the drumming of raindrops spattering on the leaves of nearby shrubs and the sound of running water seeping into the ground. I would often daydream about it as I listened to the symphony-like chorus of the rain tap dancing on the outhouse's tin roof. The sound gave me a serene sense of relaxation.

Added to the beautiful canvas of Carrefour was the pleasant sound of tweeting birds in the morning. At night I was in heaven with the chirping of a lonely cricket, the ribbiting of a confused frog in the pond, or the bleating of a lost goat. Sometimes I would hear a donkey braying or a dog barking in the distance. On a clear night with a fat moon amid thousands of stars and planets, you could only guess what heaven must be like.

The sad truth was that in Avenue Muller, there was no toilet paper or sanitary supplies. If people were lucky, they would find yesterday's newspaper or a few pages of an old notebook to use. Many copies of *Le Nouvelliste*, the country's daily newspaper, and *Le Petit Samedi Soir*, a weekly magazine, became substitutes, blackening our butts with their print. Short stories about the communist boogeyman or the Kamoquins planning to take over the country found eager users.

Such hardship and adversity became commonplace for day laborers, street vendors, recent immigrants from the countryside, men doing construction work, street sweepers, and factory workers like my mother. They lived there through no fault of their own. For lack of alternatives, they made the best of this existence for themselves and their loved ones. All the while, they searched for some respite or stroke of good luck to relieve their difficulties. For most, the break from misery never came.

A few feet away from our flat, the Bois de Chène River zigzagged past the Avenue Muller neighborhood and through several others until it reached the open sea three miles away at the bay of Port-au-Prince. It was more of a hellbroth and a dump than a river, though. All forms of debris and junk—bed frames, mattresses, worn-out shoes, empty tin cans, old car frames and fenders, shabby old tires, dead animals, and stray pets—floated in the filthy water.

After a heavy rain, the dark current would rise over its banks, toppling soil and debris and carrying it into the foul-smelling mixture; it was unfit to use for anything. Its filth consisted of dead pigs, human excrement, and discharge from an old sanatorium farther upstream that cared for people who had consumption disease. Every so often, you could spot a barefoot lady who suffered from mental illness gawking at a dead woodpecker she'd pulled out of the murky water.

Once, out of curiosity, I went to see the river. As I picked my way along its edges, I became horrified. I never went again, for what I saw—dead chickens, a disemboweled donkey, rats, and even a trapped cow—revolted me. It stank in all seasons, wet or dry. I began to wonder why Mom couldn't find a better place to live.

It must have been through divine mercy that a plague did not descend on all who lived near this hellhole. When the water rescinded after heavy rains and the day turned hot and humid, the corpses would float along the river like Styrofoam planks. Soon they began to blow up as though someone had pumped air into their bellies like tires. After a few hours under the burning sun, they would burst. Flies would swarm around the stinking carcasses, then carry their germs to unsuspecting victims. When the stench became unbearable, people would avoid coming through our neighborhood altogether during the day. Only the infirm, the homebound elderly, breast-feeding mothers, or those with small infants would stay behind.

People called it "The ass of hell where they brew the stew of Hades."

And Mom ended up there with five sons and two brothers.

"Madeleine, how can you take care of your family and yourself without breaking down?" asked Madame Montperousse, one of our neighbors.

"I don't know," said Mom, her jaw tense as she struggled to swallow her wrenching tears. "But the good Lord will show me a way, Madame Montperousse. I don't know what else I can do. I go to the Caressa Rawlings factory five days a week and sometimes six when they have a rush order. I work nine to ten hours every one of those days to survive making less than two dollars a day. By the time I get my salary, I already have more debts owed to friends than the devil owes to God." She pushed a chair out of her way and sat on the edge of our squeaky old cot.

"This seems the fate of all those who toil this land, who sew the baseballs at the Rawlings factory or the shoes at Step-Over, who water the plants and feed the livestock for the Ti bourgeois. Yet, they have less to eat than before the sun climbed. They toil and toil until the sky turns gray. The scorched soil hardens like a fouled cracker. Then the night animals walk over to desecrate it without a drop of water for their misery," Mom reflected plaintively.

Mom often confided in Madame Murat, the neighbor who lived two buildings down the lane. With courage, Mom would tell her, "Sometimes people like me find relief only when they get themselves six feet under." Then, shaking off her concern, she'd stand tall, her shoulders braced, her head high, and say, "But I can't die now. These children need me."

At my young age, I did not know much about political events. Later, I wondered why a powerful dictator with financial resources would allow his citizens to live in the filth of Avenue Muller. Daron Acemoglu and James A. Robinson are correct in their assessment in their best-selling book *Why Nations Fail*: "Nations fail economically because of extractive institutions. These institutions keep developing countries poor and prevent them from embarking on a path to economic growth. The basis of these institutions is an elite who design economic institutions to enrich themselves and perpetuate their power at the expense of the vast majority of people in society." This book was published in New York by Crown Publishing Group in 2012

I know the people who lived on Avenue Muller wanted a better life for themselves and their loved ones. The mother and the father who bore the pains of that quarter labored to leave its gates quickly. It brought to mind a saying: "No one was born or died in Avenue Muller. As soon as they entered Avenue Muller 'hell,' people planned their escape."

8
CHAPTER

A Woman of Courage

Look at the striking beauty of that woman's arm protruding miraculously in the midst of such desolation. Look at the powerful balance of that man's body, standing erect against the sky.

—JACQUES STEPHEN ALEXIS

I must admit I did not know my mother before our encounter at the courthouse. After the court ruling, Mom was thrust into raising her five boys. From the conversations I overhead Mom have with her lady neighbors, little by little, I gained a vivid picture of what a strong and resilient woman she was. In addition to her working long hours, six days a week, when she got home, she cooked, did the laundry, and cleaned the apartment. I came to admire her for her courage and strong faith that our lives would somehow improve.

The few snippets I learned from Mom's mother, Grann Bébé, gave me a limited picture of who my mother was. I never got a chance to ask them any personal questions. Then, when death took grandmother at the age of ninety-three in the spring of 2010 in Ti Mouillage, there was no way she could tell me anything about Mom's early years. Mom met a tragic end herself at eighty-two from Alzheimer's after a long life of continuous hard work. She was buried at the Garden of Gethsemane in West-Roxbury, Massachusetts, on February 3, 2019.

I regret that even when Mom was sick for two years in the early 1980s, I never took the time to learn about her past struggles. I was too absorbed with my own life to find time to ask her about hers. Given her reticence, I doubt she would have told me much. After she moved to America in the eighties, she would empty her soul during intense devotional prayers, and my half-sister Sherley Thibaud-Reese was able to hear of some of Mom's deep-seated pains and fears. The morsels of information I gathered over the years gave me a deeper understanding of my mother's grief, although it fell short of the full picture I would have liked to have.

Her stepfather, Ramsès Jeudy, a sailor, could ill afford to send all three of his children to school. In those days, two years of schooling was all a parent in the countryside could provide for their children. Public education was nonexistent for the average peasant. Even most parents in the cities couldn't afford it. Since Mom was the oldest child and female, she had to accept that the education in her family went to her brothers. For a person who loved school and learning, this contributed to her misery.

As for my father, I learned that he felt rejected by his own father. This neglect made Dad a perennial, disagreeable bully. His assertive self-doubt, pugnacious penchant, and conditional love made him difficult to live with. I saw his moods shift from sulking to temper tantrums a few times. How could a man who knew so little about himself care for a woman he failed to understand? This combination of missteps and misunderstandings made a miserable ten years for my mother during their living together. They were never married.

With all the personal demons Dad faced, it is no wonder all three of his marriages ended in bitter divorce. Like all humans, Dad was a man of many contradictions. He was generous, affectionate, hard-working, romantic, and progressive. Above all, he was a visionary. He lived most of life with gusto, but his last twenty years were marked with anger, paranoia, and depression. He became a single again at the age of eighty-five and would die a lonely man seven years later in Boston. He was buried in Port-au-Prince at Parc du Souvenir in October of 2019. I remember him more for the devoted father he was than his latest infractions in life. He is missed, just like my mother.

From my mom's paternal side, any help was out of the question. The fact that she never mentioned her father's name prevented me from raising the issue in the first place.

All those years, I failed to ask this courageous and stoic woman for her version of the events. What kind of man was Mom's father, Josaphat Thibaud? How long had he lived with Grann Bébé? When had Josaphat moved to the Dominican Republic? How many other children did he have? These questions would remain a mystery, though it was evident Mom's father had forsaken the family and faded away. Why had he abandoned them and never contacted his daughter or Grann Bébé?

There were rumors that Mom's father was among the thirty-five thousand Haitians murdered under the order of Dictator Rafael Trujillo in the Dominican Republic. According to historian Bernado Vega, many were stabbed or shot in early October 1937.

All these questions remained unanswered for me. Meanwhile, our family struggled to find some way of coping with our less-than-desirable surroundings on Avenue Muller.

Most days, Mom cooked the same meals. If it wasn't thick grits with tomatoes and black herring, it was cornmeal with black-bean soup. We were always on the cusp of going to bed with our bellies empty. Rice was a scarce staple in the Haitian diet back then. It was reserved for well-to-do families. From time to time, Ton Ramil would bring rice he obtained from the naval corps at a reduced cost. Mom would cook the rice with some beans and meat if she had money.

The meager income she made from sewing baseballs could only buy one or two staples for dinner, not three. On rare Sundays, if we were lucky, we would have chicken legs for meat.

There is one event from October 1969 that stands out in my memory. My brothers and I watched as Mom cooked millet and beans and a tasty sauce of codfish. The aroma of the stew filled the air and made my nostrils crinkle, which made Rock and Marco laugh. We sat at the table, eager to eat. Mom said, "Wait, we need to pray to give thanks to God for the meal."

We all bowed our heads, said grace, and picked up our forks. Mom asked everyone to wait again. I started to get impatient because I was famished. I watched as Mom went around the table and removed some food from each plate, then scooped the food into an aluminum plate and said, "We have to share this meal with Uncle Bastien." He lived with us, and she set the plate aside for him.

My face went blank and stiff as I watched Mom remove food from my plate with her large cooking spoon. I wanted to protest because I felt she had taken too much. I became so upset I decided to give all my food away. I shoved it onto Rock's and Marco's plates and began bawling out of control.

My brothers paid no mind to my outburst. Instead, they got giddy at the sight of their fuller plates and scrambled to finish their meals before I could change my mind. I stared at them, my anger growing, as I watched them dig their spoons into the stew—my stew.

Soon Mom noticed my crying and said to Rock and Marco, "Give Ti Milliardaire that food back." By then their plates were almost empty. All I got from them was a few scraps. That night, I went to bed angry. I thought about returning to Carrefour to be with Dad. Little did I know he would soon be out of hiding and leave for America.

Mom's one-room apartment was shared with a neighbor and divided by a cardboard sheet to give them privacy. Always curious, I peeked through a hole in the corrugated pad. I saw a woman with small shoulders standing and moving her index finger toward the tin roof ceiling. She lived alone. Suddenly she walked toward the cardboard sheet. My heart sunk because I thought she saw me peeking through the hole. I expected her to expose me and slap my head, but that was just a young boy's active imagination. I breathed a sigh of relief when she walked back into the room, paying me no attention.

As she was responsible for a religious gathering, she rearranged the chairs in her tiny room before her church family arrived for the service. I stayed quiet as I watched about twenty women and men squeeze into her cramped apartment. Some of them sat close to the cardboard, almost leaning against it; others on the mattress; while others stood outside facing the Bois-de-Chène River.

At last, the pastor and his cohort arrived. He was a short man with a big voice that shocked me. The first hymn they picked was "Jesus Saves Today." They sang several more hymns. Soon the pastor read several passages from the Bible and gave a sermon, which I didn't understand.

They kept the service going until midnight. I stopped peeking through the hole in the cardboard sheet and slipped into the shared banana-leaf-straw mattress. I lay there and wondered why they'd chosen to praise the Lord at midnight and not earlier in the evening. The noise of their prayers and songs and hymns could be heard at least one hundred feet away. It was quiet everywhere else. Why would a God-loving people make such a racket at night? They were preventing me from sleeping. I knew Mom was exhausted from her long hours at work, but I guess she was too wound up to sleep.

At last, she stood up and said, "God, you know everything. Help and keep my neighbor safe as her visitors go to their homes and hear all their prayers before the night is over. Amen!" She said it so quietly only we could hear her.

I laid my head down and went to sleep.

Meanwhile, Rosanie continued to drop by from time to time to help Mom cope with all her difficulties. She helped Mom stay sane and strong by sharing personal stories. Together, they found the strength to face the challenges of a world they found hard to fathom.

One of the ways they comforted each other was by sharing their religious beliefs. They meditated and knelt in prayer. Sometimes I would hear them praying that a loved one recover from a fatal illness. They begged God to help them find a job or improve their living conditions. It gave both a simple way to have a sense of community and spiritual satisfaction. At least they dared to hope their lot in life would improve.

Another problem Mom didn't need had to do with our schooling.

Schools began on the first Monday of October and lasted until the end of June. She didn't look forward to the school's opening day and would have liked to put it off for another month.

She had to explain to the headmaster and others more than once why her older three boys' last names were Thibaud and the younger two Syverain.

The headmaster asked, "Why do your children have different family names?"

I cringed.

Mom answered, "Their father and I had five children together. The first three have my last name, Thibaud. The last two have his last name, Syverain."

The headmaster looked confused. He asked, "Since you are both the parents of the five children, I don't understand why three are Thibaud and two are Syverain."

Mom said, "You will need to talk to their father. It was his decision."

Dad's explanation for this confusion was that he was still married to his first wife when he had the older boys. Thus Jean-Etienne, Jean-Wilfrid, and Pierre-Rock were Thibauds. Once the divorce with his first wife (who was the mother of my oldest sibling, Marie-Fernande Syverain, nicknamed Marie) was official, he gave his last name to Marco and me.

While this explanation seemed to please Dad, it caused much confusion for the rest of us. It was another reason Mom and the five of us children felt betrayed by Dad's inability to recognize what a rogue life he led.

An even worse hardship for Mom came from the school's demand that we wear uniforms. Lycée Toussaint L'Ouverture was one of a handful of public schools that catered to the lucky poor. It offered education from primary grades to baccalaureates I and II. To buy uniforms for all of us put a terrible burden on Mom's meager income.

Another problem came as a result of the school not having enough seats for all the students. To correct the situation, school administrators divided the day into two sessions—one in the morning and one in the afternoon. Out of habit, they clumped family members together in the same session, using a lottery to determine which families attended the morning session. As my mother could ill afford to have Rock and me in the same session, she went to the headmaster and pleaded with him to allow me to attend the afternoon session.

The headmaster was annoyed. "Madame, it makes more sense for your children to attend the morning session. This way, all your children would return home together."

Mother sighed. "Sir, you are right," she said. "But my situation is different from most parents." Holding her emotions in check, she added, "Our lives are very different."

The headmaster noticed Mom's embarrassment and said, "Bring me their father so I can explain to him what I have in mind. I would appreciate it if you follow the school rules."

Struggling to stay calm, Mom explained, "Their father and I are separated."

"I'm sorry," said the headmaster.

Mom went on to explain. "My two sons, Rock and Milliardaire, both wear the same size-six shoe. I can only afford one pair, so I need to have them share the same pair of shoes for school every day. The only way it works is if they attend different sessions."

The headmaster lifted his chin, looked at the sky, and shook his head. At last, he said, "I understand, Madame Thibaud. I will make the exception, in your case, for your sons to attend separate sessions."

"Thank you," Mom said, then left the headmaster's office. When she got outside and far enough away from the schoolyard, she burst into tears, feeling ashamed.

Of course, as children, we did not understand the full implications of Rock going to school in the morning and me in the afternoon. We had one hour between sessions to accomplish this feat.

Rock had a bad habit of never passing a rock, empty can, avocado seed, or any hard object on his way to and from school without kicking it; that caused wear and tear on the pair of shoes. That created a problem for me. If he daydreamed or spent too much time kicking canisters or playing tag on his way home from school, I would be late to class and get caned for my tardiness.

I was also guilty of abusing the shoes. Five days a week, I imagined myself as a sort of sprinter and would dash from school to home and back again, putting more wear and tear on them. Soon they were scuffed and torn. It's amazing they lasted until May of 1970, when Dad came and took us back to Carrefour before he left for America.

Although it frustrated Mom to see how Rock and I abused those shoes, she seemed to appreciate that boys needed to have an active life. On many Sundays after Mass, Mom would take me to a small supermarket nearby. She allowed me to help her pick out chicken legs for dinner. I enjoyed every minute of her company, hoping to make up for lost time. I dared not ask any serious questions. My mother's life was too complicated, with too many unknown answers.

She confided in Rosanie about how her dead-end job sewing baseballs at the factory paid so little it made paying living expenses almost impossible. Mom told her of the indignity she'd suffered when Dad had slapped her many times and finally thrown her out, penniless, one night in 1963 in Port-au-Prince. She'd had to fend for herself in a city where she knew almost no one. She'd found herself living from corridor to corridor and in the passageways of rickety tenements. She had few prospects in life, and she knew it.

Above all, the one thing that helped Mom keep her spirits up was the passion she had for her children. Still, when the family court forced her to take us all into her one-room apartment, she became despondent and desperate because she lacked the means to support us. Every day became a battle to find food and to buy us school uniforms and shoes. Everything became a struggle. At times, she was on the brink of mental collapse. Time and time again, the world she grew up in treated her with cruelty and undeserved punishment.

When I was three years old, I got the chickenpox. My first night was miserable as the rash and itchiness made it impossible to sleep. In the morning, Mom brought me some relief in the form of cornstarch and a few ounces of alcohol. She mixed the two ingredients and poured a few ounces into her mouth for lack of a sprayer, then sprinkled it all over my skin. The concoction created a cooling, soothing sensation and helped me cope with the itching.

She must have repeated this spraying dozens of times. In those days, this solution was a common household skin remedy for measles, chickenpox, and other childhood viral skin infections. She endured all this and more under the most challenging circumstances. There were countless nights when she never closed her eyes while caring for us. What is greater than the love of a mother?

The first week of May 1970, Mom watched Jean-Etienne, Pierre-Rock, Marco, and me leave her apartment for the last time. Her eyes were full of sadness and glistened with tears. My heart surged when she hugged and kissed us. Wilfrid remained behind with her as he had in previous five years. It was at that time I began to understand that though my mother was a small woman, she had been a giant and a refuge in our times of need.

A week after we returned to Carrefour in May of 1970, I heard rumors that Dad would be leaving for New York. Somewhere inside me, I sensed better days ahead. I began to imagine I would be able to have my own pair of shoes. I could bring Mom a surprise gift. Somehow I would make it possible for her to find relief from her financial obligations.

In school, I began telling a few kids that my Dad was moving to New York. One of my schoolmates, Didier André, said, "I heard when people move to New York, they become rich. Your dad is going to be rich."

"I don't know if my dad is going to be rich or not," I told him. "But I do know when he gets to New York City, I will be able to play hacky sack with money. I am sure of that, and so are my brothers."

PART THREE

9
CHAPTER

Getting on Edge

And children's eyes
Full right up to the eyelids
With the horror of a world
Empty of all compassion.

—MARIE-CELIE AGNANT

In May of 1970, Dad fled Haiti to escape possible detection by the murderous militia of Haiti's dictator, Francois Duvalier. None of us knew what Dad did for a living while he was in search of a better life in America, but we were thrilled as he managed to send us money for food and a cushy place to live.

Although our financial situation improved, we had more immediate problems.

The problem came when Yvette decided to leave for Boston to be with Dad and arranged for her mother to watch over us in their absence. It's hard to imagine how Mrs. Castor's character was so different from her daughter's.

Lucifer didn't have any formal schooling, and she'd never learned how to relate to others or the respect that comes with group activities. Instead, she had perfected the art of humiliating people. That made my brothers and me convenient targets for her viciousness and spiteful domineering. I began to grow quite worried. The Bible says in Jeremiah 17:9, "The heart is deceitful above all things and beyond cure. Who can understand it?" If that was true, what were we in for?

When Lucifer arrived, we welcomed her, expecting her to care for us the same way her daughter had. But before long, our house had turned into a bubbling cauldron where she concocted a brew of painful punishments meted out for the slightest misstep.

Her coming to live with us in Carrefour felt more like a curse than a punishment. She trampled the floor whenever she awoke, making it impossible for any of us to sleep. She talked like she always had something important to say. She had great difficulty sitting still because her body was often in high gear. If she wasn't stomping her feet, the ominous sound of her voice had us making every effort to avoid her.

Our small home became Lucifer's labor camp, and the work assignments began in earnest. Cleaning up the yard, watering the plants, scrubbing the family room, and picking up the fallen leaves became my responsibility. Running errands and raking the yard belonged to Rock. Climbing and plucking from the breadfruit tree scared Jean-Etienne, but he had to do it. Lucifer excused Marco because he was too young and skinny.

One evening, I gazed at the fading sun, the sky masking to a deep gray. As the darkness swallowed the day and the thick gloom of night surrounded me, I had a sinking feeling that matched the growing shadows. It was then

I realized that Lucifer had come here to stay, to torment us, and to quash our spirits.

She became furious when she had to remind Rock and me to do our daily chores. Her hostility during her tense interrogations had a do-or-die seriousness, and she would grow wet with rage when Rock and I took too long to complete a task.

Her inkling grew when she heard that rumors were being spread about that someone had cast a spell on her. She took her rage out on us with beatings and other painful punishments. At times, she would wake up early and pick one of us for the flogging regardless of whether we had done anything to deserve it. She never attempted to hit Jean-Etienne because he was a full teenager. But for unknown reasons, Rock and I would get walloped even for playing marbles in the yard. And if we forgot to do our daily work under her watchful eye, we could expect to take extra thumpings. Lucifer took delight in scarring the backs of two young asses.

Before long, our home became a plot of land full of trouble and anguish, a den where a fiery lioness leapt at will. On her meanest days, as a warning to us, she would pull the cowhide whip and electrical cord off the hook on the kitchen wall and place them on the dining room table. For reasons known only to her, her mood would become sour. Her voice would shatter the silence and splinter into a screech that threw everyone off balance. She would scream as if some demon had seized her and possessed her to smack somebody before the sun went down. She invented infractions big and small and justifications for why Rock and I should get hammered. At least that was the way I saw it.

"Ti Milliardaire, I am going to flog you today," she would say, and my skin would prickle in anticipation of the incoming drub. I would clean the yard in a timely fashion, water the plants, and scrub the floor. I would stay at home and behave politely. Still, I would get clobbered. She used a vacuum-cleaner cord folded thrice. We had no carpets at home, so I could not imagine where she got that weapon for her arsenal of pain.

Sometime in March of 1971, I came home from school hungry and tired. I quietly crawled into my room and laid my school bag on the floor while I slouched on a nearby cot. Word of my arrival quickly reached Lucifer. She wanted to know why I made no effort to greet her upon getting home. "Ti Milliardaire, I am going to break you to pieces for failing to feed the dog yesterday. You knew well what you have done, and now you are trying to hide."

I rushed outside to hide from her for fear that she would dismember me. She had that short electrical cord tied to her waist on one side and the cowhide whip tucked into the other. She held a martinet in her right hand and was caressing its strips with the fingers of her left, ready to crack the straps across my back. She was armed and squirming like a squirrel looking for acorns. She had the urge to beat someone badly.

She began pacing the yard, putting me on edge. The knot in my chest tightened as she got closer to the trees. I looked around and made sure all the leaves under the almond, breadfruit, and soursop trees had been picked up and adequately disposed of. I had spread dry corn feed on the ground for the doves. I had also scrubbed the walls of the family room until they looked bright and clean.

In hopes she might find some charity for my thoughtfulness, I placed a bowl of grits before Tang, her pet dog. I crouched on the ground, peering at Tang as he devoured the grits. My fingers pulsed like a ticking timepiece as I quietly prayed that Lucifer would allow me some peace. As she peered down at me, her stern look gripped me with panic. It was pointless asking any questions, much less offering a whimper of protest or a curse. It was a fait accompli. I still got whipped later that day. The wallop made me feel like a hounded captive in the grip of a depraved, prowling master preparing me for a midday lynching.

A few days later, Rock watched from twenty feet away and winked at me while I stood before Lucifer. I had my right forefinger in my left ear, my head bowed, my eyes averted. Rock approached Lucifer. "Excuse me, Mrs. Castor?" he said and stood up straight. "Is there anything else you would like me to do? I did all the chores you have asked of me this morning." He blinked his eyes.

"Stop interrupting me. I am talking to Ti Milliardaire. Wait till I finish," she growled. "These boys have no manners."

I shuddered.

Rock trembled before her as if asking for mercy. "Oh, I am sorry. I am sorry. What was I thinking?" I stayed there, raised my head, and looked at Lucifer's vacuous eyes as they bulged from their sockets. Then she walked away.

Thank you, Jesus, I thought.

"You are lucky today," Rock whispered to me. "She was about to beat the crap out of you. You owe me one. I saved your butt."

I managed a laugh. "I guess you did. Thanks. I wish Dad could be here— but not before she could trounce you once more." We both laughed, making sure Lucifer could not hear or see us.

The chores never stopped. As mentioned, Lucifer had chosen Jean-Etienne, who was sixteen, as the breadfruit-tree climber. Lucifer liked breadfruit because it added variety to our meals. You could eat it after boiling it by peeling away the cover. It had a sweet, creamy, aromatic quality. Lucifer also liked to cut the breadfruit into slices and bake it. Sometimes it became our main meal; sometimes it served as a side dish.

Climbing a thirty-or forty-foot breadfruit tree could be dangerous, especially for someone not used to being so high above the ground. When Dad had lived with us, he'd hired an experienced tree climber and paid him in breadfruit. Although the climber was cautious, I dreaded seeing him high up, hanging from a branch. Now that job belonged to Jean-Etienne. Any mishap meant my brother would plunge to the ground. He could break an arm or leg, or worse, his neck, and die.

Jean-Etienne had grown tall for his age. While he had a modest, well-built body, he was a gentle soul and polite as a monk. Those twenty minutes he spent high in the tree, stretching out to pluck the breadfruits terrified me. Reaching the breadfruit could be easy, but handling the rough texture could create some problems.

Every so often Jean-Etienne felt more confident and jumped from one branch to another like a cat. I hid my eyes, afraid he might fall. But he managed to push, pull, and twist the breadfruit free of its branch. Then he'd drop the breadfruit to an attendant below while clinging to the trunk with his other hand. At times, he would look down and realize how high up he had climbed, and I could see that a kind of fear had overtaken him. I would say a silent prayer, hiding from Lucifer's menacing eyes, for God to protect Jean-Etienne's life.

Then, one day, the improbable occurred. Lucifer stood outside the house and glanced at the breadfruit tree while Jean-Etienne arrived. She shouted, "Jean, we need some breadfruit for the cooking today. Go ahead and collect us some."

Jean-Etienne grew pale as he stepped toward the tree. For a while, he stood looking around. Then he put his hands to his ears, stared at the tree trunk, and then up at the blue sky—perhaps to delay the dangerous climb as long as possible. He cracked his knuckles, rubbed his hands together, and wiped them on his pants.

He reached out, did the sign of the cross, and touched the tree, perhaps to make a connection with it, before slowly climbing up. I knew he'd had very little sleep, like the rest of us, for our wooden bed frame kept coming apart at night. Eyes downcast, lips screwed tight, eyes squinting, he put his right foot on a stem and gazed up. At first, everything went smoothly as he continued his climb. Soon, he had pulled a stem, plucked a breadfruit, looked down, and dropped it. He adjusted his body to the trunk and blindly placed his right foot on a weak branch. Suddenly, the tree seemed to make a screeching sound as the branch bent under the weight of his body. Realizing he might fall, he shifted his left foot to another branch below and wrapped himself tightly around the trunk.

My heart raced, and my palms began to sweat as I looked up at my brother straining to hang onto the tree. I wondered, *How can he wrap himself around a tree trunk wider than a small car?*

Jean-Etienne tried in vain to maintain his equilibrium, but his hands began to lose their grip. The thought of plunging to the ground made him break out in a cold sweat.

Meanwhile, Lucifer's eyes grew cold, and she strained her neck, looking up to see Jean-Etienne hanging onto the tree. She seemed to be gloating and gave a quiet, sarcastic laugh, as if she were merely watching Jean-Etienne performing circus theatrics. She turned her head and winked at me as though we were coconspirators in a secret scheme to put a hex on Jean-Etienne. I bent my head down and glanced sideways, not daring to look at him in such danger. It was my overactive imagination, but it seemed like the breadfruit tree gave off another terrible screech, as if some unnamed force tormented it. The fearsome noise came from the branch Jean-Etienne stood on as it broke away from the trunk. I watched in horror as my brother plunged from one branch to another, making a desperate attempt to grasp one to stop or slow his fall.

He dropped to the ground with a loud thud, tumbling as though he'd landed with a parachute; it knocked the wind out of him. How he survived with only slight bruises still amazes me!

I hated Lucifer with a ghoulish disgust. I wanted to see her dead every day after that. It didn't matter how she died—in her sleep, zapped by lightning, hit by a tap-tap taxi, run over by a donkey, or some other divine way. I just wanted her gone.

The next day, she showed signs that my secret death wish might become a reality. She woke up with a throbbing pain across her abdomen that gave her cramps at regular intervals. She writhed in agony, her face sagging, her eyes gone dull, and her lips turning from gray to blue. Then she stood up and scampered to reach the front door while grabbing her stomach as though a boulder was bursting into her bosom. I chuckled in secret. Her end was near. At last, she was on her way to meet her master—the real Lucifer—not her maker. I was going to be free at last.

But Lucifer sat down, closed her eyes, and pawed at her forehead, which was drenched in sweat. She grasped her stomach while crouching in bed like a baby in a crib. *Is she going to die?* I asked myself. But she didn't die.

By the time I was twelve, I must have recited the Lord's Prayer more than a thousand times with pleas for Lucifer's demise. Often, I varied my prayer in creative ways. I wanted God to punish her, chase her from paradise, make her lame, or dim her sight so she stopped smacking Rock and me.

Most often I prayed for heaven to deliver a mortal blow to her every weekend. A fact that was not missed by all who lived in our house was that everyone had received the Eucharist except for Lucifer and me. In those days, I believed my moral wickedness and blemishes kept me from receiving Holy Communion because I wanted to see her dead and gone. Sometimes I felt guilty and found myself praying to God to take back my wish.

One hot, limpid day as the sun rose in the sky, she carried her mattress outside the house and laid it on the ground. She raised her flailing arms over her head and began circling the mattress and cried several times, "Kill me today or send me away!"

Send her away? Where? Did she want to go into an asylum? She'd put the mattress outside not because it was wet or filled with bedbugs or needed disinfection. No! She'd laid it there to shock her stubbly, gouty body so she could die. For at least two hours, she slouched and squirmed there, trying to kill herself by rubbing her skin against the mattress. She said she wanted to die. She was angry with her daughter-in-law, the wife of her first son, who had come to live in a rented house across from us only a few weeks earlier.

I felt a momentary pity as I passed her and looked at her eyes. Why in the world would a grown-up feel so impotent, so hopeless? She lay under an infernal, blazing midday sun, away from any shadow, to die?

She slumped against the hard mattress like the house dog dozing off at the trunk of a mango tree. It was the first of many instances where Lucifer acted like a child. But no child I knew growing up had ever said they wanted to die.

Was lying in the sun on a mattress the only weapon available in the house? Had she forgotten about the long rope in the living room that held the curtain? It would be strong enough for her to dangle. I couldn't stop thinking about the breadfruit, mango, and soursop trees and how their long trunks and branches would be a perfect place to hang the rope. One of the house chairs could serve as a platform for her to stand on and the rest would be history. It would have been quite an eerie scene. Had she forgotten about the kitchen knives? Jesus knew that, occasionally, I needed some laughter at Lucifer's gates.

Somehow she survived, at least for the moment. I looked at her and felt some sadness. After all, even with all the pain she caused us, she'd kept my siblings and me alive. If she died, what could happen to us? We couldn't return to live with Mom in the city because she still struggled financially. So we stayed put, hoping to get rid of Lucifer by attrition or some fatal accident. It would be a long, living nightmare before she was gone.

10
CHAPTER

Darkness in Paradise

*My decision to destroy the authority of the
blacks in Saint Domingue (Haiti)
is not so much based on considerations of commerce and money,
as on the need to block forever the march of the blacks in the world.*

—NAPOLEON BONAPARTE

Lucifer began displaying the gamut of her skills as though darkness bewitched and cloaked her soul. Perhaps she'd witnessed the slaps and beatings her husband had received during his political arrest in 1957. Surely she'd heard about the French savagery against the Haitians during Haiti's war of independence in 1803. I doubt she'd heard about the Armenian genocide, the pogroms, the Jewish holocaust, or the plight of the Palestinians, but she'd likely heard about the slave trade in the Americas and the Middle Passage. Perhaps she had been angry since the day her husband went to prison and felt powerless in finding justice.

She knew about the horror stories coming from Fort Dimanche, a political prison of the Duvalier era. She would serve us food daily in a single aluminum bowl, the four of us having to share. Within a few months, we were all emaciated. Marco was always sick, but the rest of us withered away too. Meanwhile, her children, Julienne and Zagalo, were plump and jolly while their mother groaned with gout.

On a good day, Lucifer could be cheerful, caring, and attentive. On one occasion, she took Marco to the doctor. Another time she inspected my bruised body after a fall and took me to the Diquini Clinic. On special occasions, such as Christmas, Independence Day, and Easter Sunday, she would provide us with enough to eat, but not to surfeit. Her soul would be ready to enter paradise though she was oblivious to the fact we lived in hell.

How did a lady as cunning as Lucifer allow herself to use her hands for beatings and punishments where love and leniency were needed? Why had Dad put her here with us?

Soon, Marie, Dad's first child, would come to live with us, and Lucifer would have to get herself out of this conundrum alone—for out of this new arrangement grew a power struggle.

One languorous mid-afternoon in the of spring 1972, Lucifer was leaning on our sad living room window, watching the weather in the sky, the wispy clouds foretelling rain, when a stylish young woman brushed past our gate. She had mistaken the house number, breezing through and leaving a few of our neighbors staring at her back. She turned back and stopped in front of the house as Tang, Lucifer's favorite pet, sauntered up to her, smelled her, and then began barking at her like a ravenous dog.

It was my half-sister. She slammed the gate behind her as she winced at me. *Marie will be our rescuer,* I thought. Tang rubbed his nose against Marie's legs, smelling her again, then crouched down, whimpering and shivering like a donkey chasing ticks from his buttocks. Then he yawned, stretched, and quieted himself.

Marie glided into the yard, a small tin suitcase in her hand, and came face-to-face with Lucifer. Stunned, Lucifer gulped like a goat, drew in her shoulders, and creased her lips. She flashed a toothless grin as her cold eyes took in the legitimate daughter of our father.

I sprinted toward Marie and gave her a tight hug, pawing at her caramel-brown skin. She looked like a younger version of Bernadette Boncoeur, my paternal grandmother, with her long nose and beautifully shaped teeth. She wore a blue satin dress and a leather belt with a large buckle that looked like the one Lucifer had once smacked me with. She strutted, her thin frame elegant, slapping my shoulders, patting my head, and repeating my name. I liked her smell—a concoction of alcohol and talcum powder like the perfume My Dream.

Marie had previously lived with us for a few months around 1967 or 1968 and soon returned to Jacmel. She left the house after Dad criticized her for her lousy cooking of a black-bean soup. She had soaked it with too much baking soda, and no one could eat the meal that day. Soon she returned to live with her mother.

Now Marie asked after our brothers. She told me Magrann and Tante Orica sent us greetings. She clutched her suitcase in one hand as she entered the darkest room in the house. She dropped it and let it hit the floor with a hard thump that startled Tang, who made a grunting sound as she opened up Dad's former closet, inspected it, then sat down on the edge of the bed. Her eyebrows came together as she raised them, and she peered up after noticing Lucifer behind her. Lucifer seemed annoyed as she stood behind Marie. Her nervous tic flickered as she followed Marie. *Go on*, I thought. I took a deep breath and held it for a few seconds to see how I felt. I hoped to see a fight or a fuss. I badly wanted to see someone beat Lucifer.

I stood there waiting to hear an argument, but my hopes were dashed. Lucifer was never a fool. She scurried away with her hands akimbo. Her wingless shoulders dropped as she folded herself, slouched into the sofa, and rested her head on her right arm like Tang did with his head on his paws. She brought her hand to her lips and cupped her face like a saint begging heaven for an oracle. She wobbled, then sprawled out again on the sofa, her tight fist into her cheek.

Lucifer sensed a new dawn approaching, and I wondered if she wished she had never come to live here. She was quiet that day but poised for whatever would happen next. How could she be so serene in the face of such a big change?

My sister seemed to have come for a fight. She intended to challenge the status quo and wrest control of the house.

Marie, with her mohawk of black hair trimmed above her shoulders, was on a mission. She'd come here to dislodge Lucifer. She wanted payback for what Lucifer had done to Tante Orica when she came to watch over us one year earlier, dislodging Tante Orica and forcing her to return to Jacmel.

"You have got to call Yvette," said Julienne to Lucifer, "and tell her that Marie has come here to take over the house. She ought to tell you in a hurry how to handle this. Besides, you have done a good job with these boys. When you came to Carrefour, you left my dad behind to raise Milliardaire's children, and it would be crazy for you to leave this place now. You've let things get out of control for too long. You tolerated Orica too much when you didn't have to. Now this heir comes here to kick you around like this."

My breath became heavy and my heart sank as I listened to them talking about Tante Orica in such a disheartening way. Lucifer had "tolerated" Orica? Hell, no. She'd evicted her. She'd chased Tante Orica away from here. I still relished the thought of seeing a fight break out. It gave me peace and pleasure in paradise.

The next afternoon, Julienne took her mother out and went downtown to Téléco, the country's public telecommunications company, to speak to Yvette. When they returned home, any shreds of civility and cordiality were gone. The house seemed on the verge of a fiery explosion between the parties. A nightmare of a different kind had taken over our lives.

Julienne was cocky but quiet when it came to Marie. "Marie, you know something?" she said, "my mother isn't going to leave this place. You must have known this already. You need to understand that without her presence, your brothers would get lost here. She is the beacon that keeps this place lit and the only compass that can bring the boat to shore. Besides, Marie, why give yourself trouble about your half-brothers? My mom is doing a better job than their mother could have ever done raising them. Let's patch this up and pace ourselves and paddle this thing together." She'd asked for a truce.

Menacing as she was to Lucifer, Marie was a sweet woman. She cared about people. She struck up a friendship with Julienne and trusted her. In one conversation they had, Marie said, "Why did my dad bring these tots into the world? After I was born, if he had had any sense, he should have stopped there with one child."

Julienne shook her head. "I understand, Marie, that you are your parents' firstborn and their rightful daughter. That's correct for you to say that." I giggled under my breath at the thought of being a window listener. "But you have no right to dictate what your dad should have done. He is your father."

"Julienne, you need to look at it this way. How in the world did he expect to raise all these boys when he couldn't take care of me and Gertha and Bernadette or any other daughter? He left them with their mothers and forgot about them too," said Marie. "Besides, in a country with high illiteracy, disease, hunger, poverty, and a low chance to move upward, why do parents think they need more than one child? Why create more misery? Why?" She paused, the veins in her neck pulsating. "People like him have the weird notion that they need more than one child. One child is more than enough for any Haitian family to care for."

"Well, I guess my parents made a mistake by having me too," said Julienne. "I am the fifth child and their last daughter. I shouldn't have been born. I am a mistake."

"I don't mean to disrespect your old folks. By golly, why have so many kids if parents can barely survive? Look, my father had to care for your first sibling by marrying her."

"Marie, how old you are now?"

"Let me see. I will be twenty-four years old next month."

"So you expect your father to take care of you, right? If that's the case, how long do you expect him to do so?"

"Well, I didn't ask to be born. My dad needs to care for me until I can do for myself."

"Won't you agree that's wrong?"

"There is nothing wrong about that. That's called 'manning up.'"

"You mean well."

"Right, where is your responsibility in all this?" Julienne asked. "What have you done for yourself at your age?"

"Hmm, well, I guess I am doing my part."

"What's your part, Marie? You said your father has not done much for you? Please tell me again. What have you done for yourself so far, Marie? You mean coming to live here in your dad's house at your age is normal? You have it wrong, my dear."

"Well, if he didn't have all these jackasses to care for, things would have been better for him, for my mother, and for me."

"Where is your mom?"

"She is in Cayes-Jacmel," Marie said. "Why do you ask?'

"Didn't you have a good bed there?"

"Sure."

"Didn't you have at least two good meals a day there?"

"Yes."

"But why come here to this crummy, cramped place?"

"Are you trying to tell me I shouldn't be in my father's house?"

"I am trying to understand where your anger is coming from."

"In a different world, the government would have imposed a one-child policy per family and I would be well treated."

"But you were well off in the country. Don't you think so?"

"Well, don't ask me that. My dad divorced my mom to marry your cute sister."

"Was it my sister's fault?"

"Today she is a nurse. My mother has no purse." Marie breathed hard. "My mother was his first wife. Why didn't he help her to go to school like he did Yvette?"

"Marie, don't you think your parents may have married and fathered you too young? Don't you think they could have waited a little longer before they had you? You would have felt differently about your dad today had they waited a little longer. Some people spend all their time grumbling as if it is a fait accompli, like there is nothing they can do to improve their lot. They walk on the ground as though they have no ambition. I know you are different, Marie. You must have great ambition. Otherwise, you wouldn't trade your place in the country settling here for naught."

Julienne had led a life of repressed romantic feelings. She spoke to my sister about her desire for elopement. "I have dreams like everybody else in this house," Marie said. "Soon, Toto Nécessité will marry me, and I will be forever happy. He is a great musician, and I know that he loves me. Sure, I am no different than anyone else. Today your mom, even at her age, dreams of going to New York someday." Julienne leaned toward Marie and looked at her with a puzzling gaze. Marie returned her look.

Julienne abruptly changed direction, as though she realized she was walking in quicksand. "Have you heard of the story of Toussaint L'Ouverture?"

"What's that story about?"

"In eighteen months, he had turned the country from its former colonial economic glory in 1801. He did that through discipline, integrity, persistence, trials, failures, honesty, hard work, and intelligence. King Henry Christophe demanded these virtues from all the former slaves." Julienne smiled. "These are values that many today consider outdated. Do you believe that too, Marie?" asked Julienne. "We need the old values back."

Marie shrugged her shoulders.

"The colony provided one-third of the French economy then. It was called the Pearl of the Antilles. That was something," Julienne said. "For the last two centuries, our country and its people have ceased to care. They have stopped being accountable." Marie stared at her, unseeing, and seemed lost in thought.

"The man from Breda stressed personal responsibility, caring, honesty, discipline, and integrity. He was the first person to rise at dawn and the last to be in bed. In creating Haiti, he also pushed us to use our brains as an untapped source of economic power and spiritual rebirth. You may ask why I am bringing Toussaint L'Ouverture into this discussion. Last week in school, we had a talk about self-reliance. No nation has ever moved forward on handouts. If you want any help, you need to start helping yourself first," said Julienne. "The Europeans, when they came to America, begged no one but grabbed everything they wanted instead."

"What a great nation we are!" Marie shouted and smiled with a hint of satisfaction.

Julienne paused and looked around as she tried to impress Marie with her knowledge. "I am sure you've heard this before. Had it not been for the Haitian Revolution and the French defeat in Haiti, France wouldn't have sold Louisiana to the United States and the United States wouldn't be what it is today? Haiti is a great nation with an unequal past. In February 1806, on the order of Jean-Jacques Dessalines, Magloire Ambroise received Francisco de Miranda in Haiti (the Latin American leader who first took arms to liberate South America from Spanish rule), gave him munitions, and men to fight the Spaniards. Within a month, the Venezuelan flag was born in the harbor of Jacmel. The red and blue colors of the Venezuelan, Colombian, and Ecuadorian flags symbolize the allegiance the founders of Venezuela made to the Republic of Haiti in 1806. When Simón Bolívar asked the Europeans and the Americans for help in the liberation of South America, all doors were shut in his face. He knew better when he turned to Haiti, a free fledgling nation. In 1816, Alexandre Pétion (the Haitian general who murdered the founding father of Haiti, Emperor Jacques I) did what Toussaint L'Ouverture, Jean-Jacques Dessalines, and Henri Christophe would have done. He provided Bolívar with all the arms—pistols, guns, bullets, Bayonets, rifles—and food and Haitian soldiers he needed to free South America. As he left through the Port of Jacmel, Bolívar knew his people would see the light. He freed South America. Bolívar wrested the continent from the hands of the Spanish Empire, bringing Spain to its knees in the Americas. Sadly, when the new South American countries held their first continental conference in 1831, they made no effort to invite Haiti. Likewise, the Cuban Revolution failed the black people of Cuba. The American and European continents' debt to the Haitian people can no longer be ignored."

Marie listened attentively.

"When Libya sought independence from Italy in 1949, Haiti provided the last vote in the United Nations to make it a free nation. We have a story to tell if we go back to the old ways. We are a beacon that can't cease to shine. We have much work ahead. Haiti was a lion in liberation! It's greater than the world can appreciate. Did you know our president Jean-Pierre Boyer helped Greece snatch its independence from the grip of the Ottoman Empire in 1822? Did you know that Haitians fought along the Americans against the British twice, in 1776 and 1812 wars"?

"No, I never heard that before," Marie cried.

"Again, history is not destiny but repeats itself," Julienne said. "When Greece began its struggle for independence against the Ottoman Empire, its European sisters wanted no part of it. France, England, Spain, Holland, and Portugal—all the players of the day—got scared of the rumbling Ottomans and refused to lift a finger to help the Greeks. Again, Haiti came to the rescue by providing coffee to them to sell for hard cash for weapons procurement. Greece fought and liberated itself. We are the descendants of men and women of valor and great courage. Two thousand years earlier, the Greeks invaded Kemet (translated as "the Black land"), changed its name to Egypt, and killed its former inhabitants. Yet, Haiti, a black nation, had come to Greece's rescue in the nineteenth century. What a turn of events!"

Marie's face glowed. She'd heard that Toussaint L'Ouverture, military genius, tactician, and prophet from Breda, was always calm. He was a thoughtful leader who'd committed his life to creating an independent nation. Marie beamed. L'Ouverture understood that the noblest things for any human being to strive for and achieve were freedom from want and liberation from all anxiety. That sounded like Bredaism to me.

Lucifer rushed into the living room, and their conversation quieted down. I continued to sit quietly in the yard on a tree stump below the window on that muggy day, hoping they would restart their conversation without noticing me. *That Breda business sounds good to me*, I thought.

As I tried to sleep that evening, I recalled a different part of the conversation. The thing that struck me more than anything else was that Marie had called us four little jackasses. Did my sister hate us too? No, I knew she didn't. She had always come to our defense. I knew it was for some other reason that she was upset, not us.

"Every month, my dad sent money to care for us," she told Rock a few weeks later, "but Mrs. Castor spends each dollar on herself and her children and feeds us the scraps."

"Marie, don't let her hear you," Rocked said. "She could get angry. Who knows what else she could do to you? You must be careful around her. She is a mean lady. When she wants to act, she can be terrible."

"Who cares?" Marie shouted. "She comes here and acts like the Queen of Sheba and seems ready to forget her benefactor. I must teach her a lesson that I belong here in my father's house. She will remain a visitor forever. I am shocked to watch how much she has discarded the humility she had in La Cour Desrosiers shantytown. Back in those days, she wouldn't even look us in the eyes. Well, for her those days are gone. Her first daughter is in Boston. I am left here as my father's first child to dance a merengue through no fault of my own and whose music I despise. Life isn't fair."

"Tell me, sister. Who are these people?" Rock demanded. "How in the world have they fallen in Father's lap? It seemed ever since that it became Father's obligation to sing them lullabies."

"Ti Milliardaire, are you okay?" she asked.

I nodded silently.

"Your father is a failure. He never cares about any one of us and lives only for the woman in his life. Since Yvette is by his side, he won't give a spit."

"Marie, how do feel living here?" She looked somber and lost in thought as Rock asked the question. Lately, she had begun to cough sporadically, bringing up copious gobs of blood. It was clear she was very ill. She had lost all her fat. Her hips had disappeared, and she walked with a lethargy that worried us. She plopped into bed for the best part of the day, leaving only when she had to go to the outhouse or take a bath in tepid water. Her eyes inside their empty sockets showed a hint of fear. Something had begun to brew in her mind, something that frightened her. She looked terrified. It was as though she was on the cusp of an impending disaster or even death in the dark days she had seen.

One afternoon, I came back from school and stumbled upon her in the backyard. She was squatting on a pile of rags and running a high fever, with beads of sweat as big as raindrops on her forehead. She was a courageous woman nonetheless and still recognizable. She lay there with a thin drape wrapped around her body and shook violently from time to time. Her eyes alone seemed alive; they were huge.

"Brother, aren't you scared sitting that close to me?" she said. "I am tired." Her voice had lost its spunk. "How was your day in school?" She began to sweat again and looked lost in thought.

"Good," I said. "But things change every day, and nothing ever seems the same once the morning comes." Her legs jerked briefly. Talking exhausted her. I handed her a cup of water. She had little strength to hold the cup to her lips. I helped her keep the water to her mouth until she swallowed it and quenched her thirst.

A neighbor a few houses down the block heard Marie was sick. He came to our place at a gait somewhat faster than a trot and bent close to Marie, who lay on the ground, drenched in sweat. Marie greeted him as she always did—with indifference. He stepped back, approached Lucifer, and whispered a word to her, which was followed by a gasp. The man thought Marie had typhoid. When my sister began to cough and spit up blood, he thought differently. He knew my sister was very sick. He wasted no time hollering for another neighbor to help take Marie to the general hospital, where they diagnosed her with tuberculosis.

As a teenager, I knew Marie's illness was contagious. It reminded me of Rock's bout with typhoid soon after we had moved to Carrefour. My stepmother, then a nursing student, had instructed us all on how to take the proper precautions to protect ourselves. She'd administered injections of a yellow substance to Rock—chloramphenicol, I suspected. Marie had only five feet and a few inches on her small frame. She smiled only when she heard an amusing story, but now her dimples were no longer visible.

Marie continued her treatment for tuberculosis until April of 1973. By then, the tension between Lucifer and my sister was tangible. Marie resented her presence in the house and again asserted that we didn't need Lucifer here much longer. She felt qualified to watch over us as an older sibling. She disliked Lucifer for subjecting us to her feral interrogations.

Lucifer continued to keep her silence, but not before she let go a long white thread of saliva after Marie had passed close to her in the yard. Her silence frightened me, and you would think that someone had placed cotton gauze inside her mouth. In any event, I did my best to stay out of Lucifer's way.

"Look at it. Look at it. Come and look!" howled Marie. "It is here on the ground. Do you see it?" I vaulted over the wall and dashed over to her to look at what she had seen. I saw nothing.

"It's a green lizard. I spat it out. It's a poison Mrs. Castor put in my food and tried to kill me with so many times since I came here. Today, I finally threw it up."

Marie stood outside the front gate of the house without shoes. Her unkempt hair made her look like John the Baptist. She stomped the ground while waving her fingers at the invisible lizard and spat several more times. The whole neighborhood showed up in front of our home. I felt numb. She took off singing and disappeared before dusk broke in the fading red of the sun behind the mountain.

The truth was that Lucifer never had tried to poison my sister. As of this writing, Julienne and Marie live in separate cities in Massachusetts.

11

CHAPTER

Dungeon in the Making

Often like me you feel stiffnesses
Awaken after murderous centuries
And old wounds bleed in your flesh.

—JEAN-FERNAND BRIERRE

L ucifer had a plan for us. I too had a concealed scheme for her when a set of twins moved into the neighborhood in late July of 1973. The two boys, perhaps one year younger than I, became the de-facto presiding princes of all who chose to live in their shadow or believed in their magical powers and superstitions. People said they had seen these conniving twins hiding in the bushes or behind trees, using leaves or tree branches to tie knots and wreaking havoc by casting spells on suspicious scoundrels of the neighborhood and invoking someone's name whenever they became disenchanted. The first spell they cast fell on my next-door neighbor. She had crippling diarrhea that kept her in the latrine day and night for at least two weeks. This was what the rumors said soon after the family of the twins moved into Madame Mombrun Nelson's rented backyard room.

I began in earnest to seek the twins' friendship in a kind of rapprochement. It was quite a balancing act dealing with the magical twins. Lucifer could understand this. These precocious boys with large ears, rattling voices, and pirate tendencies scared almost everybody.

With their presence well established in the neighborhood, I obsequiously sought their counsel. For the first time in a long while, I saw an opening, a way out, a beginning, and a rebirth. Old things were past, and everything was becoming new again. If anything, I had hope; a man's best choice in times of trouble was the confidence that the pages would turn if one was patient enough. This was the secret to a man's success when the odds stood still.

Lucifer was as shrewd and watchful as a black-and-white tuxedo cat of the night. She believed the twins living next door were endowed with the gift of divination. Soon she started giving them food to curry their favor.

Only a few days earlier, Father had returned to the States after his two-week summer vacation in Haiti. Lucifer took her renfort, a little wooden shrine, out of its hiding place. The box measured one square foot and contained a vodou doll with pins stuck all over her face. The box had a tiny door but no window. Lucifer looked after the doll like a precious baby. She would utter a few words to the doll's face before returning it to the box, along with some fresh food. She would then place a burning cotton wick or sometimes a burning candle in a white porcelain bowl in front of it.

Lucifer worshiped Damballa, the Sky Father, well-known in the Haitian and Louisiana voodoo traditions as the primordial creator of all life. Damballa ruled the mind, intellect, and cosmic equilibrium. Lucifer also adored Erzulie and a panoply of other Haitian deities. These vodou spirits, or loas, as they were called in our Créole language, were believed to provide power, wealth, health, and much luck. This was one of the reasons that every Tuesday morning, she would wake up before everyone else to begin her incantations in the dark of the night. Whenever she was able, she would take a tap-tap for the short pilgrimage to Léogane, a city farther south, where the church of Saint Antoine was located. In Haiti, the Catholic Church and Vodou are one big religion. Erzulie resembles the Black Virgin Marie, or Madonna.

Rumor had it for a long time that Yvette couldn't carry a pregnancy to full term because my mother had tied her up with some loas. I couldn't say whether Lucifer's doll represented my mother or not. It wasn't a surprise to us that Lucifer had food to waste on a dirty rag doll and two young fainéants. To our chagrin, we watched this with horror, sadness, and much anger, with nothing to assuage the hunger in our bare bellies, which brimmed with gurgling sound day and night.

Suddenly, courting these boys to aid me in hemming or hexing Lucifer seemed unwise and dangerous. If she found out I had consulted the two sorcerer apprentices or malefactors, I would become the target of many verbal brickbats, blowbacks, and certainly booming whacks. I hesitated with fear of the unknown.

Finally, I turned my attention to a hougan, or vodou priest, who lived in the neighborhood. Rumors claimed he healed the sick, those the doctors had turned away, those who got poisoned, and those who could ill afford to pay a physician for their medical care. Help was needed. Maybe he had poisons to counteract poisons; that was the logic in my blind pursuit of justice and swift judgment since Marie's declaration. Perhaps a gifted potion could easily be slipped into Lucifer's morning coffee or daily cup of stomach medicine.

But people knew the vodou priest for his healing prowess, not as a killer. Besides, I wanted to believe my thoughts belonged to someone else. I heard such a priest lived in Cayes-Jacmel; he was the man who healed Marie from her psychosis after Lucifer had chased her out of our paradise. She lived with us for about a year during her second stay in 1973.

It was hard for me to accept that people like this hougan only saved lives. I wished he would give me a potion to kill Lucifer. Surely the one in my neighborhood would remain a healer and not a murderer for a fantasy concocted in the mind of a lone, reckless, and thoughtless young assassin. The idea eventually died altogether, for all I really wanted was for heaven to quarantine Lucifer because heaven knew best.

A month after Marie had returned to Cayes-Jacmel, Jozette Boyer (nicknamed Zette), Dad's seventeen-year-old goddaughter came from Bel-Anse, a city in the southeast of Haiti, to live with us to attend school after her mother had died.

Around this time, I became plagued by strange nightmares. During the day I was troubled by the thought that Lucifer might be a loup-garou—a werewolf. People in Haiti as in many places across the globe are very superstitious. Many believe humans can be witches and werewolves. If indeed she was a werewolf, what was I supposed to do? One night in late 1973, I tried to leave the house in my sleep. Looking back, I believe I was unconsciously trying to run away from home to prevent her from killing me. My mind was trying to help me find a way out of the abuse and starvation and doing it in a way that fit in with the stories and traditions of my culture.

The nightmares afflicted me the rest of the school year. One night, I saw a figure appear in my sleep. I tried to hide from it while relieving myself behind the coconut tree in our yard in my dream, but instead I awoke around four and found myself in a pool of urine. *What shall I do?* I thought. Surely Lucifer would deliver me another whipping in the morning. I stood quietly without stepping outside into the dark because I was afraid of going to the outhouse.

I reached out with my right hand, searching for the chamber pot below the bed. I bent down and tried to crawl out of sight onto the floor to hide from a shadow I spotted, but not before I felt a tug around my shoulders. I raised my forearm, trying to wrestle with it as I tried to run, but I bumped the pot against the bed and spilled urine onto the mattress. The shape copied my movements on the wall as I sat down and pressed my shirt against the mattress to soak up the urine. I wanted to scream. I closed my eyes to mollify my nerves. I dropped the shirt onto the floor, then took the bedsheet, rolled it into a square in the dark, and pressed it against the mattress. I repeated this exercise at least five times, but it soon became clear that I was wasting my time, and so I resigned myself to lay at the edge of the mattress. The rest of the night brought no sleep, no peace, and I felt my heart quiver every so often until dawn. The mattress I shared with Zette needed drying in the scorching and raging sun of that early fall morning. That could work in a cinch. But how could I do that without drawing Lucifer's and Zette's attention?

After a night of seeing wolves, jackals, and rabid dogs, I woke up and quickly dressed without looking at the kitchen countertop. I doubted I'd find anything to gulp down anyway. I trekked the customary five blocks before catching a tap-tap to take me to school in the city. I was late for class. That morning, I forewent my small cup of roasted peanuts and the peeled orange from the street seller for lack of money. In class, I felt rage welling inside me. At recess, I sat down in the shade of an acacia tree and watched other students playing *lago-kaché*, a Haitian hide-and-seek-and-tag game.

Weekdays normally revolved around a sameness that became all too familiar with time. That Tuesday dared to be different. For reasons I couldn't recall, the argument from the day before with a set of classmates, Frantz and William Jean-Baptiste, began again. This time I thought I had a better grasp of the situation. I had discussed the incident earlier with a truculent acquaintance. Not only that fellow and I lived in the same neighborhood, we also attended Lycée Toussaint together. I had asked him for his assistance, meaning for him to break up any fight I got involved in with these brothers, but with a stern warning not to intervene if I got into a brawl with the chubby Frantz alone. I felt I could take care of him on my own. My evil neighbor promised to do just that. Only I forgot that some students would do or say anything to see a brawl last much longer.

Frantz came around and kicked my feet as I squatted on the ground. I had crouched there because I was too hungry to stay standing for the fifteen-minute recess. The boy dared me to do anything about it and called me "dog dung." I felt feral. I stood and jumped on him and began to hit him like a madman, throwing angry blows at his head. A struggle ensued, with punches flying to and fro. My lighter weight provided me with a degree of freedom the overly fed Frantz sorely lacked as my blows landed on his huge head. I was in bliss and resisted the feeling of seeing the fight stopped as I pounded the fellow on the ground and scratched his face. In my delirium, I noticed stunned students beginning to gather, clamoring, "*Roué roué!*" Now encircled by a vociferous and murderous crowd who wished to see the fight continue, the lad and I backed up until we were a foot apart. It felt good. I was driven by the deafening roar.

Within a minute or so, I felt a tug around the waist of my short khaki pants and the board-stiff collar of my school uniform. Someone had seized me and pulled me away. As I turned my head away from Frantz, the assailant landed a tomahawk punch to my neck, making me gasp for air like a hanging goat. I saw lightning before me. After repeated blows to my torso and head and neck from the twins, I realized I was near the ten-foot below ground patio wall of the music department hall. The brothers held me up, ready to slam me into the concrete forest below me. In my agony, amid the crowd, I heard a smart-aleck shout, "Hang him up! Hang him up!"

Only then did my neighborhood brat lift his right hand, shirk the brothers, and ask them to back off and spare me the plunge. Though I thanked him for saving my life and some broken bones, I resented the fact that he'd stood nonchalantly by during the skirmish, enjoying the fight until the brothers had resolved to crack my skull open.

That afternoon on my way home, I felt like a condemned prisoner as I contemplated Lucifer's reaction when she noticed the trace of golden pee left on the mattress that morning. She would motion that I follow her into her dungeon. I swore then that I would never deal with the twins in school and in my neighborhood, for evil or good.

My preoccupation with the thought that Lucifer was a loup-garou warranted further vigilance. Whether the term was used as a figure of speech or literal mattered little to me. It was true that she was neither the friendliest nor the most unpleasant gruff in the neighborhood; she was just herself. Lucifer blurted things out and meant everything she said.

If she had tried to kill Yvette when she eloped with Dad, she would be bad for us. I sat in the corner of the yard pondering whether I was going to be around much longer. Was she going to kill all of us? I had never seen a werewolf in my life, much less in the house. Could this be a lie? Besides, Dad knew her for a long time, and surely he would have taken the proper precautions by not marrying her daughter. Well, he was known for his gaffes; therefore, such a thought was no comfort. In any event, I wanted to be around much longer and to outlive her in that residence. But when I returned from school a day later, I got my wake-up call.

It was two weeks since the last pee debacle when I went to bed early one evening only to wake up three hours later trying to unlock the front door of the house while reciting a monologue about how I would soon be out of the house for that night. Zette became the only line of defense between me leaving and walking the streets at midnight in the darkness.

"Where were you going last night when you tried to leave the house past midnight?" She asked.

"I tried to leave the house last night?" A long pause followed. "Did I?" I asked.

"Why did you tell them you were coming?" she asked. "Didn't you hear the commotion in the streets?"

I gasped.

"Did you realize that there was a band Zobope passing by?"

"You mean there was a *rara* passing by."

"Yes, I meant Rara, the folk-music band of the country. You almost became their new band member." She laughed.

"Well, then, what's wrong with me?" I began to wonder. *Could it be that Lucifer is trying to sell me to the vampires?* I heard many rumors, though I didn't always believe them. As with everything in Haiti, rumors sounded like facts. I heard stories that Lucifer had revisited a hougan. Two years earlier, on the morning Zagalo and Rock sat for the national exam, I saw her giving them a bath in the yard using scented water. They both passed.

The next day, she woke up, combed her matted hair, wrapped it in cornrows, and placed a blue turban over her head. Then she put on a long purple satin robe, tightened up her sandals, and began to sing the songs of Papa Guédé and Guédé Nibo—the two vodou spirits responsible for taking souls into the afterlife. She seemed possessed. I wanted to giggle out of fear because she was going crazy. As her singing rose in pitch, she began to dance and make sideways motions, her torso jerking back and forth, eyes closed, head resting on her shoulders, and whirling. With one foot up, she began gyrating faster on the other, belly dancing and wailing while her hands flapped. She had high energy. Ten years later, I would witness Rock doing these same shenanigans in Boston before he would have a manic breakdown.

In her excitement, she slipped on the ceramic floor of the living room only to catch herself, but not before she knocked an empty pail near the corner of the sofa bed and it rattled like a fork. She glittered like an exploding star scattering its light and acted freer than a bird in the sky.

Suddenly, I opened my mouth to let out a hoot. She turned her head my way and almost caught me laughing. That day, I knew I was safe from her wrath whenever she called upon the ancestral vodou spirits to bring her good omens.

She was kind to us on the days she invoked the dead. Maybe it was out of fear that the spirits roaming around would cause her harm—so she had to be kind, genteel, and caring. She would even give us the fare for a tap-tap to school.

In time, my nightmares faded. The vicious jackals of my dreams became the donkeys of Ti Mouillage. The tigers looked more like the dogs of my grandmother, and the scorpions were tamer than the flies that buzzed around. The dark images and fretful spirits became a distant memory.

One morning, in November 1973, I stood up, hungry as always, and took a few steps behind the kitchen window, from which the strong, warm, appetizing aroma of sizzling herring wafted across the yard. I sniffed the fragrant air. Breakfast for sure, I thought. If only I could get something to calm the demons in my empty stomach. Whatever our grudging gingerly master doled out to Jean-Etienne to share with us would satisfy no one.

Already I felt my belly churning with a hunger pang that choked my guts. For Lucifer, it was a dramatic moment when her roguish grin caught my eye, causing me to shake in revulsion. *Why in the world are we living with such a devilish soul who reminds us constantly of how useless we have become? One who winks at kids when planning perverse things and who proffers evil?*

We were losing our lives to a slow death blow.

By January 1974, with hormones raging, a revolt was in the making with dire consequences for anyone involved. Every so often, my brothers or I observed where Lucifer tucked food away for Julienne and Zagalo. After much deliberation and agitation in our growing bodies and gnawing bellies, Rock made up his mind to go for the jugular and do just as Haitian slaves had done to their French masters. He reminded me of Dutty Boukman's insurrection: *"Koupé tèt boulé kay,"* which translates as "chopping off heads and burning their homes."

As John Steinbeck clearly says in *The Grapes of Wrath*, published by the Penguin Group in New York in 2006, on page 236 it reads: "How can you frighten a man whose hunger is not only in his cramped stomach but in the wretched bellies of his children? You can't scare him—he has known fear beyond every other."

We were tired of going hungry all the time. As Rock grew taller, he became a savvy teenager riding the advent of adolescence—and with that came a more creative mind and a keen instinct for noticing life's absurdities as never before. He had decided that he was going to do by force what occupiers usually did. Except we were occupied and had to do what we couldn't get done peacefully in our father's house by breaking into the cabinet where Lucifer stashed food and goodies. We were about to seize everything.

Lucky for us and favorably for Lucifer, a truce was near. A flight of doves dropped onto the roof of the house, scrabbled the bits of corn feed, and flew off like a twisted tornado. The resulting rumors that she would leave for America proved to be truthful. The news of her imminent departure came in time to temper our resolve and lock up the swinging grenade before it took off and blew up like a bomb.

12

CHAPTER

The Ghost Gone

To change masters is not to be free.

—JOSE MARTI

"Ti Milliardaire, did you hear the good news?" Rock asked in his crafty way one afternoon of the spring of 1974.

"What news?" I asked. I was too tense to stew over such a silly question.

"Did you hear Mrs. Castor is about to leave the country for America?"

"Is that the new gospel according to Pierre-Rock Thibaud, the confabulator?" I asked. "I know you are a genius who helped Marco jump two grade levels after kindergarten. I am not too sure you know what you are talking about."

"Go find out!" he growled.

"Stop being a joker. You are always fooling around."

"You don't believe me? Well, too bad. In the meantime, I am having a blast and a swell time, and I don't want you to spoil it for me, comrade."

"Wait, wait, are you telling the truth?" I asked. "Or have you just cooked up a story as usual? I am afraid that soon you are going to tell me you see Lucifer ascending to heaven."

He looked at me and said, "Do you want me to swear by the Haitian thunder that trembles in the sky and on earth?"

"Uh … I don't think that's necessary," I said. "Where did you hear that fanciful wish?"

"Zagalo told me," he confessed.

"Well, if Zagalo told you, it must be the truth," I reassured him. "He is her son, so he must know something." Suddenly, I recognized that joy and sorrow were one and the same and that in a moment like this, I needed conviction.

In school, I mocked my friends each time they asked me to go inside the Port-au-Prince Cathedral before a final exam or national exams or any school exam. Some of those same students barely studied throughout the trimester or school year. I wasn't an agnostic or an atheist. I told them no amount of prayer could extricate them from that quagmire. "If you failed to touch your books since October, there is no God in heaven or on earth who could come to your rescue from that crooked tangle," I told them. "God helps those who help themselves." I grinned.

"If you want anything worthwhile in life, you must begin working toward it today not tomorrow," Magrann used to say. "And it's never too late." The students wriggled their necks as though my statement was an abomination.

They gave me crummy looks. They looked forlorn, like some of my fifth-grade classmates did while fixing their eyes on our teacher for the Sunday bulletin-board report.

Many called me a heathen and heartless, someone without kindness, justice, compassion, or faith. But my grandmothers had often talked of a gospel of responsibility, perseverance, integrity, respect, faith, honesty, and caring and taught me to own my failure without blaming others for my mistakes—even when there was a cause. Magrann once said to me that whatever I did, it would be me who did it—not my parents. I believed that a just God must be pleased with due diligence, fairness, and hard work. Magrann was right.

That mid-June afternoon, the whole house was in a festive mood. Even the food smelled and tasted differently. Rock took a guitar and began playing an impromptu song, "Vada Retro Satana." I hadn't taken Latin in school yet, but I liked what I heard. A few years later, I would learn from the Bible the story of Jesus chastising the devil for tempting the Master. I asked Rock to translate the song for me.

"Well, you need to wait until Mrs. Castor leaves the country for me to do that," he said. I was satisfied with his promise only enough to ask him the same question again. A slave unshackled was never free if his master lived.

But heaven had finally come down to us. The day she was to leave us, Lucifer looked chic, harmless, and forgivable. She wore a white flannel blouse with brown embroidery along its edges, a brown skirt, white mini heels, and a salmon scarf. She was close to sixty and good-looking when wearing her false teeth. She stood from the living room sofa and strode out to the front porch, impatient to leave to be with her first child and to improve her financial status. But then she strutted back inside the house like a sergeant carrying out her drills in a final inspection. With her two suitcases in the trunk of the car, she took the front seat and fastened the seat belt, which was unusual in Haiti, where seatbelts were not often worn. The rest of the household huddled together in the back of the vehicle as we joined her on her way to the airport. I wanted to witness her leaving the country. She made me nervous when she glanced in the rearview mirror as I tried to adjust my rumpled shirt.

"Ti Milliardaire, are you going to miss me?" she taunted.

"Of course, Mrs. Castor. How could I ever forget you?" I lied, knowing full well how much I hated her for calling me a good-for-nothing slacker.

Only later in that evening did I realize the full impact of my answer to her, because she was still in the country. The car pulled over to the curb across from the airport entrance, a pigeon on the curb hopping away. The driver got out first and swung the door open for Lucifer, extending his right hand to help her out. The door creaked on its hinges, and I could smell the gasoline the driver had used to oil it. We quickly got out of the car. A small ramp led to the airport entrance. Inside, the lights were dim, and a few boards were propped against the wall with names like Caribbean Airways, Pan Am, Air France. I walked around the large room looking at everything, especially the polished steel countertop, which gleamed in the feeble light.

Finally, it was time to say goodbye. We hugged her. She nodded, touched my head, and then grinned before bursting through the departure gate and walking across the tarmac to the airplane ramp. As she trotted up the ramp, she turned around and looked at us with a nervous stare for fear of flying; she waved shyly as we stood on the second balcony of the airport tower and waved goodbye to her.

Once more I thought about Rock's new creation, "Vada Retro Satana," and quietly looked away, awaiting the thrumming of the plane's engines. Soon, the tarmac was jolted with the rumble of the engines. The noise rose to a crescendo pitch, then stalled before her plane could rise into the air. The motor came to a screeching halt and died. We all looked at each other in silence. We waited and waited, and still the plane squatted on the tarmac. I wondered whether my brothers had begun to worry like me. After more than an hour, the airplane door opened and the passengers stormed off the plane.

The flight was canceled due to engine problems. Lucifer returned home that evening and looked more anxious than ever, but she was oblivious to us. "Even if the engine had started working, I would not have taken that flight today," she said, "I can always fly another day." She did not comment on our song during her farewell party, even though she must have heard it.

That night, before bed, I sat down below Dad's bookcase with my leftover meal on my lap, paging through one of the books. I became puzzled and frightened by the thought that Lucifer might never leave the house. But in the words of Cesar Chavez, as said in his address to the Commonwealth Club in San Francisco on November 9, 1984, "You cannot oppress the people who are not afraid anymore." I felt that way somehow.

But the next day, we did the same things we'd done the day before—the drive to the airport, the waving goodbye, the watching from inside—and this time the plane did take off. She was gone. For good.

Upon returning home from the airport, our neighbor, Madame Mombrun told us not to rejoice too quickly because the whip that had struck us wasn't entirely gone. Nevertheless, all four of us were full of hope with the world of possibilities that lay ahead and a hundred plans to choose from.

It would have been a complete joy to see Lucifer dead upon her arrival in Carrefour. But she had thrived instead. She'd lived to torment us until that clear summer day of 1974 when she left the country. I stood there thinking that I must pay the miscreant in kind for all the terrors she had put us through.

Looking back on the whole morass, I wanted to call Mrs. Castor "Lucifer" in her presence, but I was too scared of the consequences. She had no right to treat the innocent like the guilty. One wonders if it isn't true that the executioner of the death penalty is more culpable than the victim in deciding who lives and who dies?

Ivan Turgenev, the Russian writer of *The Execution of Tropmann*, said it best when he wrote in January of 1870, published in *The Art of the Personal Assay* on page 324 by First Anchor Books in New York in 1995, "And anyway, who is not aware of the fact that the question of capital punishment is one of the most urgent questions that humanity has to solve at this moment?"

13

Origins

*In overthrowing me, you have done no more than cut down the
trunk of the tree of the black liberty in St. Domingue—it will
spring back from its roots, for they are numerous and deep.*

—TOUSSAINT L'OUVERTURE

As Magrann said, we were the people from Montagne Lavoute. When Dad was fourteen, his right leg got infected from his shin to his ankle due to a mosquito bite, and it was natural that Magrann saw this as a rite of passage and an experience that would serve the youngster well.

If Dad wanted to take a long view of that incident, it began before 1850 with my great-grandfather Manassé Syverain. If Manassé had remained in Montagne Lavoute, a mountainous region where my great-grandparents lived with Dufrène Syverain, my dad's father, perhaps Dad would not have developed his severe image problem as a good-looking man. Thus Dad could say that his father Dufrène committed a big mistake when he came to live on the beachfront of Ti Mouillage instead of remaining in Cayes-Jacmel or even in Montagne Lavoute, near the city of Jacmel. He loved his parents deeply, which was why he gave his father's name to one of his sons and his mother's name to one of his daughters. But in life, nothing is ever as simple as it looks. Maybe if Dufrène had remained in Cayes-Jacmel, Father would not have been born.

Dufrène Syverain was born sometime around 1860. He was a stern man who became a major in the army, La Réforme, because the country had become so disorderly. For most of the country's extended period of independence, the oligarchs had selected only old illiterate men to be presidents. These mostly octogenarians could be controlled and did the bidding of the oligarchs. That led to the near collapse of Haitian society in 1915 after the country had its fourth president in two years, giving the US Marines a lame excuse to land in Haiti on July 28. Throughout its history foreign interference made Haiti's problems worse.

Dad's parents had migrated to Ti Mouillage upon completion of their thatched hut and in the wake of the deaths of two of their children from suspicious circumstances in the village of Cayes-Jacmel. Along with Orica, their first child, they had left that village and moved to Ti Mouillage, where Ilfrène, Milliardaire, and Princina were born, in that order. Grandpa believed in bestowing glowing names upon their children: Gold, Billionaire, and Princess.

Grandma Bernadette Boncoeur knew about life's hardships even before the loss of her second and third children. Her mother had died when she was only five. Her father, Espèno Boncoeur, an amalgam of a former Haitian slave and French master and a heartbreaker, was very much absent in her life. He traveled and populated every town he crossed, like his father before him, having many children with many different women. My grandmother married late; Grandpa Dufrène was thirty years her senior and had several other children before their marriage.

Dufrène always reminded his children not to confuse education with knowledge. He told them that God endowed humans with all the intelligence they needed and that it was up to them to use it wisely. Sadly, he treated Dad with suspicion, forcing him to leave home at sixteen.

Dufrène went even further and questioned whether my dad was his child. He thought Dad would one day embarrass him, somehow believing he would make debts that couldn't be repaid and gamble away everything the old man owned. Perhaps he would sell Grandpa's farm before he checked out. My grandpa spoke to Magrann about his angst regarding their youngest son.

"Bernadette, I met your man this morning, and it seemed that he wanted to beat me bad," said my grandfather. "He took off his hat and slammed it onto the ground, scared me with his gleaming white teeth that he'd finally had it with me." He stopped for a moment while his neck glistened with sweat, then gazed at Magrann. Then he spoke to himself while retrieving his pipe from the small table on their front porch and putting it into the corner of his mouth while adding more snuff. He continued the conversation, awaiting Magrann's reaction. He spat on the ground, then shook his head. "I almost got myself into trouble," he said.

Magrann leaned against their small dresser and opened the latches of their living room window to let fresh air enter their house. "Capitaine, you know that you are the only man I ever had in my life," she retorted. Grandpa had worked as a ship's captain sailing the coast of Haiti for many years, carrying coffee for the wealthy merchants in the southeastern region of the country. When he got old, he spent most of his time tending his fields during the day.

"I mean Milliardaire, your favorite child," he said.

"Capitaine, you know that Milliardaire would never do such a thing. He takes after you and is a fine gentleman."

My father had removed his hat in deference at the sight of his father, but the hat plunging to the sandy backyard ground had given my grandfather the impression that Dad was angry at his old man. Magrann couldn't corroborate the story since she had died in 1989 in Ti Mouillage.

Dad followed in his father's footsteps and left his family compound. He chose the life of an oarsman with the intensity of his father and the tenacity of his mother and refused to take no for an answer. Soon, the death of his father at eighty-six brought dejection to the family. Perhaps Grandpa's worsening alcoholism had caused it.

My father was already looking to the future with uncertainty. Soon, when he was alone in the world, he would discover the measure of a man. His boldness—or madness, as some called it—soon became apparent. After they witnessed a series of setbacks and failures in my dad's life, many of his friends kept their distance. He borrowed money to grow coffee. Then a drought came in and destroyed the crops with a ferocity that ruffled the young man as he sought a risky future.

He was healthy, handsome, and worked harder after his father's death in 1952. He was married and had already had a child, Marie, my half-sister, so he felt he needed to prove himself before his siblings, who may have doubted him. He became the first person in his family to move to Port-au-Prince, the capital city, seeking its promise of fortune.

Before he left the countryside, he took driving lessons on the rough, rutted road, kicking up dust for the twenty-kilometer drive and climbing the hills between the city of Jacmel and his hometown of Ti Mouillage. When an acquaintance of his saw him in the driver's seat, wrestling behind the wheel of a 1930 woebegone GMC truck, the man swore that Father could only be trained to ride a fat ass and not an automobile anywhere in the country.

Dad separated from Marie's mother after a scuffle where she hit him in the head with a chair and told him to go work instead of staying home playing bingo. He subsequently turned his attention to the teenager who became my mother. She lived five houses down the block from my paternal grandparents. By the time Father had exchanged the beach town of Ti Mouillage, with its meadows and brooks, for the noisy streets of Port-au-Prince, he had fathered four children with three different women.

My mother had bushy, furrowed eyebrows, brown eyes, a petite frame, and dark, cropped hair. She was not yet seventeen when she gave birth to Jean-Etienne.

Mother never returned to Ti Mouillage. What had she seen or heard or suffered there? Something tormented her, I suspect, but she chose to keep it a secret. Dad insinuated that Mom wasn't always sincere, but coming from him, how much weight could I give to his statement? As for my part as a child, Mom would say, "Leave me alone," when I asked certain questions. She kept private whatever ailed her until the bitter end. Though the world can always keep our secrets private, certainly it can't postpone our pain.

I spent the summer vacation of 1972 in Ti Mouillage, a charming town where you could hear the silky swoosh of the hulls of the canoes hacking through the water and the grumbling waves lashing against white, sandy beaches. The butter-yellow clusters of coconuts on the trees, the fishing, the greenery of the coastal range, and my grandmother's fried red snapper made this place unique. The grits with coconut milk and black beans, my aunties' warm hugs, and my cousins' charcoal-stained teeth from eating grilled corn on the cob made me laugh often. The fishing on the reef, the bird hunting, and the memorization of incantations soothed me to no end. The learning of all kinds of prayers, like "Protect me in the dark and keep away all evil," gave me a sense of safety. The mangos of the small family farm, roaming through town after town, and swimming in the sea from dawn to dusk, made for a happy existence.

The water glinted, the breakers foamed, and the waves crashed. A flock of gulls flew above as two groups of a dozen men, each bare-chested and wearing faded khakis shorts held up by a string, began to set out a net while standing across from each other. One hundred yards away, a fisherman at the helm dragged a dugout into the water and made a U-turn toward the beach, spreading the net. The women, most fully clothed but barefoot, and children, some naked and younger than I was, stood in parallel lines, waiting for the holding and pulling and rolling of the net onto the shore, hoping that the day's catch would be worth the wait.

They were seining—the peasant's safest and quickest form of fishing and an excellent way to scoop up schools of fish with neither bait nor boat. A canoe would do. If you saw seining and didn't understand it, you would think someone was drowning and that a rescue was needed. Once the line was fully spread and secure, the men would walk back to the beach in slow motion, each hanging on to its end and pulling until they could wrap up the net on the shore and collect their windfall.

My brothers and I arrived in Ti Mouillage in hopes of a respite from the brazen summer heat of the city. The ocean looked calm on the surface, though we knew it was blue and secretive at its core. We longed for sand in which to curl our feet. We took off our shoes and let the soft white sand silently warm our feet and tickle our sweaty toes and ankles. This corner of the island seemed like a fairy-tale garden with its light green hues, coconut trees, and various other tropical plants bowing over it. The road that twisted and paralleled the deep blue sea became more and more familiar with every footstep we took on it. A few yards away, fishermen took baby strides, watching and waiting for schools of sardines before casting their nets.

Every time a man smiled, but more so when he laughed, he added something significant to this fragile and sacred existence. Yes, this place! The Arawaks and the Tainos and my forebears had walked it centuries ago, just as my brothers and I and the villagers did that day. My waiting was worthy of all the smiles in the world. It paid to be amongst your own.

The crescent beaches of Ti Mouillage were the only playground available to the children who lived in the town. The ocean's proximity to the people's dwellings provided superficial, underground, clear water that helped feed a limited aquifer system where each family dug their well to provide water for showers, cleaning pots, and perhaps boiling some food staple that needed a tinge of saltiness.

As I lengthened my stride and inhaled the saltiness of the sea, my love for this place, this paradise, suddenly returned. The dry, fine, sandy soil is among the best in the country for coconut growing and very different from the beaches of Maui, Mykonos, Tahiti, and Cancun. The Eden-like, sandy beaches of Ti Mouillage allowed for gazing up at trees swaying, hugging southerly breezes and looking off in the distance at the blue, tortoise ocean and the backs of the Quisqueya Mountains. Gone were the nightmares of Carrefour.

This rich, serene swath of land stood as an oasis of cool away from the cruel existence and scorching heat of the capital. Ti Mouillage became my refuge and my salvation. Without me knowing it, this place provided me with the slow pulse of its meditative powers and a spiritual awakening.

The aroma of the beach village of Ti Mouillage was a blend of freshly cut green vegetation mixed with cow dung and diffused ocean spray. The village had its own scent, and upon my arrival in my childhood years, there was always the return of that pleasant odor.

Memory is a drug, and without it, we are nobody and might as well be extinct. Perhaps it is the singular reason why I keep returning to this place time after time.

Ti Mouillage was generally breezy and fair during these summer months. Le Massif de la Selle, the highest peak in the Quisqueya Mountain Range, was bathed in a thick, dense forest that shadowed the coastal areas below with a green hue. The mountain crossed the corridor, protecting the towns south of it from the suffocating, searing heat that affected Port-au-Prince on the other side of the range at the peak of summer.

In the evenings, my eyes searched the sky for everything that moved or glittered in the vast darkness of the countryside. I would gaze upward at those sudden streaks and flashes of light and shudder or have goose bumps and say "ooh." I'd shake with fear and wonder when someone suggested it was a sign of someone having died nearby. Many a night, I begged heaven to prevent that calamity from falling upon any of the roofs nearby, be it my father's family's house, or my mother's, or any of the aunties' or uncles' homes along the track.

On clear nights when it was all beauty, I would hurtle across the beach for a celestial view until the horizon, the sky and I became one. The stars looked closer against the vast expanse of the ocean and southern horizon and away from all the modern amenities of the city—honking cars, electricity, power lines, generators, flashlights, or the revving of an engine. All was quiet except for the distant barking of a lame dog and the squawking of a lone chicken.

The nights were pure, like a Nubian princess, the stars shining more brightly when a bright moon was absent. On rare occasions, streaks of light would move across the sky before they disappeared on the lower horizon. Many came from airplanes drifting through our sky on their way to South America or America. For a Haitian boy like me, it was a big deal to see a bird streaking across our night sky at altitudes greater than our highest Quisqueya mountain peak.

Each day in Ti Mouillage was a new adventure that drew me in like a rock cod to fish bait. At dawn, the thumping sounds of the fishermen dragging their canoes and oars from the shore to the bay and the splashing of their nets on the water made an echo of slumbering peace in the quiet of the rising sun. The smell of freshly caught smelts in the misty morning air would bring the village back to life as the locals gathered to haggle for lower prices as the fish splashed in buckets full of water.

Sometimes my cousin Toto (Desparbès Syverain) and I went swimming at the nearby coral reef. Timidly, I would crouch down and hold the scraggly, rocky part of the reef to avoid the crashing waves that threatened to sweep me into their deadly currents. The quieter the tide, the more pleasure I derived.

One evening, Toto took me walking on the beach, but it was not long before I tripped on the roots of a coconut tree growing past our yard, thinking I had seen a white colt in the pitch-black of that moonless sky.

"Cousin, are you all right?" he asked. "Remember to make good use of the prayers I taught you."

"I know. This beach is spooky at night. I have heard that monsters and werewolves roam it frequently, and you don't even tell me."

"Cousin, where did you learn this? Have you seen Papa Noël before?" he asked.

"No, I haven't. But monsters do exist. You may disagree with me, but I know they do."

"How can you be so sure? Have you met one in Port-au-Prince? You seem to know something that we in the countryside have yet to discover. Have you had some experience with the underworld? You talk about bakas, zombies, loup-garous, and zobope all the time. Has uncle Milli taken you to places where werewolves creep?"

"Why are you mocking me? You know I haven't lived with my dad since he moved to America."

"Then you are learning this from Tante Madou."

"I don't live with my mom, either. My stepmother's mom takes care of us."

"But who is she, then? Cousin, you know too much for your age. The things you talk about don't exist here."

"You know something? That lady I live with is a devil and a real werewolf."
"What?"

"Believe me, she is a werewolf, a real loup-garou. She tried to sell me before, and, once, I almost vanished in the night."

"Ti Milliardaire, let's return home. That story about vampires and ghosts scares me a great deal. You must have heard already how my mother died here in the countryside. A mistress of my father became jealous of her beauty and poisoned her. You know that each of my father's three former wives died around here. That's why when he remarried he decided to live in Thiottes, not in Ti Mouillage anymore."

I hurried and scurried, following Toto's footsteps on our way to Magrann's abode to rest for the night. Perhaps Grandma would have already lit the kerosene lamp. She would hold the light up, the glass globe as clear as limpid water, the wick glowing in the dark and dancing on the walls, the straw ceiling filling with the faces of people and trees and animals leaping. With one hand a few inches away from her face, she would look like a chalice figure and inspect each child before she retired to bed.

But before we arrived home, we continued with more stories of ghouls and ghosts in the stillness of the night. I was shaking like a coconut branch with goose bumps, my jaw tight and tense. When a soft breeze wrapped itself around my withered legs, my breath could be heard a mile away.

"Cousin, are you still scared?"

"I thought someone had come to put a rope around our necks to harm us." Panting heavily, I tried to hasten my pace as our place looked farther than it was. Barefoot, I wanted to walk faster but without stubbing my toes, bumping into a tree, stepping on a log, or worse, running into what I was running away from—the white horse amid the rustling coconut trees.

The sand was still warm under my feet, and yet I couldn't tell whether the rustling was coming from the galloping of a horse or the motion of trees bending and caressing the beach behind me. My arms were shaking, my throat was dry, and my feet felt like lead as I took several giant steps in the dark.

The faster I sprinted, the slower I seemed to be moving. Help was far from coming. Toto tucked his hands in his pockets and shook his head as we got home safely, but I was not of sound mind.

The longer I stayed in Ti Mouillage, however, the more my phobias of the dark retreated in the face of my carefree existence.

Magrann was the first person to teach me how to pray. At bedtime, she would call all of her grandchildren for prayer, and we would stand before her 10-by-5-foot bedroom. She would choose one child to hold the scapular and ask us all to kneel and close our eyes in adoration. Every time I would close my eyes, I was left to wonder, *how can I see God if I close them?*

Talking about evening devotion and prayers made Grandma happy. It was the only time she interacted with us, for she spent most of her daytime dealing with the clients who came to her small apothecary. She warned us that we should remain devout Catholics unless we'd resigned ourselves to going to hell. To save our souls, every night, she recited with us the Seven Virtues, the Seven Deadly Sins, the Act of Contrition, the Seven Sacraments, and the Litany of the Blessed Virgin Mary, amongst other religious recitations. She recited, "*Mea Culpa and Je vous salue Marie, pleine de grâce; Le Seigneur est avec vous. Vous êtes bénie entre toutes les femmes et Jésus, le fruit de vos entrailles, est béni. Sainte Marie, Mère de Dieu …*"

Some words were hurled at us in Latin and remained opaque to me. She told us to remember our history as a race who'd come to America hundreds of years before Columbus had set foot in the new world. For us, that world existed when our forebears came from Africa and built pyramids like the ones in Egypt in Mexico and throughout the Americas.

Bernadette Boncoeur Syverain reminded us that we were kin to an elite group of people who suffered and shed their blood and died so that we could be here. "Hence, Haiti must remain active in the struggle for liberation across the globe," she said. The name of the first ship they boarded off the coast of Ghana was called *Jesus*, after a dark-skinned man who came to save the world. King James II of England financed that ship in 1660 to propagate the slave trade instead of the Gospel. These kings were bent on making a buck at whatever cost, even at the expense of the Sermon on the Mount, and they had no intention of proclaiming it to free the captives or sending away the prisoners.

In the words of Martin Gray in *Le Livre de la Vie* on page 19 published by Éditions J'ai Lu, Paris, France in 1985, "Then I shouted at the Nazi officer. Yes, I am a Jew. And you can't kill me, you won't be able to. Yes, I was proud. For, if beasts in human forms could hit us, we Jews. If executioners could torment us, it's because we didn't belong to their race. Thank God for that." Were we to raise a holocaust museum for all those who'd died at the hands of these brutes during the great crossing or the Middle Passage from Africa to America? It would bear no name but would have a series of anonymous entries arranged over twenty million lines. They were people from the motherland—Africa, the cradle of all civilizations and cities—which gave birth to all the races and mothered all men, even those who turned on it as in the matricide of Greek tragedy. Africa has given us Timbuktu, the Nubian

Valley, the Great Empire of Zimbabwe, as well as Egypt, with its Sphinx and large broken nose. Just like today, no aborigines trod the soil of Haiti. "If Africa dies, the world would stop whispering at once," said an African sage.

As the ships cruised the thousands of square miles of the Atlantic Ocean, the sea became a burial ground for many of my ancestors. They were forsaken, but they are not forgotten. When they became sick—their captors fearing the loss of the whole cargo and blood money—they were thrown overboard even if they were not yet dead. Still, death was preferable.

My great-great-grandparents were among the few who made it across the Atlantic having embarked on ships off the coast of Africa with shackles on their feet and necks and chains on their wrists, en route to the new and terrifying world that awaited them. They were brought to South America, North America, Central America, Mexico, and all the Caribbean islands to grow sugar for the master race, a race that refused to toil the land in its laziness.

We still have families in Africa and cousins in the Americas. We live to bear witness for them with the obligation set before us that those who perished in the Middle Passage didn't die in vain—we, the sons and daughters of the less-than-strong tribes, given to the new continent for hard labor and sweat and blood. We enriched the Americas and Europe.

"There are seven qualities that one must acquire to overcome adversity: acceptance that life is unfair, hard work must go on, patience to endure, integrity in all circumstances, the humility of knowing that the tables will turn, assistance to those in need, and forgiveness to wrongdoers." My mother told me this once.

"The strongest people in the world are not those most protected: they are the ones who must struggle against adversity and obstacles and surmount them to survive." This was written on the back of a photograph of a group of slaves in 1861, on which also was inscribed the word *strength*. "The lynching of black folks, the raping of our mothers, the murders of black men at the hands of the oppressors, the use of a corrupt justice system to inflict hopelessness in a people pursuing its path, the violence against our children, the genocide against all others but whites, and the pathological fear provoked in white people when they meet black folks. However, black people are much forgiven as made by their Maker." Said Dad once.

14

CHAPTER

Payback

*Your eyes were a sea conch in which the heady battle
of your fifteen-year-old blood sparkled.*

AIMÉ CÉSAIRE ON EMMETT TILL

Ton Ilfrène's mouth dropped open as he listened to Magrann. His lips wrinkled as he swallowed his saliva. His head cocked as he learned about the misconduct of his son Toto's last twelve months. "Desparbès, pass here!" my uncle shouted. Toto was standing a few feet away when he heard his name. His spirit plummeted as he tried to grapple with his father's command to come forward. I stood near him, listening to the drone of a woodpecker working its magic on the trunk of a coconut tree. My uncle had no patience for a rebuttal, wanting payback instead.

Twenty minutes earlier, Toto, and I had returned home from our daily outing. Of course, the boy was frightened at the imposing presence of his six-foot, four-inch father. Uncle Ilfrène didn't look upset or menacing, but he was annoyed. My cousin stole furtive glances at him, smelled the air, and, like a cub eyeing his predator, chose to keep at a safe distance.

"Desparbès, I am calling you. I don't have the whole day to wait for you." My uncle heaved a sigh and went inside the house to talk to Magrann.

My uncle peered out at him like a lion on the verge of pouncing, veered in his direction, and lurched at him, but Toto escaped in the nick of time. Meanwhile, Josephine, one of Toto's older sisters, busied herself, her head down as she fanned a small blaze and fed it dry timbers. Soon, the fire flared, and jets of red sparks flew like rockets from the midst of white smoke. She blew on the small fire, hoping to turn the flames as hot as a furnace in preparation for the evening meal. She was in cahoots with her father, tracking Toto's every motion.

A large cooking pot was placed above three triangulated large stones. Josephine used dry coconut skins, timbers, and leaves to keep the fire going. She fanned it until the flame raged and fed it with new skins as needed until dinner was ready to serve.

Ton Ilfrène cleared his throat while crossing his lips with his finger, then walked to and fro inside the house and glanced out the window. As evening closed, my cousin got hungrier, so he pulled the casement window open and peeked inside. The smell of red snapper, black-bean soup, and grits wafting from the straw kitchen into the yard had become irresistible to the boy. Next, he stuck his face through the door and scanned the food on the table. I couldn't help him even if I wanted to. Toto turned to the left of the house and tried to enter through its backdoor but hesitated for a few minutes. He'd resigned himself to his fate because he needed to eat. My uncle hid behind the door, awaiting his prey. As Toto entered, my uncle went silent, his thin frame hunched over, until he could lunge at him. Toto was caught by the neck from behind.

My uncle then dragged him by his shirt collar outside the house. I feared for my cousin and I was afraid that his father was going to whip him the way that Lucifer walloped me many times in Carrefour or the way the French chafed slaves in Saint Domingue before 1793 I used to see in our history books.

Not wanted to witness what could occur I sprinted toward Grann Bébé's home, my maternal grandmother, a few houses down, gasping for air. "Are you all right?" she asked. I told her about what I was afraid of. She reassured me I was safe, even at Magrann's. It was fortuitous that I lived in both grand-mothers' houses.

Early the next morning, I crossed the street from Grann Bébé's house and walked up the beach. I went into Magrann's house through the back gate and found Ton Ilfrène sitting in the back of the house, looking pensive. "Good morning, Uncle," I said cautiously.

"Good morning, nephew," he said.

"Are you all right?" I asked softly. "Could I get you some water, Uncle?"

He raised his head and smiled. "I am well, nephew," he said. "I thought about what happened last night and what would become of Toto." He scratched his throat. "I didn't mean to frighten you. In the past, young men like him could have gone to Île de la Béate to earn a living in the fishing industry. They wouldn't be here making their grandparents' lives difficult. For the past half century, our neighbor, the Dominican Republic, has taken control of that islet. A country Haiti had occupied from 1801 to 1844. They did it under the pretext that their border includes it. Yet, from Les Frères, Le Fleuve Saturnales, La Baie de Neybe (Neiba Bay), the Bahoruco Mountains in the Southeast, all the way to the Massacre River (Fleuve Dajabon), in the north of the country, encompassing La Plaine de St. Jean, Roquille or Étang Salé, and Les Montagnes de Monte-Christi, which are among the most fertile part of the island, all belong to Haiti historically and eternally. To understand this better, you would need to look at an old map of Haiti soon after its independence. Or read about Le Traité de Bâle and the Treaty of Aranjuez, ratified on June 3, 1777, between Spain and France."

"You mean Haitians could no longer frequent our islets?" I asked.

"Yes, I mean none of us could go there as its rightful owners," he said. "But most of their border was moved westward, meaning the Dominican Republic took two-thirds of Hispaniola."

I gasped. A quiet man by nature and full of wisdom, Ton Ilfrène said, "From the most southern part of the country—Navassa Island, the tip of Tiburon, Les Cayemites, Île-à-Vache, Île de la Gonâve, Île de La Tortue, Île de la Béate, Cap de la Béate, Rivière Sèche traveling eastward to Punta Cana, they all belong to Haiti. Remember," he scoffed. "If our ancestors with flintlock muskets and other guns seized from the French could wrest Haiti from them and kick them out, what or who could keep us from regaining our land and islets again?" His face tightened. I knew little of what he was talking about. I wished only to see him go back to Thiottes, where he lived. Toto and I needed to go rummaging in the rustic plateau above Le Massif de la Hotte. If he stayed here, Toto could go nowhere.

"In life, the strong dictate the rules, but the weak live under them. For the weak, not having a sharp knife, like a nuclear bomb, is an invitation for the Goliaths of the time waiting and readying themselves to shackle our legs again. Haiti needs to be and stay strong." He wiped his mouth with the back of his hand. "They will one day apologize to you without paying reparations. How can you trust them?"

"But, Ton Ilfrène, Magrann said that the last could also be first."

"You said it well, nephew. If the last begins to work today with a vision and without asking for permission to be first. He shouldn't wait for tomorrow," he said. "We need to stop being fooled by our people who become agents of the enemy. They bend over backward instead of creating an inclusive society with inclusive institutions. Haitians need to choose their leaders well, in line with our forefathers who were courageous people daring to confront the invaders. Our armed forces should be there to deter the Dominicans from stealing our land while protecting the interests of Haitians. Then you will see that Haiti, the Pearl of the Antilles, reclaims its name. Quisqueya, our motherland, will be made whole; never again will invaders trample her. Remember our proud motto since 1803: 'Liberty or death.' Our mountains will be green. Our hills will be ripe with mangoes and corn husks. Our ravines will overflow with water, and our children will walk on the grass for ages." He looked above the roof of the hut and said, "Remember what the French did to General Louis Delgrès in Martinique in 1802. Eight years before, a slave descendant born in Jeremie (Haiti), the best warrior France ever produced, General Alexandre Dumas, the father of a future celebrated French writer by the same name, once fought a cavalry squadron by himself, commanded 53,000 troops across the Alps making France victorious in its Second Italian Campaign against the Austrian Empire. Napoleon nick-named him "the Horatius Cocles of the Tyrol."

Had I heard him correctly?

"Méfiez-vous des étrangers," he said.

Should we always mistrust our neighbor on the east of the island? I wondered.

"They could only slow us down, but can't stop our marching." He said, "Remember, the time will come where there would be a voluntary Haitian commando with the unique task of neutralizing at home and abroad those who prevent Haiti moving forward and block the uplifting of its people."

His statement rang hollow at the time and remained so until years later when I stumbled upon a French map of Haiti made in 1811. It read, "Carte Possessions Françoises Dans L'Isle D'Aiti, Communement Appellée Saint Domingue." At Stanford University Green Library in the rare books section, this map sat as if few hands had touched it over the last two centuries. But it was a reminder that what I had considered the fables and fancies of an old man were facts. It was vindication, for he dared to speak the truth and recall the past.

The rest of that summer vacation was drama free. What he'd said to me that morning about Île de la Béate was ominous for Haitians. No matter how one looked at it, Haiti should reclaim every inch of the territory our ancestors had passed down to us. Some say Haitians should at least popu-late their claimed territory. Sadly, the saga of Haiti (Quisqueya, Bohio) was one of foreign betrayal and graft in what became known as "the nightmare of Quisqueya."

Perhaps the Arawaks should wake up from those Baruhuco Mountain pits where they were slaughtered and buried at the hands of the Spanish conquistadors under forced labor and disease to take back their land from us for having given it away. In the meantime, Magrann's donkeys and goats and dogs continued to stomp the ground, making it flat and hard.

A week later, Grann Bébé and I went to the city of Jacmel, a three-hour walk from Ti Mouillage, to buy goods for her little store. It had rained hard the day before.

Her small house sat halfway below a shallow hill heaped with sugarcane trees. We left around four o'clock that morning so we could arrive when the stores opened.

At dawn, the air had been crisp, a fine spray having fallen through the mist, keeping us comfortable until the scalding sun peered in. Grann Bébé's straight back was outlined by her clean white cotton blouse as she plodded along. Her long, wispy, salt-and-pepper hair was tied up above her neck and flirted with the morning breeze. Making this round-trip on a hilly, muddy road under the hot sun was too much for a fifty-five-year-old person and would be a feat for a city boy, but I wanted to join her because I had a question.

Rue Stenio Vincent was the main artery connecting several towns and villages in southeast Haiti. In those days, it was a stretch of rocky mess. When it rained, the road was unsuitable for driving and worse for walking. That morning, Grann Bébé didn't give it much thought, for she had to run her errands. We simply left the stairs of our hovel, and soon she took the lead. At times, she slowed down, each step slurping up the mud. It smudged the back of her blouse with brown slush; her shoes were coated, the dense sludge moving toward her calves, her feet as heavy as two dumbbells. We lifted our legs like pulling logs uphill, pushing ahead despite shoes sodden with blobs of mud. Finally, I said, "Grann Bébé, what was that religious ceremony we attended last week about?"

She paused and peered into my eyes. "When you get old enough, you will understand what it all meant to us," she said. For the rest of the trip, I dared ask no further questions about that Assumption Day in Ti Mouillage. On August 15 of that summer, many family members had gotten the Crisis of Possession. Ton Bastien had swum in the water, boarded a mooring cargo boat, then climbed its mast, head down. Earlier that day, the big family cow had been killed, its meat cooked and served to family and friends. Most adults and children had joined in a chorus with dancing, singing, and prophesying. Family members trekked from our three farms located in Nan San Nom, Passe Candio, and Nan Télé to converge on the beach of Ti Mouillage.

Grann Bébé didn't answer my question, so I began walking ahead of her. We stopped along the way to drink from a stream. We stood under the shade of a large acacia tree to cool ourselves when the sun began to dance above our heads. Soon I began to develop a blister on the lateral aspect of both ankles. The wounds seemed to have opened and eaten almost to my bones. I had to stop walking for a while. The rubber shoes I wore could no longer withstand the heat created by the midday blaze. Grann Bébé advised me to take the shoes off to reduce further injury. We finally made it to the city and bought sugar, flour, indigo, soap, and spices, and then turned around to head back home.

She usually traveled this road within three hours each way, but that day, with the massive bog on the road and my foot injuries, we did not return home until early evening. It was worth it, however. I learned for the first time that I had been born near the city of Jacmel and spent my first two years with her. My mother had left me in her care after my birth so that she could return to tend to the older boys with Dad in Port-au-Prince.

Grann Bébé was sweet and even-tempered. Every day I had two breakfasts and two dinners. On some special occasions, Gran Bébé's younger sister, Tante Tabo (Eritha Pierre Dextra), would provide me with a fifth meal.

It pained Grann Bébé to see us go back to Port-au-Prince. Sadness overtook me each time she began to sing from her veranda while staring at the sea so that we wouldn't notice her tears. Her longing songs and mellifluous voice soothed me.

I thought about what I was leaving behind as we returned to Port-au-Prince at the end of summer: the overpowering scent of her brown-paper sugar packets, the shriveled sardines, the flanks of boiled plantain, and perhaps her akasan (fermented cornmeal porridge) served in warm milk with sugar. My hands would tremble as I brought the small brown paper bag to my nose—the last scent of the sea. Life often escapes us at our moments of weakest disposition.

As the summer wound down, Grann Bébé began preparing for our return to Port-au-Prince. The last evening before our departure, she sat in her rocking chair and softly teetered back and forth. She sang in her sweet, plaintive, sonorous voice one of my favorites, "Pran Kouraj Pa Febli O, Min Bondyé Nou Kap Vini O." She wept and sang while telling us to be courageous. Then she cried. My heart was near the breaking point. Each time she sang, "Be courageous for God is on His way," I felt carried away to a distant place where our forebears had gone.

Outside the yard, some Hispaniolan Trogon birds (Haiti's national bird) sat on an acacia tree branch and jabbered, "Tweet, tweet, tweet!" She had been good to me, and so was my mother. A poem I wrote says it all.

The Departed

I am the departed of these hundred homelands,
I have left my stars, my moon, and my thousand flowers,

    The sun of hot summers and my soft tarlatans,
The cold morning showers of my steamy rivers,
The dance and the drum that carry my prayers …
I dwell among your hearts where the sun soon to rise.
I am the departed from lands of misfortune
For which time can attest that my love never dies.
I have left my friends in search of good fortune,
Hoping to meet again all the known departed.
I am the emigrant of old town farm roads
Where people go barefooted in winter
As well as in summer.
Step by step, together they go to the rivers.
Over there I have learned to talk and smile.
So I knew then how to sing our songs.
Now I listen; I do not understand,
Neither knowing how to laugh
Or when to smile
Strange, isn't it?
Alas!
If earth is for us all, our eyes are windows
With no frontier in sight.
We all can meet again where life grows.
I have seen the rainbow right above in the sky.

15
CHAPTER

Confessions

I have known rivers
Ancient dark rivers
My soul has grown deep
Like the deep rivers.

—LANGSTON HUGHES

ucifer went to America in mid-1974, Benjamin, her third child, became our caretaker. Something had gone wrong. It was a bad choice, and it soon became obvious.

When Benjamin became our guardian, he was given complete license to molest, harass, and rape any woman who wasn't his relative. He even had the temerity to echo his mother's statement: "Even if I kill you, your dad wouldn't care." When Tante Orica stayed in our house, she lived in constant fear for her two teenage daughters' safety because of this twenty-five-year-old libertine roaming around. I learned this in 2000.

After Lucifer's departure, strange things began happening in the neighborhood. The dogs barked loudly, the cats meowed more forcefully in the house next door, and the crickets stridulated as if tomorrow were their last day on earth. Even the babies nearby cried as if they had the worst bout of colic they'd ever experienced.

Without being asked, I appointed myself mayor of the house, whether out of fear or folly. Perhaps Benjamin would be pleased that I had become a house detective if I didn't follow him. I began to watch who was going in and out of our home, whether pets or humans. So when Julienne started dating the cat-faced, bony-headed man from the city, I had a fit. I began to savagely tease this man every time he came into our backyard. I teased him for having a bow-legged posture and a tall, scoliotic spine. I teased him because every so often, spittle would fly from his lips with each word he uttered. But what business did I have bothering Julienne for dating this poor fellow? The guy seemed decent.

By now, Tang had died. For five months after his death, I wanted to get a dog. I wanted a mean dog. The house needed a dog who could chase people or take chunks from the fainéants' legs. I wanted a dog who could chase Julienne's boyfriend out of our yard for good. Of course, it would be justice. Yet caring for a dog was hard work. A friend who had heard me talking about dogs assumed any pet would do. I kept the reason why I needed a dog to myself. I finally told him that cats had always scared me as I was superstitious about cats while living in Haiti.

One sunny morning in 1975, I noticed a gray cat creeping between me and the custard apple tree in the backyard. Its flat tail lay still, then twitched a little; it looked like someone reaching for a revolver. It had long whiskers below a broad nose and grimaced at me as the cat curled herself inside the massive hole in the trunk of the custard tree. It looked like a lynx, and the thought made me shiver. Soon it began to hiss at me from that cave like dwelling, crouched and hiding away from the daylight. I thought the devil had finally appeared in the form of a demonic cat and wanted to do me harm—something Lucifer had tried to do many times but failed. I had heard plenty of church sermons. I had attended many religious services about the devil. The sight of the cat in the tree was an omen of things to come. For, sooner or later, I would find out where evil lived.

I ran to the back of the yard, grabbed a long, hard stick, and brought it back to the tree. The cat huddled, then arched its back like a caterpillar. I tried to dislodge it while shouting, "You devil, if death is your desire, then you will meet your master today!" The cat shrieked a crescendo pitch and licked its lips. It washed its face and rinsed its whiskers like a man in a creek. Then it screamed a sudden meow, sending me off at a quick gallop. It was all the proof I needed that it was the demon in the body of a cat, as mentioned in Revelation. Could that cat be Lucifer ferried from Boston to Haiti? Its eyes haunted me, watched my every move, paralyzed me with fear and dread. I was afraid of touching it, but it scratched its back against my legs earlier before flexing its paws.

It growled at me again, my stomach heaving and my heart racing. I hopped back and prayed the cat would get out and give me the peace I sought, but it backed farther into the hole, raining thunder into my gut. I stamped my foot against the trunk to scare it, but it screeched and retreated even farther. I gasped when it curled its tail and flapped it toward me. It turned its head from side to side and cocked it at me, then hissed and dug itself deeper into the tree, its widened pupils staring at me. This cat was a menace.

I raised the stick again and rammed it full strength, only for the cat to swerve and raise its paws at me, shrieking even louder, its eyes glistening like crystal water under the sun. A cold sweat ran down the inside of my arms, drenching my khaki shirt. No one was home to help me. I backed away from the tree trunk and once again ran to the back of the yard, where I located an empty bucket and filled it with water. I sprinted toward the tree with the bucket in my right hand, then lifted it to my waist and began to throw the water at the creature to dislodge it. But the soggy cat stayed put and purred away. Then it hissed and raised its paws at me again. It looked like the carnivore I thought it was, but I was no mouse or rat for this cat to feast on. I stopped and thought for a moment. I'd never expected to meet the devil right here in the backyard.

I grabbed the stick again and tried to thrust it at the beast, shouting, "In the name of Jesus, I am going to kill you, Satan!" With full force, I struck the cat on the head; it screamed and withdrew inside the tree again. I continued to ram the stick into the poor animal until it stopped wiggling and emitted a faint meow. Its sputtered once more as scum spilled on the wet bark floor and its paws stretched out from its limp body.

If I'd had a BB gun or an arrow or a Winchester rifle like the kids in America, the killing would have been faster and less tormenting but bloodier. The poor animal lay still, with not even a ripple in the air. Neither a fly passed by, nor a lazy bee buzzed. I grew cold and hot, with large beads of sweat dripping off my face. Suddenly I felt as if someone had been spying on me. I felt like a condemned man doing forced labor. My right hand began to shake. I had killed a cat. Something was wrong with me.

I wanted to bury it without bringing attention to my crime. I could throw it over into Madame Mombrun's yard. I scanned the yard, then took the stick and wedged it under the cat's midline, lifting it up. I sent it to its final resting place.

For the rest of the day, I went on with life but with a heavy heart. I felt some angst about the callous act I had committed. Was it true that the cat was the devil? I wondered. My conscience began to question my actions. Often, I thought of the limp body of the dead cat with its red eyes staring at me. I went to bed that night trying to forget the whole thing with some confessions made in my heart. What had I done? I had become a cat killer. Did I accept that the cat was Lucifer's ghost?

Early the next day, Madame Mombrun wasted no time in walking over to my house. She scorned me for carrying out such a riotous act and for trying to bury the evidence in her backyard.

A month later, Rock was brought home drunk. He wore a green headband made from part of a faded T-shirt. He acted as if he were a member of Greenpeace, giving everyone he met the V sign. All the while, he rambled on in French as though a rabid dog had bitten him. He had a mahogany acoustic guitar slung over his shoulder and shuffled past our entrance gate. One hour earlier, a Good Samaritan had rescued him from drowning in the ocean. He'd pulled Rock to shore after Rock had guzzled a pint of whiskey at a beach party ten blocks away. According to the Samaritan, his friends had laughed while he was drowning. They'd thought he was joking.

"People lack common sense these days," my neighbor said. In the words of my great-grandfather, Manassé Syverain, "Is it any wonder that the world is clogged up with misery? For few truly appreciate the gift of thinking."

Two weeks later, I was inside the house sitting down with my face in my hands.

"Wake up! Why are you so pensive?" Rock asked. "Are you well?"

"I don't know if I am well," I said. "Does it make any difference?"

"That's your business if you miss the devil!" he said. "As for me, I am having the best time of my life." He jostled me. "I am in bliss, as Voltaire says: 'I love luxury, beauty, and all types of arts and any honest man feels that way.' Do you feel that way?"

"What? This has nothing to do with Emperor Henry Christophe, General Toussaint L'Ouverture, or Emperor Jean-Jacques Dessalines," I said. "But it has everything to do with us and where we go from here."

"Well, think about it," he advised. "As for me, I am living the life I want while you think about it. Remember my song: 'Vada Retro Satana,'" he said. "Hope she never comes back to break your neck again." Rock stumbled out like a drunk leaving me ruminating about a recent disappointment at a tailor apprenticeship.

I lay in bed in my blue shirt and khaki pants as though I was grieving. I stayed in bed the rest of the afternoon, thinking about how freedom had its price. I had a sense of foreboding.

Three days before, the neighborhood tailor had muttered to one of my friends that he thought I belonged anywhere but in his shop. It had taken me the whole afternoon to sew four buttons on some purple fabric—fabric I had purchased to make what looked like a shirt but was rather a mish-mash wrap fit to dress a donkey.

"Yes. It's true that practice would make anybody but you better here," the tailor said.

He pedaled the sewing machine while the needle ran smoothly over the sleeves of a shirt. He stopped and made a notation in a ledger he kept in the drawers. Soon he stood, went to a cabinet, pulled out some fabric, and brought it to a chair close to the sewing machine, where he stacked it. He raised his head and shook it, looking at me. I stood there frozen and feeling confused and bewildered but said nothing.

I turned back and looked at that sewing machine powered by its wrought-iron foot pedal. The tailor's head was bent over it. I then understood that he was right.

"Ti Milliardaire, what makes you believe you could be a tailor?" the tailor asked before sending me home.

I said, "*C'est en forgeant qu'on devient forgeron.*" It was practice that made things perfect. I repeated that mantra, telling him of my desire to prove myself worthy of his time. I could learn only if I could practice. I tried to keep myself busy when these words leapt from my lips as though I didn't believe them myself. *Well said,* I thought. Borquière, my tailor teacher, didn't buy it and had a retort. He wanted to trap me, for he said it with such fury and exaction. I thanked him for that lost opportunity as I exited his one-room shop two blocks from home.

I walked home, defeated, a lump swelling in my throat. I promised myself I would not cry from the humiliation. That afternoon, I felt like a water-boarded prisoner ready to be pounced upon by General Jean-Baptiste Donatien de Vimeur de Rochambeau's imported angry canines during the Haitian Revolution.

16

CHAPTER

The Clouds
Came Crashing

When history sleeps, it speaks in dreams:
on the brow of the sleeping people, the poem is a constellation of blood.

—OCTAVIO PAZ,
"Toward the Poem"

On a bright Saturday morning in the summer of 1977, Rock was outside in the yard and began his day with a rambling talk. As soon as he sat down, he would stand up again. He did it several times. He'd had bouts of the jitters in the past, but that day was different because when he hollered, one could hear him a block away, even with all the noise of pedestrians and traffic. He finally strode inside the house. Benjamin was the only grown-up present that day.

Three days before, Zagalo had returned from America for a two-week vacation in Haiti. He became a sensation for the neighborhood youth overnight. "Pretty soon I will be able to build my house in the States. It will pivot on hinges and provide me with a 360-degree view of the city. It will be a house on a hill." Zagalo continued, "My brain will be stuffed with the knowledge that allows me to read anyone else's mind." The kids there were fascinated but skeptical of his deliberations.

Hans Semelfort, my protégé, with his brown moccasins in tow, confided to me afterward: "If he could read everyone's brain, how much can he read his own?"

Rock began to miss school. He wandered the streets of Port-au-Prince most weekdays instead of spending time in the classroom. He pocketed his school tuition. No grown-up gave it much thought until one day in late June he came home drunk and strumming his guitar. His friends had brought him to us since he'd gotten confused about finding his home.

Rock ran toward me and, with fear in his eyes, began screaming, "My heart is itching in my chest, and I am dying!" I had no idea what he'd ingested that morning. As he walked, he writhed with a jerky, unsteady, to-and-fro motion of the middle part of his abdomen and let out another long, piercing howl. He stood, hunched over and pale, holding onto a chair before sitting down and sobbing. With his left hand, he motioned for me to come over. I walked back to the living room and dragged a chair over, sitting down next to him and thinking that he was leaving us for good. He was the smarter boy in the house, and it would be horrible to lose him.

"Comrade, I am dying. I am dying. Put your hand on my chest and tell me what you feel, brother," he begged.

I approached him and placed my right hand on the left side of his chest, looking for the faintest sensation or pulsation. "I don't feel anything," I informed him.

"Put your hand again. Don't you feel that it is beating with a slow tick-tack?"

"Well, I don't feel it at all."

His eyes twitched. "I knew it. I am dying."

I looked at him and wondered if it was going to be the last time I saw him alive. "Stay here," I said and went outside the house, sweating.

A car engine roared down the block. I peered through the open gate to spy on the passing vehicle. Benjamin's friend Crapo sat behind the wheel of an old Volkswagen Bug. The tailgate dragged on the floor as the car zoomed by at full speed. It passed our gate before coming to a screeching halt. Crapo swung the car door open and sprinted inside the backyard, asking, "Where is Benjamin?"

I told him he was in the living room with Rock. Together, Crapo and Benjamin lifted Rock and sat him in the car to take him to the general hospital.

After twelve hours, the hospital sent him home. When he came back, he was as calm as a clam but forlorn. He sat in a corner, looking at the wall with a blank stare and barely moving his head. Benjamin said nothing. Though I wanted to know what was wrong, no one told me.

I was embarrassed when the people gathered outside, looking at us in pity or amusement.

The morning after his hospital visit, Rock sat still, his face sullen and puzzled, and nodded at me as I passed him. He asked me in a low voice if I could call the young doctor who lived two houses below ours to come and see him. He told me he felt weak.

Dr. Kepi showed up thirty minutes later with a black bag in his right hand and dressed in a white shirt, blue trousers, and red bowtie. He sat down with Rock and asked him a few questions while examining him. Next, he pulled out his long black stethoscope and asked Rock to remove his shirt and lie down on the family couch. As he started listening for Rock's heart, two large creases popped up on his forehead. "Hey, Rock Madichon, did you get any medicine from the hospital yesterday?" he asked. "I notice that your heart is beating rather slowly." Rock pulled a small bottle from his pocket and handed it to him.

"Well, do you have glaucoma?" Dr. Kepi asked.

"No, I don't."

"Oh, you don't. But this is a glaucoma medicine you are taking."

"Could it be the reason my heart seems to beat so low?"

"I am not saying that it is the cause, but it could be."

"Am I dying, Doc?"

"I don't know."

The young doctor picked up his bag, waved goodbye, and told Rock to stop taking the medication. The night was painful. No one seemed to sleep as we all waited to see if Rock would survive and what would happen next. He wailed and kept asking whether he was dying. I wanted to know what he had done that had brought him to this predicament in the first place, but I didn't want to make him feel worse than he already did.

Zagalo said nothing. He remained indifferent of what was happening to Rock. They had been buddies and classmates in middle school. Rock survived the night. He continued to complain that his heart was itching and that he could only see things up close, and he was no longer interested in anything, not even food. Then he confessed that Zagalo had given him a powder originating in the States.

"I don't know what it was. The stuff held promise that I could travel far and back in time and I could see my life displayed before me in a futuristic sort of way. I would not need any soothsayer or palm reader to tell me anything about tomorrow." We were all aghast. We had never heard of something like this in our rustic Carrefour, much less from a family member.

Deep inside, I was angry at Zagalo for bringing drugs to Carrefour. Rock needed help for his behavior. I know Zagalo had been emancipated in traveling to the States. He had seen the world, but I couldn't understand why he would bring drugs to Haiti in his turpitude. He was likely more troubled than Rock. I felt I needed to say a prayer.

On Sunday morning, I woke up early to attend Mass after what I had seen at home with Rock. I had to say thanks to Saint Michael Archangel, Saint Peter, and even Saint Thomas. It was as though Rock had been rescued from the mouth of Crète-à-Pierrot, a famous Haitian hill, during the battle of independence.

Still, that didn't dampen my enthusiasm for attending Mass when grown-ups would invite me to come along. That morning I dressed in my white cotton shirt, a pair of navy pants, black socks, and black shoes. I pushed the front gate open and turned toward the main road. The houses in the neighborhood lay quiet. The sun climbed up, and the moon hung above it while a cool breeze succored my anxiety as I looked around. I walked the road and heard not a peep on either side of the street except for the barking of a small dog. An old man bellowed for it to shut up in the far corner of a yard I passed.

I continued my stroll and soon began humming. I took a gravel road and ran to cross the main artery in Carrefour on my way to L'Église Saint Charles at the edge of town. I needed to get to the church in time for the first Mass. As I approached Saint Charles, I heard a sudden burst of activity, along with a display of musical sounds.

A young girl came out in front of a house holding a water bucket in her right hand. As she stood there waiting for me to pass, she lifted the bucket and placed her left hand around it, clutching it to her breasts. She then began to sprinkle the dusty floor with water, a tradition of country folks. I jumped before the water sprayed my shoes, then turned and looked at her.

She told me how lucky I was for not getting wet and hoped I would do better at staying at a distance from the place. But she wasn't done with me yet and felt it necessary to open her front gate and let her crazy, scruffy, oversized terrier go after me. The dog dashed straight at me and snapped his jaws into one of my trouser legs, getting a piece of it. I panicked and cowered in the middle of the road before I shoved my right hand at his head. I should have been more cautious. Earlier, I'd noticed this dog jumping around the fence in the backyard, yapping, growling, drooling, and poking his snoot at the gate.

If only I could muffle his barking, I swallowed my words. Times like these made me reminisce about how Lucifer could pacify any unruly dog. She would feed a canine with an undercooked bloody sausage, a boudin of sorts, laced with rat poison. I'd paid the least attention to that mean-looking assassin as his squinty eyes became riveted on me. Fido meant business that morning. He gave me a good dose of attitude adjustment before I got to Mass.

The road to Saint Charles on Sunday mornings was always a lonely affair. There was a line of people standing outside the church door, spilling onto Main Street. There was a procession, so I joined them. We left the front of the church and headed right, in the direction of Mariani, a nearby town. A white-robed priest with a potbelly led the crowd. At his side were two choir boys carrying the incense lanterns, the smoke from the lanterns spreading out and pervading the air under the warm sun.

Laboring up on the hard pavement made me resentful. The sun had already dried the morning dew as well as the water that had been sprinkled in front of the stores. The sun scorched our parched lips, but few seemed to care. It was my first and last time in a procession, for I didn't know the distance the churchgoers would trudge from Saint-Charles to the next town. The old and young walked together intimately. Parents held their small children's hands. The teenagers laughed and giggled with their friends all along the route. I knew no one.

The priest dug in after having walked this road several times before I was told. The faithful continued their singing, their faces and foreheads drenched in sweat and reflecting the glistening sunrays in a cloudless sky. The crowd steadily climbed the small hill on the sparsely inhabited road. There were empty fields and small farms on either side of the road. A rooster crowed its exalted cock-a-doodle-doo long enough for everyone to hear.

Looking behind me, I saw the church had disappeared. Soon the green fields were replaced by a sparse, brown, parched land crisscrossing the heat-baked mountains, as if a fire had recently razed the place. A man sat high on his horse, strutting around and looking at us but saying nothing. He shook his head and laughed at the passersby.

"Where is Mariani?" I asked a middle-aged woman in the crowd. "Are we going to turn back soon?"

She looked at me and said nothing, until another rooster crowed, "That depends on Father Boursicot. We may be here for a while."

I gasped. "At Saint Charles, a procession is a full-day affair."

She continued. "Remember, child, that he who loves sleep would grow poor. Stay awake and you will have food to spare."

It grew hotter. Father Boursicot wore a straw hat and began to wipe his face with a handkerchief as he continued on without goading anyone or saying a word. Grudgingly, I trudged on, but soon I began to fall behind the crowd, my stomach growling. The mass of people headed straight to the rolling plains that stretched to the water's edge. On the green grass to one side of us, cattle, pigs, and goats grazed in an open meadow; horses, asses, and mules grazed to the other side. A limpid stream on a bright patch near the road babbled quietly.

The parade had finally left me. I needed to slow down and turn back. I had wasted a whole day of my life. It was time to turn back without having to worry about Lucifer. I cared only about going home.

Before I arrived home, word had spread among my friends that I'd lost my mind going to Saint Charles.

"Here he comes." My friend Hans sighed. "Ti Milliardaire, we have been looking for you all day."

"Are you all right? he asked. "Your face looks gaunt and pale today."

"I am well, Hans."

"Where have you been?"

"I went to Saint Charles and spent the whole day walking in a procession," I said.

He guffawed. "You mean to tell me you spent the entire day of Sunday walking in a procession? That's deep, my friend. Have you committed some awful sin?" he asked. "Why would you spend a whole day walking under a frightful hot sun? What did you do wrong? I can't believe this."

"I am not atoning for myself or any sin committed by my forebears. They never killed anyone. They didn't sell their brethren so that they could grease their cheeks for another day. They didn't buy anyone to slave for them. They never made people work without paying them their wages. They never lied to anybody to get them in trouble or got them thrown into prison so they could eat. They never mistreated anyone to get ahead in life. How could I atone for myself?" *I needed to atone for the cat's killing*, perhaps.

"You don't need to be angry, Ti Moléon."

"I am not angry," I said. "I wanted to attend Mass but didn't know today was going to be a day of procession."

Hans was still doubtful. Though I knew I was innocent, I felt guilty being questioned by a friend who treated me as though I were inventing things.

A week later, the other kids in the neighborhood gathered in front of my house and came to my rescue. Two feet away, Harry looked at his watch. "Hey, guys, it's time to go to Ticam playground," he said. "Ti Moléon, are you coming?"

"Of course, I am coming," I said. They all laughed. "Everybody loves a good soccer game." I went inside the house for a pair of shorts, then left for Ticam.

"Ti Moléon, let's go over there and check out that bike," Hans said to me. "It is a better Phillips than all the rest. I heard the guy who owns it is looking for a buyer."

"Let's find out," I said. "How much did the seller ask?"

"I am not too sure," he said. "I heard he wanted ten dollars for the bike."

I juggled some numbers in my head as we walked to meet the seller. At fifty cents for a fifteen-minute rental on weekends from morning until late afternoon, I would break even very soon.

"I am only asking ten dollars for the bike. It is a brand-new bike." The seller must have been about eighteen years old. He confessed he had been kicked out of Canada three months earlier. He said nothing about why they'd returned him to Haiti but admitted he wanted to sell the bike because he needed the money. It was Sunday afternoon, so we told him to wait. He looked impatient and like he wanted to sell the bike for a quick buck.

"Can you wait until next weekend to sell your bike?" I asked as he avoided our gaze. "I would be able to buy it then." I needed time to think it over, but more than that, I needed time to collect the money.

"Whoever comes first with the money will get the bike!" he shouted.

"Hans, what do you think?" I asked. "Do you think this is a good deal for us?"

Hans Semelfort was not only a friend and protégé but a financial adviser. "I think we can earn a handsome profit if we buy this bike, Ti Moléon."

I stopped, touched the two rear pockets of my shorts, and counted out seven dollars. That was all my treasure. I sent Hans on a dash to talk to our friends about collecting a three-dollar loan while I continued negotiating with the seller, my negotiation merely a distraction so no one would outbid us while we raised the needed funds.

Only two days before, I had visited my half-sister, Gertha Sanon, who ran a small grocery store in downtown Port-au-Prince, a few blocks from my junior high school, College Bird. She had given me five dollars, which I'd folded and placed in my wallet, along with my two-dollar coins. I'd thanked her and said goodbye, but not before I had surfeited myself with peanut butter and bread from her shelves. Harry Guerrier, Marco, and Hans each loaned me one dollar.

Hans cracked me up in a giggle. "Ti Moléon, now we are ready to buy the bike."

"Monsieur, does your bike run well?" I asked. "With that kind of money, we want to make sure the bike is working."

"What are you talking about?" he said. "Can't you see for yourself?"

"I know. We want to make sure it's worth our money."

Within twenty minutes, the deal was done. It was dark by the time we left Ticam playground and went home. Hans and I took turns riding the bike. I pushed the bike into our backyard and locked it inside the house.

Loulou, another kindred friend who lived in the house behind the wall that divided our dwellings, invited me to share his meals with him. After lunch, he wanted me to sample a capful of the five-star Haitian whiskey called Rhum Barbancourt. I did.

"What does it taste like to you?" he asked.

"I don't know," I said. "It smells like alcohol and tastes like my grandma's medicine."

He reached above his head and pulled something out from behind an armoire. "You would prefer that Prestige beer instead—the best we make in Haiti." He giggled. "Try it. If Fritz finds me drinking his Barbancourt, he will whip my butt," he said. "But I don't care."

"But what about that fizzler you are holding?" I asked him. "Does it taste like a Cola Couronne?" He offered me a swig of Prestige, the national beer. His older brother was away from home that day and wouldn't know what his sibling did in his absence.

"Why do you drink it after eating your meals?" I asked.

"I don't know. I guess it's for fun."

"Is it worth taking a beating for?"

"I don't think so."

"In any event, I come here for the meals, not the grog."

"By the way, I heard you have a bike," he finally said.

"Yes. I have a new bike. I intend to rent it on Saturdays and Sundays during the soccer games at Ticam playground. I could rent it here in the neighborhood streets too."

"Can I take a ride?"

"You can, Loulou. Do you know how to ride a bike?"

Loulou had moved to our neighborhood only a few months earlier, having lived in Aux-Cayes, the largest city in the south of Haiti, before coming to Carrefour. I took him outside the yard into the street.

"Okay, Loulou, you sit still. Hold the handlebars. To move forward, you need to pedal forward, and to stop the bike, squeeze hard on the left brake lever and move the pedals backward."

"I see," he said.

I held him while he mounted the bike, and he finally took off on his own. He returned the bike, thanked me, then jumped the fence and slid into his backyard.

Early Saturday afternoon, I rode the bike to Ticam Park to begin offering paid rides.

A day later, while we were watching soccer games at Ticam, two boys came in to rent the bike for half an hour. They each paid their fifty cents. I wanted to play soccer, so I called Hans over and told him what he needed to do. He brought the bike to the far corner of the field where the boys could safely ride it, and I hurried to join the game on the other side.

Fifteen minutes later, I heard a commotion. "Ti Moléon, hurry up!" Hans shouted. "The police have seized your bike."

"My bike?" I said under my breath. "Impossible. It must be a mistake." I raced to meet him.

The officer shouted, "What's your name?"

"Milliardaire Syverain Junior."

"And you, little boy, what's your name?" he asked Hans.

"My name is Hans Semelfort, monsieur," he said.

"You are lying," the officer said.

"He is telling you the truth." I didn't want Hans to be in trouble with his parents for my problem.

"Sir, is that your bike?"

"Yes, it is," I said again.

The officer turned toward me and asked, "Where did you buy this bike?"

The officer then asked me to accompany him for possession of stolen goods. By then, the police officer was pushing the bicycle to the police station. I followed, pleading with him to give my bike back.

"Boy, you mentioned that you bought that bicycle last week. Could you tell us where you got it and how much you paid for it?"

"Well, I purchased it on the soccer field from a gentleman."

"Do you know his name?"

"Oh no, I forgot his name."

"So, you are telling me you bought this bike from somebody you don't even know." I knew then that he had good cause for suspicion.

"We are going to lock you up for stealing that bike," he said.

I protested to no avail.

"Wait, officer!" Hans said to him.

"On our way here, I saw the guy who sold us the bike a week ago standing in front of the Cric-Crac Ciné Theatre."

"Could you take me there to meet him while your friend stays here?"

That afternoon, I knew that my tail was on fire. The sale has gone sour. How had I gotten myself into this mess, I wondered? They'd arrested me for having a stolen good.

Hans and the officer had already dashed out of the police station looking for the bike seller.

Meanwhile, I sat on the bench in the lobby near the front door, hoping for the best. At least I could try to escape. I looked at a sea of people all dumped into one room and huddled upon one another. *My God! What am I doing here?* My head pounded, and my heart raced. The two officers inside the station pulled a welded wire door behind them and leaned on the back wall. They talked among themselves.

By then, groans were coming through the open back window. *Jesus, how in the world did I find myself here?* I thought. *If Jean-Etienne comes home and doesn't find me, I am going to be in trouble again.*

It was thirty past five on Sunday afternoon. My heart quivered every time an officer arrived. *Are they going to book me?* I asked myself as I sat on the bench. Inside the station, the noise got louder, and an old man shouted, "Let me go home, you young rascals! Do you have any respect for the old? I could be your father, Officer. Do you have any conscience? What did you learn from your parents?"

I feared the worst. I would be in jail tonight. That would be too great a burden for my older brother, Jean-Etienne, who by now had become our caretaker since Benjamin had gone to America. I never knew that blessing and burden lived in the same quarter. I wished Lucifer were still in Haiti. I would have been home instead of roaming the streets trying to make a few bucks renting a stupid stolen bike.

After about an hour of waiting, Hans could be heard talking with the investigative officer. The officer pushed the front gate of the police station open, the bicycle seller in handcuffs beside him. We came face-to-face. I turned my head away from his mean stare.

Hans craned his neck inside the police station and motioned to me that it was time to go. "You may leave now!" shouted the police officer. "I got the real thief."

I thanked him for his diligence and bolted out.

Neither Hans nor I spoke on our way home. My nerves were rattled as I entered the gate of my house. Hans walked away and pushed the wooden gate of his family's ground, which sat at an angle to mine.

"Oh, wait, wait, Hans. I forgot to thank you for finding the thief," I said. "I will see you tomorrow."

It was seven o'clock in the evening. *Last week I followed a procession at Saint-Charles, and tonight I almost went to prison. So much for those prayers made,* I thought as I turned to go inside my yard.

17

CHAPTER

Watch Out

Imagination is magic carpet,
Upon which we may soar,
To distant lands and climes.

— SUN RA

With Lucifer gone, as we had no fear of reprisal and no confinement, my brothers and I started spending more time outside our front gate. But I soon discovered that not staying in the house all the time had its risks. Before long, I would be tested again.

A week after Lucifer had left the country, Marco, Harry, and I climbed a concrete wall and jumped over a fence, intending to steal oranges from the owner's farm. It was five blocks away from home. Two days earlier, we had noticed that the farm was gorged with oranges and that they were falling off the trees.

After sliding down the grainy concrete wall, we landed on the ground. The hunger pangs in our stomachs wouldn't go away. As we began to move forward, we were jolted by the sight of a fierce, skinny, tall, and mangy dog. Its tiger like jaw awaited us. We ran before it could lunge at us and clap its saber-like teeth into our bony little asses. Luckily, we escaped in one piece, flying over the fence before it could reach our legs.

I spotted a young boy my age scurrying down the corridor in front of my backyard every Friday afternoon. He was well nourished and intimidating. Every time he passed, he gave me or Harry or Marco a mean face. Every time he looked at me, he filled me with terror and I turned my eyes away to avoid his.

One Friday afternoon, he stopped by while the three of us were playing soccer in the street. Soon Marco felt a thud on his shirt and a shove in his chest. Harry's left ear was pulled, while the young thug stomped on my foot. We took off, emptied the street, and dove into our yards, shivering in fear. The boy was looking for any excuse to beat us up and shove us around. We stayed home until the sun turned a luminous pink, orange, and salmon against the deepening indigo of the sky, and then was gone as the passing wind.

Another Friday came, and when we saw him a few meters away, we ducked out of the street before he could ram us again. Soon, we stopped playing in the street in front of our houses on Friday afternoons. Every week, the boy looked stronger, bigger, and meaner than he had the last time we'd seen him. He delighted in terrorizing us without cause.

It was on one of these Fridays that I noted how beautiful the coconut tree branches in our yard had become. As few doves jostled them about, I had an epiphany that better days could be ahead.

From the back porch of my house, I could hear people passing by and laughing. I heard Madame Mombrun Nelson talking to her boys. She said, "Go take your showers before your father gets home."

That evening, I knelt and, like a wandering zombie, blubbered something like a long prayer. I did that often. I went to bed making the sign of the cross until I fell asleep at the edge of the mattress. I played inside my yard because I feared the bandit. I had a vision that I was a cowboy riding on a plain under an indigo-blue sky with a bright sun. A soft breeze caressed my face, and the hooting of hungry birds sounded in my ears. I had a lasso in one hand, ready to do battle and catch a bull.

A few weeks passed, and then, one day, for some crazy reason, I wanted out. I was tired of staying indoors, though I dreaded that something terrible would occur one of these Fridays. A nervous feeling enwrapped me, but staying in our backyard every Friday afternoon had become unbearable. It had ceased to be a viable option after a grueling week in school and with homework to complete over the weekends. A cage could be both a bulwark and a barn. To kill a kid like me in his cage would be grotesque at best and cowardice at worst.

All week, I ruminated about my plan to escape my prison. I forgot to inform my little brother Marco and our friend Harry of my fiendish plot. I plucked a branch from a small coconut tree in the front yard, peeled away its fresh twigs, and left it in the corner of the backyard to bake under the scalding sun for five days. I smirked as I looked at the perfected product, then let out a guffaw that puzzled and shocked the boys.

That Friday in school, I merely watched the instructor's mouth move. I had fallen into a trance that took me home. That afternoon, I left school with élan and boarded a tap-tap to Carrefour. Days of gaiety were a rarity in Lucifer's time, and this time in my life needed savoring before it turned gray again.

We didn't use batons, knives, guns, or clubs in those days. But a good drumstick in the hand was something even Lucifer wouldn't have objected to. My cause was just. Before I entered the house, I inspected the bare, thorny-looking branch that lay in a corner of the front yard. I let out another hoot of laughter for the third time that day. That insolent visitor, that bully, that boy with a snarky look needed restraint. He'd made his weekly presence felt.

Lunch had no appeal for me that afternoon. I put my hands in my pants pockets and went outside with Marco and strolled around the yard. Then I called Harry to join us to play our soccer game in the street.

As if by mutual consent, no one said a word. Boy Who Makes Us Run on Friday Afternoons would drop in soon. This time would be different. I kept looking into the distance without bringing attention to myself or putting fear into the boys. Around four thirty, I noticed a head bobbing about a hundred feet away. He was sprinting as though he was late for his destination. I turned toward Marco and Harry and told them the truth about the bandit's coming.

"Eh, guys, the boy is near. This time we are staying here in the street and making a line starting from Harry's to my place." I stood in the middle with my hands folded behind my back. I said, "We are going to stay still and face the lad today."

"But Ti Moléon, he is a big guy," said Harry Guerrier. "He will bang us again like he did the last time."

"Ti Moléon, this guy is horrible. He could hurt us," Marco said. "He is a cannibal." Meanwhile, I fiddled with my handiwork.

"This time is different, brother, because I have a bare coconut stick with me," I reminded them. "We can thump that bandit. This stick will make a huge difference for us today."

That was no assurance. The boys were scared, and my hands shook like a patient in shock. Though Lucifer had gone to the States, my scrawny legs and arms were still withered and weak. But I tried to stand up straight.

Like most brazen young men, this young buck didn't have any sense that danger loomed. Instead of quietly passing by on his route to go buy his grandma's snuff tobacco, he pushed me, booming, "Get out of my way!"

I became agitated. Before he could say another word or shove the others, I drew the stick out from behind me and raised it two feet above his head. I saw a flash of fear, like a nuclear explosion, in his eyes. Swoosh! Without another thought, I slugged it full strength into his face. Before the blood began to flow, a piece of flesh was scratched away from his left cheek. It fell off and exposed the white skin underneath. Then his blood spurted, splattered, and began to drip, drop by drop. At the sight of the onslaught, I threw the stick away, then froze. We broke into a run going one way, the lad sprinting the other.

We escaped home. We knew we were in trouble for hurting somebody badly. We feared that his parents or guardian would quickly come into our neighborhood with a Tonton Macoute, the dreaded militia, and arrest us all for hurting their child. I guessed that he'd scooted out looking for cover and perhaps became afraid of losing his life or an eye.

Only a few weeks earlier, I had gotten into a brawl with Harry's older sister for shoving Marco. The boys argued over calling each other names. The day after, onlookers reminded me I was too young to be fighting with students like her. The whole incident had taken place a few blocks from our homes on our way to school. I had gone overboard for a minor aggravation.

We stayed home for the rest of the day and weekend. After a week, we resumed our play as though nothing had happened and, sure enough, the boy never took that road again.

But one trouble followed another. The reality of my questionable judgment began to unnerve and terrify me. I'd promised an old classmate that I could get him a seat at Lycée Alexandre Pétion as a high school freshman. He agreed that his admission was guaranteed.

Gaining admission to public school in Haiti was difficult. All public schools were free of charge, but they had very few seats, meaning most children weren't able to go to school. Private schools were reserved only for those with financial means, and so often, the brighter ones stayed home doing chores since they had few connections and no money.

Before school started, Sauveur Pierre Étienne came to my house and brought me a twenty-dollar bill for a bribe to get his name onto the school roster for September 1977. I gave the money to Rock, who promised me that a state employee down the street would take care of it in no time. Before Sauveur Pierre Étienne's name was on the roster, I told him he could join me in class for the lectures at Lycée Pétion. The young man heeded my advice and trustingly came to school, taking his seat like everyone else.

Sheepishly, he sat near one of the enormous windows since he couldn't prove to other students that he was legally there. Five days a week, he came to class to tame his unquenchable thirst for learning. At our previous school, he'd introduced me to Oswald Durand, Montesquieu, Alexandre Dumas, the irreverent Voltaire, and Blaise Pascal, the author of the *Pensées*. With hunger pangs in his stomach, he remained relentless in studying dead

Haitian and French philosophers. You have got to respect teenagers of such caliber, drive, and passion.

Thanks to Ton Bastien's pedigree, he got me into the Lycée that year. Dad could no longer send money from Boston for my private school tuition, his salary being insufficient. My uncle had attended Lycée Pétion a few years earlier. Later on, he went to the school of agronomy at the state university. He had befriended his former school headmaster, Oxil Jeanty.

One afternoon after school, Sauveur Pierre Étienne encouraged me to read l'*Esprit des Lois* and *Lettres Persanes*. He told me one of the most significant problems of Haiti was that people with prestige and money could buy privilege and power. He confided how fearful he felt each time they called the names on the roster at not hearing his own. The classroom was packed with more than two hundred students. Many of those students, like my friend, weren't on the attendance list. These pupils could sit on the three-foot thick wall in front of the two windows of the second-floor balcony, which faced the street below. This was a courtesy of the first public school built in Port-au-Prince in 1818 and named after Haiti's president at the time, Alexandre Sabès Pétion.

Here we were in October of 1977. The school lacked the space to take all the pupils who needed a free public education. Many had to resort to bribery to guarantee them a seat. During class, the school grounds were locked behind a sizeable corrugated wrought-iron gate.

One afternoon, the weather got muggy, and in the overcrowded classroom, the students became sullen and surly. The place became unbearable, and amid a cacophony of voices, it was impossible for the teacher to be heard. So he resorted to the only thing he knew would help. He called the names on the roster, demanding that each one of them stand outside in the hallway. Sauveur Pierre Étienne stared at me. I knew then that I had done to him what Peter had done to Jesus. I had failed him with the promise made in September.

Pandemonium broke out. More than half of those present in the classroom didn't figure into the roster. Aided by the vice principal, the teacher began to whack those whose names weren't on the list with cowhide whips.

Those missing from the roster could stay inside the classroom and get whipped or jump from the second-floor balcony and face possible injury or death. Sauveur Pierre Étienne was a skinny, lanky teenager who weighed less than 110 pounds. He had vanished by the time I opened my eyes again. I couldn't tell whether he'd taken a plunge over the balcony or dashed into the school corridor with whacks on his back. I knew it was my fault for giving the money to someone who'd failed to fulfill the promise and then refused to return it. It stung when a few weeks later Sauveur Pierre Étienne asked for his money back. "When I am hungry, I take some salt tablets and wash them down with water to calm the hunger pangs. I have no right to take what is not mine."

His financial situation was worse than mine, and though he knew it was out of reach, all he wanted was an education. And he allowed himself to dream about it. He understood that an education would open doors for him. He believed the Haitian people could be there another ten thousand years if they applied themselves.

It became a puzzle to me when he uttered those words of going to bed hungry instead of taking what belonged to someone else. Must he? Unlike me, he had no one in the States or anywhere outside of Haiti. How was he going to get out of this morass?

I'd failed him when he hadn't failed himself. Today he is the author of *L'énigme Haïtienne: Échec de l'État Moderne en Haiti, Haiti: l'Invasion des ONG,* and many other scholarly works. His time in school was worth every injustice he suffered at the hands of unscrupulous teachers and school principals—those who had lost their compass for failing to assess why they became educators in the first place. Who knows? Folks like Sauveur Pierre Étienne, remarkable Haitians, indeed, could be there another ten thousand years.

Me, age 1.

Me, age 16.

Marie Madeleine Thibaud (Madoudou) , circa 1961.

*Milliardaire Joseph (Pa) and my step-mother, Yvette
Castor Syverain, January 1970.*

Grandpa Dufrène Syverain.

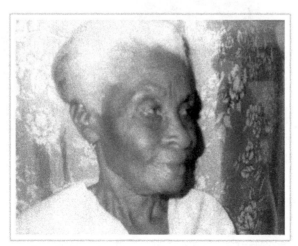

Grandma Bernadette Boncoeur Syverain (Magrann).

*(from left) Tante Erita Pierre Dextra, a family friend, grandma
Abélide Alphonse Jeudy, and me, Ti Mouillage, Haiti, 2001.*

*Marie Fernande Syverain and my son,
Milliardaire III, California 2000.*

Gertha Sanon Syverain and Jean Etienne Thibaud, 1962.

(from left) Jean Wilfrid Thibaud, me, Bernadette Sylverain, Jean Etienne Thibaud, and Dufresne Syverain, Dad's 75th Birthday party, Boston, 2003.

Pierre Rock Thibaud, Boston 1987.

Rose Marie Chery.

Pa, Taryn Jude Castor Syverain, Tracy Jude Castor syverain, Varnell Castor, and Kasseem Jude Castor Syverain, Boston, 1993.

Fabrice Pascal, Pa's last child.

Youlamou and me on May 22, 1982.

*(from left) best woman Iveline Syverin Bustros, me,
Youlamou, and best man Samuel Jeremie on my
wedding ceremony, Haiti, December 29, 1983.*

*President Jean Claude Duvalier, first lady Michèle Bennett Duvalier,
my father-in law Samuel Jeremie, Youlamou, and me at The
Auditorium Adventiste de Port-au-Prince, Haiti, December 29, 1983.*

(from left) Cousin Pierre André Syverain, me, Youlamou, my mother-in-law Vesta Paul Jeremie, Magrann, and my sister-in-law, Marie Edwine Jeremie, Ti Mouillage, Haiti, summer 1985.

Me, Madoudou, and Youlamou, Boston, 1987.

*Nephew Matthieu Syverain, Youlamou, and me,
Ti Mouillage, Haiti, summer 1988.*

*(left front row) Jerome Simon Junior and his mom Jeannie
Simon, Madoudou, Sherley Thibaud, me, Maurice
Merone, Pa, Jean Wilfrid Thibaud, and Paul Christian
Namphy, Stanford Graduation Day, June 1993.*

Me carrying the Haitian flag, Stanford Graduation Day, June 1993.

Youlamou, our son Milliardaire III, and me on Stanford campus, 1998.

Pa and Milliardaire III at Staten Island,
New York, summer 1999.

*Three generations of Syverain, the three
Milliardaires, Boston, September 2003.*

Youlamou and me at Toussaint L'ouverture Memorial,
Fort-de-Joux, France, summer 2006.

Encounter with Christ

Why should legal constraints hamper their activity? Of course, these women are not numerous, but how many men of this caliber exist? While men, even when immoral, weak, and incompetent, find open to them all doors, women, even competent, find these doors tightly shut.

— DANTÈS BELLEGARDE

he fall of 1977 greeted me with great shock and confusion. Before, going to school had been my escape; now I had my doubts. My old classmate Sauveur Pierre Étienne had vanished. Most days after school, I wandered along the streets, not knowing what to do with my life. I didn't know where to go next or whether to return home. Sometimes I found myself lacking the bus fare to get back home. Many times, as hungry as I was, I had to walk the ten miles home.

One day I resorted to begging in order to go home. A total stranger forked me a quarter. Though he failed to make eye contact with me on Grand-Rue, he gave me enough to pay for the tap-tap to get back home that evening. I felt ashamed as the man turned his head, frowning and whirling after giving me the coin.

The culture at the Lycée was different. The teaching was rigorous, the pressure to excel unbearable. In the public schools, few teachers cared about students learning. Most would get to the school campus late. Many of them worked for private institutions in addition to their work at the public schools. In the private schools, they arrived on time to ensure their continued employment. In the public schools, these teachers were paid sporadically. Sometimes they would go three or four months or longer without pay, which explained why they paid lip-service to the students at the public schools, the wretched of the city.

Whenever a teacher gave a lecture, one had to struggle to glean even a snippet of the information. Many of these talks baffled me from beginning to end. I failed to understand much of what was said.

The students became frightened when Maitre Fortuné, our mathematics teacher, came to the classroom one afternoon, a cigarette hanging from the corner of his mouth. He squinted through the smoke and babbled a few words to himself. The eyes in the café-au-lait face of this man of intensity could read my soul. He stood tall, cocky, brilliant, and confident. I cowered each time he came into the classroom. His square jaw quivered each time he spoke in his great erudition. His head shook as he tried to explain the mathematics of our ever-expanding universe. I doubted anyone grasped it. He taught us that Eratosthenes, the African athlete and brilliant mathematician born in about 276 BC in Cyrene, Africa, was the first to calculate the circumference of the earth and had been the chief librarian in Alexandria, Egypt, which became the intellectual hub of the era, surpassing Athens.

"Those who built the great pyramids at Giza were people like you and me. Yet today one could not spot anyone like us in all of Egypt. They vanished like the Aztecs and the Olmecs of Mexico or the Incas of Peru. They disappeared like the Tainos of Quisqueya. That decimation took place in less than one hundred years." He lit another Camel and paused, puffing on it a few times. "Students, if you don't study hard, you also will vanish. If you visited America five hundred years ago, you would have found only people with red skin. There was no black, brown, or white skin." He turned to the blackboard, shook his head, and wrote another equation. "What I told you—I hope you will remember it all your life and pass it on to future generations."

Maitre Fortuné was a man of gusto born of rare stock, yet his constant shifting became a cause of concern to me. I had difficulty following him whenever he did trigonometry or algebra on the board. He would whistle each time he sensed his speech getting fast. That seemed the only way he could slow himself down as he imparted his knowledge.

One day, after he had written a quadratic equation on the board, he leaned against it, digging in his pockets for another cigarette. He grasped one, lit it, placed it between his lips, puffed it, and tried to slow his quickening pace. He then took the piece of chalk he was using, tossed it in the air, and flicked it with his middle finger, like a donkey kicking a mule. Then he blew the white powder from his dry, dusty fingers. After a ten-minute lecture, he walked away. No wonder he'd warned us to study hard if we wanted to move ahead. Had he done that in the religious or private schools he taught at, he would have been sacked on the first day.

In January 1978, American preacher Kenneth Cox came to Haiti to lead an evangelical revival from January 8 to February 4. Every evening at the Auditorium Adventiste de Port-au-Prince, my spirits soared. It was as if heaven was being handed to me on a platter. Though I was confused about the distinction or the sameness of God and Christ, I forged ahead.

The interesting thing was that nobody spoke in tongues in the auditorium, so no one needed to be tied down like the lady who'd chased a clique of deacons at a church near my house a few years earlier. Then and only then had the police intervened to rid her of that spirit.

For four weeks, I scrambled across the city blocks to get there before seven each evening. On the evenings I lacked an entrance ticket, I would stay outside the auditorium courtyard listening to the voices thrumming from the large loudspeakers. On weekdays, I was the first to leave the classroom at the Lycée, and on weekends, I somehow managed to scrounge up enough for the fare to travel to the revival.

Standing to the left of the podium, Pastor Guy Valleray translated English to French and read lines of scripture. I was ready to attend Pastor Cox's evangelical crusade for the duration. It was easier to grasp the vision of the Three Angels than trigonometry or a first-derivative function. He spoke about the coming of Christ. A few of the faithful stood in a corner each night before the beginning of the program. They prayed for the crusade's success and beamed with approval. I became afraid of burning in hell.

I knew that joining my cause with Christ's could put an end to all my concerns and misery and the sooner, the better. "Prepare to meet your God," as found in Amos 4:12, hung on a large banner above the altar. I stopped when I first saw the writing. A year earlier, I had come across another passage from the same book: Amos 5:11. A colleague in school had shared it with me during a discussion on colonialism, imperialism, and communism. It read, "You trample on the poor and force him to give you grain." These two passages left me in deep contemplation.

Going to church in Haiti had been a joyful and uplifting experience, and attending church on the island three to four times a week wasn't uncommon for many. We sang the traditional hymns of repentance as we surrendered ourselves to Jesus. It would almost be a worldly woe if you failed to glorify God with lungs filled with praises. A religious people we were.

Though like most attendees I was new to the faith, with so much repetition, I had the songs memorized by the third night. Amidst the throngs of people, prayers, singing, preaching, amens, the ruckus that continued with the faithful clapping of hands, and Pastor Cox's bible prophecies, I failed to remember what Professor Fortuné had taught about quadratic equations in math class that week.

Even in the daytime, it was dim inside the auditorium. Behind the solid oak pulpit hung several cotton banners. Their inscriptions read "Maranatha," "Jesus Is King," "Three Angels Message," and "The Spirit of Prophecy." I wondered why the church had failed to hang a banner that read "God Is Love."

More than two thousand people attended each of the nightly sessions, and for twenty-eight evenings, all three daily presentations were packed. The auditorium was above capacity every night. My earthly wants evaporated as I learned heaven was near.

The floor of the auditorium was flat, with pew following pew all the way to the front. Before the evangelist began, all the lights grew dim, with only a sliver of light from the alleys prevailing. People came bathed in cologne and perfume as if this were the preparation day for their burial or wedding and tomorrow would be no more.

With lively hymns and songs of praise surrounding me, I envisioned the Messiah's return. I had found a good excuse to forgo my studies altogether. People cried and confessed Jesus as their savior. They wailed when Kenneth Cox began to read from Revelation, nineteenth chapter, verses 11 and 12: "I saw heaven standing open and there before me was a white horse, whose rider is called Faithful and True. With justice he judges and makes war. His eyes are like blazing fire, and on his head are many crowns. He has a name on him that no one knows but He himself." Those eyes of blazing fire made me cringe. That sounded like terror to me. Handkerchiefs were opened as people began to weep. They stood, clapped their hands, and swayed from side to side within the aisles as the music rose from the altar and booming voices sang, "He touched me." I joined the chorus and thought of seeing heaven that evening without the fear of being mocked by anyone who knew me.

But my heart grew troubled the last evening of the crusade. A few meters away among the throng of faithful who had accepted Christ was Maitre Fortuné. He stood before the altar, facing the assembly of that large auditorium in Port-au-Prince. What else did I need to know to accept the fact that I was wasting my time in school? Even Monsieur Fortuné knew what to do when decision time about the new faith came.

He had a degree in civil engineering. He got paid for his teaching. He was well-groomed and well-fed when he stepped into our classroom with its huddled and tired mass of students. He left the auditorium after his baptismal ceremony, and there on the street corner, Monsieur Fortuné looked right and left, then put on his *comme-il-faut*. He thumped the cigarette from its box, brought it to his lips, and lit it before inhaling deeply and allowing his thoughts to trail off as he released a massive stream of smoke. He uttered something that sounded like "For it is by grace you have been saved, through faith—and this is not from yourselves, it is the gift of God—not by works, so that no one can boast." As found in Ephesians 2:8-9. He took one last drag on his cigarette, then extinguished the smoking butt between his chalky thumb and forefinger, casting it on the ground and stepping on it, grinding it to a gray pulp as though it were his last smoke.

Only a week earlier, they'd held a health seminar before the evangelist had spoken. They warned us about the dangers and the evil of smoking and drinking. I wanted to tell Mr. Fortuné, as read in James 2:26 "So faith without deeds is dead." Perhaps he would need to remind himself of that during another crusade.

On Monday when I returned to school, he failed to show up to class, so I sat there for the second lecture of the day watching the literature teacher's mouth drop open and the quizzical look on his face upon reading a fellow classmate's abysmal essay. The teacher decided to give him a passing grade for his services to the school. That classmate of mine, Tilagris, the last student in the class ranking, had won at least four awards for being master of the bugle in the school band. Of course, he couldn't fail literature. He was good for the school. Shouldn't I have maintained my status as a vagrant student taken over by religious insanity? It would have been an excellent way to forget my problems as the absentee pupil I had become.

Even collaborating with three other students during the physics final exam, I failed. I'd trusted my instinct instead of humbly accepting their answers for the exam that Sunday morning in June of 1978. We'd opted to rest the day before, on the Sabbath Day. It was gloom all over again for me at the end of the school year. While all three of my friends passed, I had little to show for myself—not a passing grade in any of my classes. At least I had encountered Christ.

They kicked me out of the school for failing ninth grade. In the fall, I enrolled in a private school that didn't care whether I entered the tenth, eleventh, or twelfth grade. One caveat was clear: I had to make my monthly payments on time, even if I failed year after year.

Holding the purse strings in our house gave me leverage. Dad had chosen me to be responsible for dispensing the funds for groceries, for other purchases, and for paying the utility bill. So I resorted to providing everybody with less food. I shaved fifteen dollars off the hundred dollars Father sent from the States every month and used it to pay my tuition.

After waiting for Jesus Christ to come during my ninth and tenth grades to no avail, I began to apply myself better in that new school with its easier curriculum than the one at Lycée Pétion. My hard work started to pay off at the beginning of the school year. Soon the US consulate office in Port-au-Prince granted me a resident visa and I would go to America and live with Dad and my stepmother, Yvette. It came five years after Dad applied for me.

PART FOUR

19

CHAPTER

Cage Dweller

You don't leave this country.
You don't leave it
Nor even go away.

—LOUIS-PHILIPPE DALEMBERT

Children rarely forget the events that scar them. Nature had finally conspired against Lucifer, and a raging storm loomed on the horizon for her as I met her one cold evening in Boston, my mind consumed with dark thoughts.

One of my dreams had finally come true when I left Haiti on December 19, 1979, aboard an Eastern Airlines flight that took me to Miami International Airport. As my Eastern Airlines Flight 966 taxied into its terminal, I pressed my head against the thick window, my nose smudging the glass. The sight that greeted me was surreal. As my eyes took in the skyscrapers on the horizon, I got a taste of what heaven was like. That crisp, cool evening became the high point of my teenage years. Two hours after my papers were processed by agents of the Immigration and Naturalization Service, I boarded another plane to Boston. It was an airplane larger than any of the soccer fields I had ever stepped on. It was a fascinating change of events. Everything was bigger and faster than I had ever imagined.

Only four hours earlier, I had lived in a small working-class community near Port-au-Prince. Now I was in the richest country in the world. I took my seat among the other passengers, smiling at everybody I saw.

Six weeks earlier, the US Embassy in Teheran, Iran, had been overrun by an angry mob. The mood at this airport was different from the one I'd left behind in Port-au-Prince. No one joked here. It was all business and no pleasure. The immigration officer who took my papers looked somewhat somber and carried himself like a wet crane in cold weather. His hands were spread casually on the tiny desk inside his small cubicle, and he had an air of resignation. He nonchalantly looked at my papers and handed them back, telling me I was welcome in America. Was I? Looking back, I don't recall how I got onto Eastern Airlines Flight 46 to Boston.

My plane finally landed at Boston Logan International Airport after what felt like a trip to the moon in a tumbling dryer. I followed the other passengers getting off the plane and picked up my small piece of luggage in the baggage claim area. A cold draft hit my face as I came out of the gate to meet Dad. He had brought me a thick coat. I put it on, the hood covering my face like an Eskimo, before exiting the terminal. Right there, he advised me to make sure I got as much sunshine as I could in this land, though it would never be as much as I got in the Caribbean.

Dad took us on a twelve-minute ride to Chelsea, a suburb of Boston.

It was ten past eleven when we entered the redbrick apartment complex on Shawmut Street on one of the coldest nights of the month. Dad had to go to work early the next day. As I looked around before stepping through the front door, I noticed that there were no trees, no dogs, no backyard, nobody. It felt spooky, but I tried to trust my dad. The dim light softened his face. As I followed him up the stairs of the second-floor corridor, I realized that within the confines of the white walls surrounding me, there were no sounds here either—no pets to greet, not a soul in sight. I thought I saw someone poke a beaky and sullied nose through the small crack in a nearby door.

As a child, I had heard stories about ghosts and monsters and ghouls. Though I hadn't seen any before leaving Haiti, the place I stood in that night felt like a ghost town. Whether it had ghouls and monsters, only time would tell, but that first observation of America rattled me to the core. I had believed I lived in a cage in Carrefour, but it wasn't until I crossed the Atlantic Ocean that I found out how a real cage dweller felt.

For years, I'd longed to see America. In the pages of magazines, it was a country of beautiful valleys and meadows, manicured lawns and lush cornfields. It had skyscrapers taller than the Tower of Babel; I had seen the ones in New York City on television. The country had mansions with landscapes that were sometimes larger than cities. I had seen its golden canyons in the American television series *Gunsmoke* and *Bonanza*. Its beaches were loaded with sharks and its waters were as cold as glaciers.

I had wanted to see everything out of a sense of danger or fascination. But that evening, I was staring at a place that looked tired, stale, bare, lifeless, and grew old even as I gazed upon it. It looked beaten and hopeless—like the face I was about to see. Lucifer, who lived with Yvette and Dad, seemed in the grip of a great depression, an outcast left on the sidewalk.

Dad again warned me of the dangers of not getting enough sunlight. He believed the children of Haitian immigrants were dull and aloof because they lacked vitamin D prior to their births. Before my arrival, he had already planned his return to Haiti, giving little thought to leaving Yvette to fend for herself with their two spirited infant daughters, Tracy and Taryn. One of my little half-sisters almost cracked her skull open against a bedpost when she jumped out of my hands while being fed a bottle of formula. The formula must have made her hyperactive.

In the morning, I woke up and directed myself toward the kitchen for breakfast, where I opened the refrigerator. There were dozens of white eggs on the shelves. I found onions, tomatoes, sliced bread, mayonnaise, butter, Dijon mustard, and cartons of milk and orange juice. A large bottle of soda gawked at me.

I looked at all that food as though it were lethal poison. Something that abundant can't be good for me. But at the thought of scrambled eggs melting on my palate, I sighed. Finally, it dawned on me why they called this the promised land. I picked out three eggs, poured them into a bowl, and stirred. I added a pinch of salt, chopped the onions, and placed some in a skillet, then added some olive oil. I turned the gas on and cooked the eggs, then toasted four slices of bread. I slathered butter on the bread after sprinkling it with rich, syrupy ketchup. Then I placed everything on a large plate. As I sat down at the dining table, facing the street, I thought about something I'd once heard in Haiti: "America is heaven. I have found it while walking on land."

Outside, it was cold and lonely at such an early hour. The streets were empty. The air was still and menacing. The quietness of the place threatened to unsettle me, but I sat and ate to my satisfaction. Dad and Yvette watched me during all this cooking and serving, but I paid them no attention. I imagined they were happy to see me gobbling down the food I'd dreamed about back home. As I finished my omelet, Dad called me over, and I saw another lecture in the making. I was in trouble. I didn't know what I had done wrong. It was torture as I waited for him to speak.

"What do you think?" he asked. "You found everything already purchased, brought, and placed inside the refrigerator." He snapped his head to the side to look at me. "But you found it improper to prepare breakfast for everyone?"

"Well ... well ... Pa," I said. "I did not realize you would want to eat my scrambled eggs." Dad glared at me. "I am not a great cook," I mumbled. "I thought in America people only eat great food. You wouldn't eat food from someone like me. I have no experience in American cuisine." I felt smug instead of chagrined.

"It doesn't matter. Here in America, no one has time to do much besides work. Yvette and I would have appreciated you cooking breakfast today. Yvette works the night shift at Saint John of God Hospital and must care for your two little sisters when she is home. You aren't working or in school yet, and your help is much needed here. Yvette told me how you cared for her godfather, Parrain Vivi, when you were nine years old. Now you are living in America, and you seem to care only for yourself. What has changed you so fast these past years? What has happened to you since the time I left Haiti? I worked two jobs to care for you and your brothers, and now I have to ask myself if anyone cares about me." His words ended and left me looking for an answer.

"Can I make breakfast for you and Miss Yvette now?" I asked.

Dad gave me a shrug, then walked away, leaving me to feel inadequate. Here was Dad, who had given me a memorable childhood. He was my hero in many respects: he'd taken all of us boys to the National Palace one Christmas to collect toy giveaways from Papa Doc, something the president had done for poor folks like us during his fourteen years in power; Dad had brought us to Stadium Sylvio Cator many Sunday afternoons to watch professional soccer games; he'd driven us to the beach house in Ti Mouillage for swimming many summers and engaged in countless other activities with us. That day I was exposed as a fake who'd failed to prepare a simple breakfast for Dad and Yvette. I'd failed when it mattered. It wasn't out of malice that I hadn't cooked for them. I truly believed that they wouldn't eat my food. I never bore any hard feelings toward Dad or Yvette. These people had been the heroes of my childhood, and I wanted to please them. But how?

On my second morning there, I woke up inside the two-bedroom condo. It felt awkward being indoors, sealed away from the caresses of a soft breeze or a ray of sunshine. My love for the outdoors as a child of the countryside of Ti Mouillage was well known. Many times, I had slept outside along with other family members when the weather was fair and the circumstances warranted it.

Chelsea was a rude awakening. In the tropics, one spends much of their time outdoors in wide, open spaces. Children were watched after by neighbors, friends, family members, and sometimes even strangers. Here in America, I felt like a caged bird, a Hispaniolan trogon trapped inside a cave. It was disquieting. The whole thing made me nervous and provoked panic attacks on some days. It wasn't long before I began to plot my return to Haiti.

I had left Haiti with excitement and determination as never before, but now, here in America, I heard people talking but could not understand them. I saw them laugh when watching television, and I didn't know why. I felt like an alien from another planet or, rather, like the people I saw were from another world. During my first few months in America, I thought most people in the country were crazy. They walked with their heads down when they were on the streets and avoided eye contact. Or when they were inside, like in a restaurant or bar, they kept their eyes on the television screen, avoiding any small talk. I said to myself, "Here is a land of madness. It is unlike the one I have dreamed about."

As a youngster, I'd often thought of other planets and other worlds to cope or assuage my fears while dealing with Lucifer. I remember how Frère Constant, a church elder in Carrefour, once said, "Over there is heaven, and here we are in hell."

How the hell had I found myself here at such a time? It was a strange feeling. I needed to explore the country. All living creatures must learn to adapt to their surroundings, and so I tried to adjust. The first two weeks were the hardest. I found myself in a funk.

Christmas in the tropics had been an occasion filled with joy, family, and friendship. Here it was different. I saw people buying stuff. And they bought more stuff. Then they returned to the stores for refunds. For whom or why had they bought all the stuff they were returning? It baffled me. Gone were the joy and the laughter I'd always associated with this time of year. The people had given up. Were these people always depressed, desolate, and disoriented? I guessed that could be normal. What a Faustian bargain! Hell.

People hurried to be off the streets like squirrels scrambling for their ground holes. The few daring souls I saw standing in the sun, I thought amusing. The lack of sunshine felt surreal and like it was affecting the masses of wandering souls. Could this temperate and sedate climate be the reason black people suffered such high rates of cancer and mental illness? Many of the black folks I met seemed morose. No wonder people drank so much grog in this land. In times like these, my soul craved a tropical gust, a panacea to lift my spirits. I needed the scent of Ti Mouillage's sandy beach under the midday sun to stuff up my nostrils and show me a side of heaven not yet spoken.

One morning, Dad began shouting at Yvette. I couldn't tell whether it was his daily devotional before he went to work or not. I was confused as I had never seen him lash out at Yvette or Lucifer before. But he was like a gushing fire hydrant. "This La cour desrosiers will always remain an undigested food and a nightmare in my life!" He bolted from his bedroom for impact. Perhaps he wanted me to see the spectacle in its entirety.

"What a terrible encounter to have," I murmured.

"Why did I bring you and your family here?" he asked Yvette. "With your mother in our midst, I knew it would be hell for me."

I shook my head as if I had just woken up from a Haitian dream. Had my presence in Chelsea opened a can of crawling worms?

When Yvette finally spoke, her voice was inaudible. She was quiet, cerebral, and patient. She knew Dad's verbal volley would pass. She was a caring, sympathetic, wise woman whose devotion to our family was unshaken. But as the calculating first child of Lucifer, she could also plan her moves. That made her a bit unpredictable too.

Why spoil the good opinion I had of America after all? The canvas looked different. That morning, when I gazed upon the gray sky through the French door of our condo, I saw smoke spewing from a factory or power station nearby. I turned my gaze to the ground, where the snow glistened like glazed crystal porcelain, and I did not know how to react. I yearned to go outside. I felt trapped inside the apartment as the grown-ups argued.

Here was Dad, who only a few weeks earlier had had an altercation at work with a twenty-six-year-old white male, someone half my father's age. The coworker had attacked him in the factory cafeteria. A year earlier, as a cabbie, he had been chased by an angry mob of white men after dropping a passenger off Charleston. If it hadn't been for the quick intervention of the passenger, who'd tucked him away in his apartment until the police arrived, the mob could have killed my father.

Dad's memory of the history of America was full of injustice, exploitation, humiliation, and barbarity toward black people. For him, this was America's heritage. Grandpa Dufrène had told him about the abuses Haitians had suffered at the hands of the Marines during the 1915 occupation of Haiti and how they had acted like the Babylonians. Dad had grown up against that backdrop and become part of a generation that dared to think differently. He believed in fighting fire with fire and pride, even at the price of his life. He was never ready to turn the other cheek. Dad strutted his contempt for vanity and ogled it with sheer indifference. He never strived to be accepted. He felt he was authentic to the core and imparted that authenticity to us. "I would take no nonsense from potentates, prelates, or popes," he used to say.

At work one day, he'd hidden a crowbar under his large coat cuffs to guard against a man who'd threatened to follow him after work. When the guy attacked Dad in the factory parking lot, he took a victory lap. Dad was the cleverest. He used the crowbar to hit the fellow until he collapsed, but he was not dead. Dad was stressed out.

I felt numb and began to plot my return to the motherland after my short landing in America. Between the arguments I listened to in the apartment and Dad's debacle at work and the sensation of being trapped like I had been in Carrefour, I couldn't decide which was worse. The old demons of Lucifer had crept up to cast a shadow over me. I wanted out. Since I had left Haiti around Christmas, I hadn't missed any school. I would return before it started in January.

But that thought was fleeting. After Dad took me out to a hamburger joint twice to surfeit myself with cheeseburgers, fries, and shakes, I wanted no part of going back. I'd caught the disease that ails most immigrants upon their arrival in this land: "Americanitis." No matter how much an immigrant might be displeased with his or her adopted country, he or she could rarely readjust to his or her native land. He or she could visit but would quiver about staying for good. My home was America. America was more than a country. It was a thought, a philosophy, and a desire to do things differently to reach the acme of a new human civilization.

Three weeks later, Dad decided it was time for him to resettle in Haiti, even though Haiti was no longer his home. He left because he found himself in trouble with the law. He left me with my stepmother to explore this new world. I became my own guide and adviser. I soon received my Social Security number and green card. It was time to find a job and set sail for an unknown shore.

That winter provided me the canvas on which to repaint my life. I was finally coming to terms with my nightmares. It seemed a thousand bells clanged within my cortex, reminding me of past insults, taunts, and mistreatment. I thought about all the wrongs I had received at Lucifer's hands, and I swore vengeance. But I had come to America in ignorance of its customs and laws.

In Haiti, people sometimes took justice into their own hands. I entertained myself with the thought that Lucifer must pay for her past transgressions. I ruminated on the idea of acquiring a cowhide whip like the one she'd used to whack Rock and me and similar to what they used in the South for caning slaves. A friend back home would ship it from the motherland, and I would use it to deliver justice. The rekindled bitterness in my heart was mired in a childlike excitement I shared with Rock. He had arrived four months earlier and promised to assist me in this new theater that now belonged to us.

I would hide in the bushes off the curve of Spring Street near Chelsea Square at dusk, awaiting her arrival from work. From there I would follow her and at the proper time, place, and manner, deliver her a flogging—a sort of punishment the police would find it difficult to explain in case someone called them. She would have welts like the ones she had inflicted on us in the early 1970s.

One Thursday in late January 1980, I entered a laundromat near Chelsea Square to wash my clothes. Around the square, a hundred people shifted and shuffled in all directions. In their midst, a hand waved at me. Who was this? I hesitated, for I couldn't see the face behind this brown wrist. I searched for the raised hand—until I came face-to-face to Mrs. Castor. I grew dejected, but she lunged for me and clutched me to her, giving me the embrace of a mother, before letting me go. As she hugged me, I felt she wanted me to understand her and didn't want to let go. "Hey, Ti Milliardaire, come and help me carry these bags home," she said. "I know how much you like eggs, bread, and milk." I picked up the grocery bags off the floor and trotted along.

A few days before, I had envisioned revenge. Now Mrs. Castor was asking me to carry two heavy grocery bags with food she thought I would enjoy. What was wrong with this world? She'd shown me a kindness that made me want to tear off my clothes and walk like a madman I once saw in Haiti. That evening, as I sat alone in the living room away from her now-gentle eyes, humor, and pleasant disposition, it dawned on me how little I knew of her.

She had called me a slacker and a son of my father. Why? Was it because I was too slow to respond to her requests? Or was it because I had been too dismissive of her during our first encounter? Or maybe my priggish attitude had blinded my sight and made me her first casualty? My anger had quashed my spirit upon my arrival. Dad had brought me to live in a house with her again. Luckily, with the passing days, weeks, and months, I moved on and made peace. I never asked why, and I no longer felt she needed my forgiveness. Years later, I learned from Yvette that during the time Dad went into hiding away from Papa Doc's feared militia and couldn't work, it was Mrs. Castor who had provided us with food and money. Now Lucifer truly bore her name for being an angel of light.

Because of that experience and realizing my ignorance, I tried to develop a healthy and positive attitude about life in general. In any event, I forgave her and, more importantly, I excused myself. That was the blessing. I had to thank her in my heart for giving me the zest and drive to live and laugh at life ever since. She taught me not to give a hoot about my detractors. As the saying among my siblings goes, "If you had lived with Mrs. Castor in Carrefour and you didn't die, then you are cut of steel."

In more ways than not, I realized, Mrs. Castor had displayed decency and kindness: There was the time I brought myself to have her check my itchy skin when no doctors were in sight. And the night the front door of the house opened as I was about to leave for a midnight walk in the dark, sleepwalking, and she'd put me back in bed. I don't know the reasons for many of the things she did. I couldn't divine the cause of her erratic behavior, but I do know that my caricature of her had been false. The day she went to America, I said to myself, "Only two mountains never meet, and neither of us is a mountain."

Years later, during a visit to Yvette in Chelsea in September 2003, we found Lucifer sitting on a small couch near the entrance of the home. She smiled somberly as she looked into our eyes. She may not have known my son, Milliardaire Yves Rashid Kwame Syverain, III (Kwame), or my wife, Yves-Renee Jeremie Syverain (Youla), but she was familiar with Dad and me. Her hands lay quietly in her lap, as if someone had tucked them there before our arrival. I didn't want to accept what I was seeing as I bent down to hug her and give her a warm kiss on her wrinkly, soft, peaceful face. Our inevitable fate as humans isn't so much a tragedy. It's only a pause, a mirror, a reflection.

Here was a woman who'd left everything behind; just as Peter, Matthew, and Mark had in following Christ. She'd closed her small business as a street seller. A proud mother, she'd supported both her family and mine for years. Her husband had become a prisoner of the state because he failed to support Papa Doc Duvalier's presidential election in 1957. Mr. Castor soon became an alcoholic after his release. Mrs. Castor had landed in Carrefour, leaving her husband behind and giving up her small business to raise children who belonged to others and who may have been ungrateful.

I knew it was true in my case. I was a selfish brat, a bumble head, and a bully who'd convinced himself he had rights bestowed only to princes. In my hate for her, I'd sanctioned my insubordination.

I have come to believe that people in positions of power often misuse it. They squander it because of internal conflicts and poor self-image. Or they are sick. Many of the people who bully others and abuse their power have low self-esteem. They carry resentment, fear, and feelings of impotence. They feel helpless when facing their enemies, imaginary or real. Some of these people have undiagnosed mental illnesses wrapped in paranoia.

My propensity to hold grudges shocked me. Before that experience, I knew nothing about harboring old grudges. I hadn't thought about Mrs. Castor for more than five years since she'd left Haiti. My coming to America, however, had awoken in me old demons buried under a mask of smiles and self-deception. These were demons I barely knew existed, and I wondered how I would have felt had she died before I came to America.

To understand a person well, one must know about his childhood and his beliefs. Only then can one hope to see even a shadow of who an individual is.

The shocking thing for me was that Mrs. Castor had moved on. She'd discarded or buried the past we had shared—a past I had chosen to remember and cling to and relive. She wisely refused to have anything to do with it. I finally realized that it would be up to me whether I caressed, cherished, rehashed, or buried the past. It would be futile for me to try to make her feel guilty about it. For her, that past never existed.

She'd had enough on her own to reckon with or discard altogether. Who knew how much pain Rosa Celenie Esteve Castor carried with her to her grave at Cedar Grove Cemetery in Dorchester, Massachusetts, on July 12, 2006?

A few days after I arrived in America, I picked a telephone book up off the dining room table and began to flip through the pages. I was looking for a Seventh Day Adventist church to attend. To my great dismay, someone told me there wasn't one anywhere nearby. After a five-block bus ride in Stoneham, I located an SDA church, but it was a "white church"—a church for only white people, I was told. I could not make sense of what that meant. "A church is a place of worship," I said. "Churches are for believers, and I am a believer." I couldn't understand why human beings had to segregate God too.

I finally understood the need for the universe to expand. It needed space for groups to segregate. Whether one was a caveman, a cosmopolitan, or an extrovert, I hoped there was room for everybody!

I had arrived in the promised land. How could someone dare to deny me heaven now? I almost lost faith not only in human beings but also in God. If God was a segregationist, as some portrayed Him to be, what in the world did I need heaven for? I had a habit of avoiding places where folks who looked like me weren't welcome. I could never be in want of friend or foe in such spaces.

I was sure the people would have been polite had I gone to worship in that church in Stoneham. They would not have removed me from a church pew before the face of the Lord. But after hearing this, even if I were invited to come, I would have objected. In all fairness, I doubted the report was accurate. But, in any event, who needed trouble?

I wanted no complications in matters I did not understand. Besides, I spoke little English and wouldn't have understood a thing. Why make a scene with something as trivial as my physical presence between walls? God lived in the hearts of some humans. I could always pray in my heart and not in abodes made by man in need of an overhaul. That worked for me.

20
CHAPTER

Boston Goes Bonkers

Take me to another place
Take me to another land
Make me forget all that hurts me
Let me understand your plan.

—ARRESTED DEVELOPMENT

Under a cold, blue morning sky, I set out looking for a job in Charlestown. I boarded a bus in Chelsea Square, traveled three miles, and crossed the bridge over the Chelsea River to Charlestown, homeport of the USS *Constitution*. I got off in a semi-secluded area, hoping to walk into the city center as it was my first time in town. Little did I know that I was far away from downtown Charlestown. With my heavy coat wrapped around me, I stood there on Main Street, looking around, dazed, as my ears grew cold. I sensed that something was odd. A serene, old white man with blue eyes, yawning pores, aquiline nose, and freckled cheeks waved at me. He was stooped and gray from the passing years. His shriveled frame said he was in his eighties. He called me again. Soon he approached and told me in a quiet voice to stay behind the street curve closer to the storefront behind me.

I thanked him and obeyed without asking why. When you first came to America, you had to believe that everyone was working in your best interest.

He must have suspected I did not know well the town where I was and who I was. I saw no one who looked like me. It hadn't occurred to me that I had gotten lost in Charlestown. Soon I knew why he'd spoken to me like that. My gaze was drawn to the oncoming traffic, and about thirty feet away, a red car gunning straight for me. I moved closer to a storefront as the car quickened at my heels. I thought for a second that it was going to crash against me, crushing my legs, maiming me, or killing me. "Merde!" I said.

The car and its full-throated engine sped away, having missed me by inches. Two white male occupants in the car's front seat shook their fists at me, their eyes holding mine. They gave me the middle finger as their red Camaro glistened like a river of Bloody Marys flowing away from me. I panicked, not knowing what all this was about or what the middle finger meant. Sotto voce, I whispered, "Welcome to America!" I had come here to stay. I stood motionless for at least five minutes. Then I tilted my head, and my muscles tensed as I bolted toward the bus stop. I almost stumbled as the nearby pedestrians watched me.

Many saw the incident, but only one person spoke up. "I am sorry of what our city has become lately," said the old man. "You need to hurry and leave this place behind." The two demonic heads in the Camaro bobbed in and out. They grimaced at me through their rear window as the old man said goodbye to me.

Before he'd gone back to Haiti, Dad had told me how white hooligans often lurked around the greater Boston area, waiting to lynch black people in the land of plenty. I'd tried to ignore all of that. It was hard to believe. But America was in an age of violence. In a study published by A. Przeworski, et al, entitled, "What Makes Democracies Endure," scholars concluded that "poor democracies, particularly those with annual per-capita income of less than $1,000, are extremely fragile."[1] In other words, an annual per-capita income of $1,000 to $4,000 in a declining economy, as of 1996, plus a 2–3 percent annual inflation rate doomed any democracy. In *Edge of Chaos*, prize-winning economist Dambisa Moyo writes, "Prematurely shoehorning democracy into poor countries runs the risk of creating illiberal democracies that can be as bad—or worse—than the authoritarian systems they replaced."[2] America faces a different problem with its democracy today. It has an issue with race and power. America continues to fill its jails with the flesh of black and brown bodies. One-fourth of the world's prisoners live in America, but the country accounts for only 4 percent of the world's population. Can't America do better?

A rift over the issue of busing existed between blacks and whites in the greater Boston areas. The concept of busing was a colossal bust—a bad idea conceived over an issue lawmakers misunderstood. Though they likely had good intentions, Massachusetts politicians had tried to buy the issue on the cheap. As a result, it had backfired. Like the many programs self-serving politicians claim to create to help the poor and the minorities in America, it did not work out. These programs are used for short-term gains and to get politicians reelected. In America, as in many countries, few politicians have the courage to do the right thing.

One of the best ways to bring racial equality to a society that grows out of inequality is by providing top-rated education to minorities and financial support to struggling families. Ethnic minorities and disadvantaged students learn best in familiar places. Is that too much to ask? Estonia, Finland, and Singapore have set the bar for other countries to follow. No one learns well when alienated. Countries with vision invest in education. Like the medical profession, the teaching profession should be competitive. In fact, the teaching profession should be more competitive than any other. Teachers deserve the highest salaries. Countries that lack vision send mediocre teachers to needy schools in poor neighborhoods. That is an act of malfeasance and malpractice. Singapore and Japan are among the countries with the best school systems. Their best teachers instruct pupils in the most challenging institutions. "Schools can create an environment of cooperation with parents and communities."[3] Black and white people in America have been eternally engaged in a continuous dance of entanglement, though neither of them knows it.

To bring racial minorities into school communities that dislike them is wrong. Worse, it is destructive. People can't fake caring about needy kids when they don't give a hoot, and children can detect the hypocrisy. They are smart and can read between the lines. Wealthy school districts spend a lot more money per pupil than poor ones. The whole country loses when inner-city kids get an inferior education.

In *Palo Alto Weekly*, an op-ed argues that the current per-pupil expenditure cost was near $20,000 in 2019 in the Palo Alto Unified School District. On average, the United States spent $11,292 per pupil in 2018.[4]

I'd stumbled into this gothic, Celtic, myopic, schizophrenic city of Boston. It was something out of the mythology of a more primeval period. It was gnarled, repugnant, and inept. It was 1980, and this wasn't the South of the United States or Appalachia, it was a Yankee backyard. It was Boston in New England, the place where one found a university on almost every city block. Boston was the birthplace of American independence, wasn't it?

I boarded another bus leaving the town and didn't return to Charlestown until December of 2015. Today, a nephew of mine lives there.

To its credit, Boston has changed some from what it was in the 1970s and 1980s. The transformation that occured in Boston since then imbued me with more optimism for America, albeit cautious optimism. People will display their worst instincts when they feel vulnerable or threatened. Humans are xenophobic by nature because they fear the unknown.

People function on an emotional level and on basic instinct. This experience hadn't alienated me at all but, instead, enriched my perspective. Despite the problems between colors and groups that surface from time to time, America looks ahead. All significant changes must occur at the legal level. America shouldn't rely on the tip of a bayonet or a bullet to bring change, though often, this has been borne out in crisis. Change isn't often easy or straightforward.

As I got off the bus back in Chelsea Square, I noticed something new: I lived in a quite different place. In the 1970s, Chelsea was one of the most desegregated towns in America. It had received a massive influx of recent immigrants from Puerto Rico, and white people and other ethnic groups lived in propinquity. I felt safe there.

I stayed home the next day, organizing my thoughts. The mailman arrived and dropped a few letters into our mailbox. The thought of the previous day's experience roused me to go through the letter box. I needed a message from my mother or my siblings or the friends I'd left behind. The only letter in the mail was from the Suffolk County Superior Courthouse. It was addressed to Milliadaire Joseph Syverain. I dared not open it. Later, my stepmother tore it open.

Dad had resettled in Haiti because he believed he wouldn't receive a fair hearing at his upcoming deposition. He'd defended himself against an aggressor half his age who weighed more than 240 pounds.

Rock and I decided to try patching things up for the two alpha males. The young white man had attacked Dad at work. Dad was vocal about the way they treated black employees at the factory in comparison to their white counterparts. He would say, "Be strong and subtle, be serene and serious; be smart and stay black and beautiful!" So Rock and I scoured the white pages looking for a certain James O'Brien who lived in Somerville, Massachusetts. We came across several, but calling them all to find the right one was a herculean task. Besides that, calling during the day was not going to be fruitful, and calling at night would be sacrilegious as we might interrupt dinnertime. Then it occurred to us that when we left the courthouse in early January of 1980 during Dad's last hearing, his protagonist was on a paid leave of absence. So four weeks later, we tracked him down after some false starts.

"Good Morning, are you James O'Brien, the one who worked at the factory and who had an altercation with Joe Syverain?" I asked with hesitation because I wasn't sure he would understand me.

"Oh yeah, that's me. Joe and I are two nice guys, and we didn't have to get to that level. I am sorry for what happened." He was able to detect the origin of my accent. His answer satisfied me.

"Well, James, I think you and my dad need to put your differences away by not showing up for tomorrow's hearing," I told him.

"You are right. We need to finish with that nonsense, and I know it was my fault. I provoked and then attacked Joe the morning of the incident, and I told him after work that I would teach him a lesson. Sadly, I learned that lesson instead when he hit me with a crowbar as I tried to hit him a second time in the parking lot. Well, tell him I am sorry for starting the whole thing."

I was puzzled by the sincerity of his apology for creating a mess and by his willingness to own it. I'd wished I had a tape recorder.

"Okay, James, I will tell my dad. Thank you for taking my call and take care of yourself." He was relieved to find closure. He was satisfied, and so was I. The next day, early in the morning, I got up, put on my ivory suit, and directed myself toward Chelsea Square. I was on my way to the Suffolk Courthouse to find out if James would show up for the hearing.

Dad had feared losing his dignity. I knew it was proper for me to show up at a court hearing that wouldn't go well for him. I entered the room and waited until the judge called for both defendant and plaintiff to show up. Their names were called twice. Neither the plaintiff nor his lawyer was in sight. I smiled at the sense that I had finally been useful to Dad in some small way.

My stepmother calculated that she couldn't afford to rent the condo on her salary as a staff registered nurse. With two young children to support, she decided to move out and take up residence with one of her brothers who lived nearby. I followed her. We stayed in a small three-bedroom house on Shawmut Street. I could find no place to sleep except in the hallway between the kitchen, dining room, and bathroom. It wasn't out of anyone's malice or indifference for me that I ended up sleeping there every night, and it was better than the street or a pigpen. Silence came only after everyone else was in bed. With wandering eyes, I would look around the house and stare at the ceiling. I noted how the light bulbs here were brighter than those back in Haiti.

The job I got at the McDonald's on Tremont Street near Boston Common made me king of the day. I had canvassed the Manpower office near South Station for several mornings. Every evening, I would return home with no bacon. Now I had a Whopper at every lunch, with hot French fries on the side and a strawberry shake and orange juice. I liked my job and proudly wore my navy-blue shirt, black pants, and cap with burgundy visor. My duty was to clean the tables and put away the trays after customers finished their meals.

Several girls from the Temple Salem Church, the Haitian SDA church in Dorchester, frequented the restaurant during their school outings. I hated that. One day, about six of them dropped by just as I finished sweeping a table. The place was packed. They probably never even noticed me, but I was embarrassed to be in the lobby cleaning tables. Management was taking too long to train me behind the grill flipping burgers and cooking fries. There, I could be shielded from view. I had my old mindset from Haiti that the job was beneath me. But I needed the money.

When I came to America, I wanted to stay polite and amicable, the way my folks had taught me back home, but the time spent waiting for the bus to take me home each night after work proved the undoing of my good intentions. At Haymarket Station, I picked all kinds of words, words that seemed to inspire laughter or excitement among others. Normally, no one got upset or overreacted as they exchanged greetings with me, and things seemed to be going well with my new vernacular. However, my interaction with a stranger one evening brought everything to a screeching halt.

In my eagerness to show off how much of the language I had acquired in the briefest time, I shouted, "F— you!" to a beautiful young lady passing by. It stunned her. She rolled her eyes and looked piercingly at me, then her face paled, and it was as if a light inside her had just been switched off. She hurried away. Her behavior had me thinking, *Maybe she didn't understand my accent.* I bellowed a monosyllabic "Sh—" in the same expletive family as she dashed away to make up for lost ground. She said nothing. By then, the young woman looked disgusted and a mile away.

I waited at the station before my bus arrived. It finally came. I boarded the bus, lowered my backpack, and sat down. I retrieved my transistor radio from my pocket and wondered what I had done wrong. The snarly look the young woman had given me troubled me. I promised myself to do better next time by using the English words I had learned in school in Haiti. I ceased to use the language gleaned from the wild streets of Boston.

The transistor radio was my sole companion as I went home each night. It provided me with the only songs on that came close to the hymns I'd listen to in church in Haiti.

Everything about this place was strange: the smells, the songs, the people, the colors, the scenery. I needed to calm my angst as I found myself in a sea of confusion each day. Honestly, in the literal sense of the word, I was a foreigner, a stranger, an alien, just as my green card stated. I would turn the transistor radio dial to a family radio station that broadcasted Christian programming to several cities across the country. The eleven o'clock nightly program of religious music was my favorite. I listened to it as I ruminated about the need to learn a skill to survive in this promised land.

One night in late April 1980, I arrived home around eleven thirty from my $3.10-an hour job at McDonald's. I gently opened the door to avoid waking my two baby sisters, my stepmother, and her brother Manny, who had lived with us since Dad had returned to Haiti. As I pushed open the door and furtively cocked my head, I was met by a medium size, rigid shadow—a ghost of sorts—behind the door that startled me.

My stepmother popped out and pulled the door open wider, letting me in. Before I could say, "Good evening," she began. "Ti Milliardaire, I need to talk to you." She shook her head. "This is very important." I collected myself. "Do you know where your dad is? Please give him that letter since I don't have a forwarding address for him back home in Haiti." Something was wrong, and whatever it was, it must be inside that envelope.

The house was quiet and dark except for the dim light coming from the bathroom. I followed it, got undressed, and put on my pajamas. As I brushed my teeth, I felt a searing pain at the back of my head. Was she going to ask me to leave? I felt like a boat losing its moorings, floating toward deeper waters and tossed sideways in the undercurrent. I left the bathroom and found my cot in the corridor. I felt sick and found it hard to fall asleep. *What's in this envelope?* I took a deep sigh, and after a while was carried off to dreamland.

Early the next morning, I awoke, washed up, and hurried to get dressed. I put on my navy-blue pants, buttoned my beige shirt, and grabbed my green sweater, pulling it over my head. That morning, I didn't think about my three scrambled eggs and four slices of bread.

Something had deviled me all night, but I was unable to imagine what it could be. There was no need to reproach myself for being timorous or cautious that morning. I often blamed myself for falling short. The trash can was overflowing with spoiled foods and soiled diapers. The can was one foot away from my head, but it hadn't bothered me a great deal that night. In the past, I'd had to cover my nose with a kerchief to deter my gag reflex. I needed to take the trash to the dumpster. But that thought had never occurred to me.

I picked the letter from my stepmother up from the table, then sat on my cot. I removed the letter from the envelope and spread it open. I began reading: "The Commonwealth of Massachusetts …" I stared at the page and grew numb with disbelief. I was sweating. Waves of shock, confusion, and loss washed over me as horror, denial, pain, sadness, and grief set in. I rested my head between my hands. I thought of the country I'd left behind. Then I surprised myself by laughing as I read on. "Um, this is a divorce letter," I said. "If that is the case, what in the world am I doing here? Whatever knot tied us before is now broken, and how can I still live with her?" I wrapped my clothes into a ball and tucked them into my backpack. I placed my other pair of shoes, a small French-English dictionary, and my toothbrush, comb, and small transistor radio into a bag. I was ready to crawl out quietly.

Perhaps she was bitter about the way Dad had gotten himself into the predicament with the bully at work. He likely hadn't thought about how his actions would lead to his leaving two infants behind. Why did my stepmother have to hand me the letter for him when they had lived together for nine years in America? Was she afraid of what Dad's reaction might have been? Like when Dad got Madame Klebert arrested and jailed at the Penitencier National because of the comments the old lady had made about Yvette shacking up with him, the way John the Baptist had complained about Herodias's behavior with Herod Antipas?

My stepmother and I had always been on good terms. Yvette was the sweetest woman. Early in my life, I had mistaken her for my mother. She was a force of good in my family, and her counsel had saved Father's life on several occasions. She'd left Haiti when I was still a kid, but she would return with Dad each summer.

And when they came, they would take us to drive-in theaters to watch movies in the open air. Those days gave me a sense that life was beautiful, sweet, and joyful. What I liked best about those excursions was the food at the drive-ins. It was delicious and gave us a taste of middle-class life.

During one of these summer vacations, Dad asked me to clean his rental car with a rag. I also did something else—I hid in the hatchback of the rented Mazda by lifting the latch and pulling it down. When Marco passed by and saw me, he wanted to join me, but I signaled for him to stay away so as not to bring attention to my presence. He acquiesced. Dad and Yvette were distracted as I crawled into the back of the car. I breathed softly during the entire trip to Port-au-Prince. I so badly wanted to be with them. As they got out of the car, my stepmother noticed me first and called Dad to look in my direction. They both laughed.

Their squabble in the winter of 1980 almost left me a homeless vagrant in Boston. Did I have to be part of their outbursts? Why pollute our relationship? Why did I have to become a witness to the grown-ups' interactions? Why did she have to wait for him to return to Haiti to muster the courage to give him a divorce?

Shouldn't immigrants from traditional societies receive psychological counseling before they leave their homelands? Or soon after they arrive in America? Shouldn't they be taught about the pitfalls and stress of the hectic and fast-paced life awaiting them? Shouldn't they also be educated about laws, norms, and expected behaviors? Shouldn't they be warned about the danger of isolation? Shouldn't they be informed about the signs of depression and other mental disorders? They were forever changed.

Many immigrants never adjusted to America. That was sad. Was my stepmother being passive-aggressive? Who could blame her for the mess she found herself in? Was my father a saint? One need only recall that Dad could be a curmudgeon at times.

I put on my shoes and gathered my belongings. What could I say? This was the stepmother who had been such an important part of my life all those years, who had given me wise counsel over the past three months, who had succored me when I was sick, who many times had helped Marco and me, especially when we fell from the stairway of the apartment on Rue Montparnasse. This was the woman who'd pleaded with Dad on our behalf and contributed so much to our lives, the woman who'd sheltered me in her house even though Dad was living a continent away, the woman who'd kept Dad sane all these years. What could I tell her for choosing me to deliver the message of her divorce to Dad? In truth, I harbored no ill feelings toward her, none whatsoever. She had been my second mother. To paraphrase Voltaire, "If God did not exist, it would be necessary to invent him." Well, if it wasn't true, then I invented it. I had only gratitude for her for not leaving Dad when we were young. As I vacated her brother's house that morning, I hugged her and said, "I understand."

She was worthy of my admiration and love, but I was losing a part of myself. I slung my backpack over my right shoulder, pulled the door open, and stepped out. I clutched the handle for a few seconds, but took a deep breath and walked away. It was a chilly day outside. Without delay, I went to a telephone booth and placed a call to my aunt, Tante Princina Syverain

Romain. I explained what had just happened, and she reassured me it was time for me to move in with her.

That night, I took up residence in a different household. I was only four months out of Haiti, and I had changed homes three times. It is a ritual many immigrants experienced upon their arrival. My aunt was gracious in inviting me to stay with her.

In my head, I knew I was on my own and had to grow up fast if I was going to discover my compass in America. I began to see America for what it was: neither hell nor paradise. But it could be brutal at times. It empowered me to know there was no reason to whine or to blame anyone else.

I woke up the next morning resolved to make good use of what life had handed me, no matter what. "Auntie, what do I do to go to school?" I asked.

She looked at me, puzzled. "You have to work for at least ten years before you can attend school," she said.

I balked. "Well, if that is the case, I might as well go back home to complete my studies before I give up."

"Do as it pleases you," she remarked. "That is my observation in the last three years I have lived in this country."

Though I appreciated her insight, I had my doubts. By nature, I have a contrarian attitude. I resolved to become the exception.

Temple Salem became my beacon. I attended their Sabbath services every Saturday. To my great surprise, I found a cadre of college-bound young men and women who were more than willing to offer me a morsel of their wisdom. They attended Boston College, Boston University, Boston State College, and the other universities nearby. I was hooked. I couldn't wait to get there each week to listen to their academic tales. I craved their company.

One young man, Jean Robert Cenat, who was a psychology major at the now-defunct Boston State College, became my mentor. Perhaps he had noted my desperation to attend school. What I liked about him above all else was his positive attitude. A positive outlook is a man's best friend in times of great turmoil. Former chief of staff general Colin Powell says that optimism is a force multiplier.[5] Jean Robert Cenat wasn't one of those jealous and pessimistic losers I had encountered on my journey. With him, everything was possible. "If you want to become an astrophysicist," he once said, "that it is within your reach if you are willing to do the work and jump higher.

Or better yet, be a nuclear scientist." This young man was my Toussaint L'Ouverture, a man of progress, my true Bredaist.

What made him so authentic was the fact that in his youth, on his road to Damascus, he had made some bad choices. For a while, he had forsaken his assembly, smoked, and drank before he became a psychologist and man of purpose. Now he was in a better position to counsel others, giving them advice born of experience.

On Sunday mornings, many of these students came to Temple Salem's basement to study. They also tutored those seeking help with their schoolwork. Whew! These sessions mesmerized me. I had never seen so many large, bound books on subjects like chemistry, mathematics, biology, and human anatomy. Their books were bigger than the largest dictionary I ever laid eyes on in Haiti. Looking at these books and their bearers left me feeling giddy. Many in the group were premed students, and I gravitated toward them like a magnet. One of them, a first-year medical student, once brought a large femur bone during a health seminar. To me, it was like something from the Wizard of Oz. The students' presence at the church gave me a thirst and a yearning for knowledge—knowledge that could help the world move forward.

I became restless and impatient to enter the twelfth grade in September. The basement was always cold in winter, no matter how hard the boiler worked, but the mass of bodies moving from book to book made up for it with human heat and indomitable spirits. I regarded them with awe.

Kathy Desrosiers looked a little older than she really was because she was so serious about her schoolwork. She had a creative brain that contained every word found in *Webster's*, and also had a self-assurance rarely seen in youth her age. Where I had doubts, KD offered guidance. Her father had deserted the family or had mental illness and couldn't care for them. She lived with her mother, who worked two jobs to support her and her two younger siblings. KD's demeanor attracted me like a moth to the light.

I spent much of my time talking to her about the different classes I needed to take in September and how to best prepare for college the following fall. She once said, "You told me you want to go to Dorchester High School in the fall. But I notice that you spend most of your time peeking at college-student materials." I pretended not to hear her. "Well, young man, remember first things first, always. Please don't go bonkers in Boston."

21
CHAPTER

Finding an Anchor

What better way to enslave a man, than to
give him the vote and call him free.

—ALBERT CAMUS

Another month passed, and by the spring of 1980, I was edgy as I looked ahead. KD must have noticed my agitation. "Would you like to enroll in a school?" she asked. "I could assist if you want me to."

"Oh, sure! I'd love to go to school," I said. "You could help me fulfill my dream of going back to school. I stopped attending in December."

KD was a stellar student at Boston Latin High School and was preparing to attend college in the fall. Like her, I wanted to be a doctor one day. As a child in Haiti, I saw people die due to lack of medical care, and I thought that one day I would bring medical care to the sick and the poor. I had dreamed of becoming one since I was eleven years old, but I had kept that dream a secret out of fear of rejection, ridicule, or bullying. I had angst about people killing my dream.

She directed me to the Codman Square Library on Washington Street in Dorchester. I had never been into a library in my life. Back in Haiti, neighborhood or school libraries were nonexistent. The first day I stepped into that library, I became absorbed in thinking about all the books on its shelves. I saw doors opening for me if I learned the invaluable information contained within their pages.

Thousands of books sat on the shelves. How fortunate this poor neighborhood was to have such a rich collection. What more could a poor immigrant ask for in his new, adopted land? I had all kinds of manuscripts at my disposal and plenty of time to read them. Who needed television when one could gain knowledge from books? "All wealth comes from knowledge," Dad had said.

As winter began to wane in Boston, the cold mornings, frosty evenings, and frigid nights finally melted away. The petals of daffodils grew bright. Green orchards and white lilies blossomed under the heat of a suspended blue sky. Spring was in the air. Yes! Life was good, and I had finally found a better job—another gift from heaven.

I'd never felt like anything was against me. There was no need to blame a person, state, or system. In Haiti, all people were in the same boat, and that boat was sinking. It was always up to the individual to swim against the current. But when I came to America, I got my lucky break. To quote the pioneering neurosurgeon and father of cervicomedulllary decompression, Dr. Ben Carson, "Poverty is in part a mindset and to a large extent a state of mind."[6] I agreed, though sometimes, I knew, it was impossible to get out of it without help.

In late March of 1980, I showed up for work one morning at a factory located in East Cambridge, near the Lechmere train station. The foreman handed me a pushcart packed with a large roll of fabrics. It weighed at least three hundred pounds. Pushing it from the factory's weaving-loom area to the shipping area was out of my league. The cart veered off with the roll and jerked the whole thing toward me. I attempted to secure it with my body, but I quickly sensed my weight couldn't counterbalance the giant roll. As the cart pressed against my chest and began choking me, my breathing became shallow. Yet I pushed on, thinking I could tame the cuckoo cargo, only to realize I was still gasping for air. With resignation, I did a ninety-degree turn, dodging the cart that was now chasing me like a bullet. I let the whole thing crash to the floor. The supervisor had been tracking my movement without me knowing. He called me and told me to follow him to the human resources office. There, he asked the bookkeeper to cut me a check on the spot for the four hours I had worked.

Before I left the factory, a compatriot who had worked there for fifteen years pulled me aside. "Young man, I am glad you are leaving this job," he said. "Of the few of us who are still working here, half are crazy from the toxic fumes we've inhaled over the years, and the other half can't tell you what day it is." I thanked him for his honesty. I sure needed a job but not at the cost of going nuts.

As I waved goodbye to the crew with my paycheck secure in my pocket, I felt confident I was in America to stay. I had come to discover lost paradise or heaven or hell or whatever else loomed ahead.

After weeks of fruitless job searching, I became despondent. I would have returned to the linen factory had they been willing to rehire me. The country was in the midst of a deep recession with inflation running high, like a mad bull in a bear economy. People seemed distant. Many likely asked themselves, "What's wrong with America?"

I filled out many job applications throughout the city of Boston and in the surrounding areas. But I heard nothing. I finally found a part-time position at the McDonald's on Tremont Street across from the Boston Common Park. It was a godsend. The office manager, Ed Wob, was a decent man. When he hired me, he must have seen my plight as a "just come"—what we Haitian immigrants called ourselves back then. I was at my wit's end. My mother's annual lease on her small room in Haiti was due, and I had promised I would pay her rent. Haiti was still a place to raise a family and roam its streets safely. Today, the oligarchs have their gangs and so do the politicians. They work together toward the common goal of terrorizing, kidnapping for ransom, intimidating and killing people among the middle class and working class. Many of the wives and children of these politicians live overseas. Nearly all young Haitians want to leave, and they no longer trust the country's corrupt and dysfunctional legal system. The older folks are nostalgic of the Duvalier dictatorship. Haiti is fast becoming a mafia state. Democracy has failed!

The night assistant manager at the McDonald's, Mr. Jemison, was a morose man with stooped shoulders, as though burdened by haunted memories. He would ask me to carry loads of garbage that weighed more than I did. He would make me clean the bathroom after everyone had left even though there were night janitors to do this work. His eyes were sad and his gait diffident. This man could have been a father or even an uncle to me. His forebears had been brought to America four hundred years ago, shackled like mine before boarding a ship and chained below deck. They'd been put in iron cuffs, thumbs screwed under the ship's bridge for the duration of the torturous three-month voyage. They landed on the shores of America to till its soil without pay, never thanked for having made America great and wealthy. This man was my family. Our people had come from Africa. More than half of our forebears had died at sea, many having had the courage to commit suicide instead of accepting their lot. Many died before making it to the auction parlors in the South. Many of the survivors were crippled for life and tossed into the streets of many plantations and left for dead.

As Ta-Nehesi Coates states in his book, *Between the World and Me*, "It is easy to look away, to live with the fruits of our history and to ignore the great evil done in all our names. You and I never truly had that luxury. I think you know."[7]

This man was born in a country that had stolen from black folks for centuries. America had gnawed upon their marrow for years. How could he have the energy and the means to stop the plundering of its "Dreamers," as Coates called them, if not to suck a bit from me, making him an accomplice? I was young, and my marrow fresh as warm milk from the udders of a healthy heifer. This man lived in a country that butchered black babies before they could ask questions. Black folks couldn't begin to comprehend how they'd even gotten into this predicament. What gods had they angered to have had such a seal placed upon them for the marketplace? America is still wealthy. America refuses to pay a dime for reparations. America is the richest country in the world today, but it doesn't want to meet its obligations toward those in its midst that have been exploited for centuries. Black people in America must be saints; otherwise, they would have imposed forfeiture to America or have self-destructed with the country.

James Baldwin says in his book, *The Fire Next Time*, that America holds a quarter of the world's prisoners within its dungeons. They are dungeons, not correctional facilities. China has four times as many people as America. "A civilization is not destroyed by wicked people; it is not necessary that people be wicked but only that they are spineless"[8]

The prophet Habakkuk asks God in Habakkuk 1:2-8, "How long, O Lord, must I call for help, but you do not listen? Or cry to you, 'Violence!' but you do not save? ... Therefore the law is paralyzed, and justice never prevails."

It says in Habakkuk 2:8-16, "Look among the nations and watch—and be utterly amazed. For I am going to do something in your days that you would not believe, even if you were told ... Then the Lord replied, "For indeed I am raising up ... a bitter and hasty nation ... to possess dwelling places that are not theirs ... They fly as the eagle that hastens to eat ... Because you have plundered many nations, all the remnant of the people shall plunder you ... The cup from the Lord's right hand is coming around to you, and disgrace will cover your glory."

My father brought me to America. Our forebears inherited the island of Quisqueya. Millions before them died for their beautiful blue blood. France imposed an indemnity of 150 million francs—money they received in gold—in 1825 to Haiti for a war they lost. It would be absurd for the United States to impose an indemnity to Vietnam for having lost the Vietnam War or to Afghanistan for having spent 2 trillion dollars and 20 years of occupation there. Today, that amount is equivalent to several billion dollars. In other words, the French gutted the Haitian treasure with dire consequences for a fledgling nation.

However, to compare myself to my evening boss bore no justice. He'd had no choice in that matter. My ancestors, when they had been brought to

Saint Domingue, had no say in the devil enterprise either. But they wrested the land from the French. The deck had been stacked against Mr. Jemison from the start. It bore witness to this man's hard work, and many like him never had a chance to come close to my fortune.

This man's forebears received no reparations for having had their bodies plundered and their labor unpaid. Yet Germany paid the state of Israel upon its foundation up to $4 billion in reparations for the Jewish Holocaust. President Lyndon Baines Johnson once argued as quoted in the *Washington Post* of November 13, 1988, "If you can convince the lowest white man he's better than the best colored man, he won't notice you're picking his pocket. Hell, give him somebody to look down on, and he'll empty his pockets for you."[9] African Americans never received compensation for the free labor they gave to America over the years, and more than any other group in America, they continue to suffer the brunt of mistreatment and abuse. Furthermore, they still can't afford their bail when thrown into jail for parking violations.

Where are the reparations for African Americans and their descendants? Their children are being tossed into the gulags of America every night, and few notice. Where are the amends for the descendants of the slave living across the globe? Is that justice, or is it predation?

"By our unpaid labor and suffering, we have earned the right to the soil, many times over and over, and now we are determined to have it," said an anonymous author in 1861. The backs of black people built this world.

Mr. Jemison was born in a nation that has denied him and millions of black people the basics of life. He didn't have a place or land to call his own. His living wage couldn't afford him a decent place to sleep. He likely lived in a neighborhood where police harassed him. He couldn't roam without the shadows of racism and discrimination chasing him. In the words of an urban studies expert who helped create the New York City Housing and Development Administration, Charles Abrams: "Instead, the Federal Housing Administration adopted a racial policy that could well have been culled from the Nuremberg laws."[10]

My coworker had the right to feel indignant and irascible. How can one not be when born under such inauspicious conditions? He lived in a country that did everything it could to dismiss his manhood.

"It is in vain to allege, that our ancestors brought them hither, and not we," Yale President Timothy Dwight said in 1810. "We inherit our ample patrimony with all its encumbrances and are bound to pay the debts of our ancestors. This debt, particularly, we are bound to discharge: and, when the righteous Judge of the Universe comes to reckon with his servants, he will rigidly exact the payment at our hands. To give them liberty, and stop there, is to entail upon them a curse."[11]

With their free labor, my coworker's forebears propelled America and England and the world toward the industrial revolution. By 1840, the cotton produced by black slaves in the Southern states represented 59 percent of the country's exports. "Whoever says Industrial Revolution," wrote historian Eric J. Hobsbawm, "says cotton."[12] Not surprisingly, before the Civil War, the Mississippi Valley had more millionaires per capita than anywhere else in the country. And all that wealth was gained on the backs of black people and free labor. America knew how to milk black folks. It still does.

As *New York Times* best-selling author Michael Eric Dyson says in his book, *What Truth Sounds Like*, "Recently, as bigotry resurfaces, symbolized in the events in Charlottesville in August 2017, the lie is put to the belief that 'this is not American, this is not us,' when, indeed, it truly is. We do not want to acknowledge how true it is because it makes us look complicit in prejudice we thought we had gotten over. Donald Trump is far more representative of the nation than many whites would like to admit."[13]

In Quisqueya, the only thing I lacked was plenty of food. I had the good fortune of being raised by parents who gave me a head start. I inherited a soil to call my own. There were no forced partings or nuclear family destructions once the ex-slaves revolted and routed France off the land, unlike what happened to Henry Brown's wife and his children during slavery in America. I had neighbors who watched and cared for me as their son. Teachers prepared me and instilled in me early on a love and joy of learning. And even a fallen angel like Lucifer found it impossible to undo what my parents had instilled in me at an early age—my sense of self and resiliency. Like the African proverb says, "It takes a village to raise a child." A village raised me, and I couldn't have had it any better. I had everything I needed as a teenager in America because I knew who I was. As Magrann would say, "We are the descendants of princes and princesses, of kings and queens. We give life to an elite community where love unlocks a world of beauty and serenity. We must remember who we are wherever we are."

By the time I arrived in America at age nineteen, my mind was made up.

Though I felt a bit confused at first, still my priorities were as clear as day-break, and no one was able to shake my foundation. An individual can only be destroyed when he stops taking stock or gauging his situation. Instead, he must accept the path traced for him by others for a journey he is ill-equipped for. The culture that made my night manager what he was had stacked the odds against him. America didn't want to face the truth, redress this man's grievances, or give him justice. If anything, that man's plight had grown over the years and would burden him until he slipped into his grave. If it weren't for some good old Negro spirituals on Sunday mornings, folks like this man would have some good and legitimate reasons to go crazy while clinging to their bazookas. God isn't dead! I know.

As I thought about this middle-aged man's dilemma, I wondered, did he have a choice? It would be easy to criticize him for his heavy handling of me, but that would have been unfair to him. I had more options than he did. I was young, alert, aspiring, observant, and I had no family to care for, so to speak. I had no moral duty to care for others if I couldn't care for myself.

One evening, I found myself dragging a large trash bag outside the restaurant. After several attempts at throwing the trash bag into the dumpster, I collapsed. So I quit. I found a part-time position at another McDonald's. Soon I began looking for a school. I need to acquire a skill.

The next Saturday afternoon, I met Jacques Eusebe Sr, a well-respected, middle-aged man of the church in Temple Salem's basement.

"Hey, Jacques, I am told you work at the CETA office. Can you help me enroll there?" He was a sort of troubleshooter for new Haitian immigrants and knew how to help me apply at the Comprehensive Employment and Training Act Office.

"Well, drop by Monday at the Roxbury office and ask for me at the front desk," he told me. Then he gave me the address.

Early Monday morning, I took a bus from Chelsea to the Haymarket Square station. At the station, I went downstairs and boarded the out-bound Orange Line to Roxbury Station. As the train emerged from the underground passageway and onto the suspended railroad tracks, I peered through the windows at the maddening traffic below me. The train lurched and screeched as the conductor applied the brakes on the grinding metal rails and slowly made a turn. I thought the clattering metal and the train would hurtle off the tracks and onto the street, so I jerked to the opposite seat. Then the train finally came to a squealing, wheezing stop. I exited the doors and walked onto the platform of the terminal and crossed Dudley Street, where I directed myself to the CETA office.

At the office, I was given a basic algebra test. Thirty minutes later, I returned the paper with all the right answers. I was admitted and thrilled to finally have found a school in America. When the young female receptionist told me to return the next day to start training, I saw before me a dream of infinite possibilities. I loved America. I was to become an electronic technician.

Tuesday morning came, and I was ecstatic. I was back in school, sort of. I wasn't waiting for KD to help me enroll at Dorchester High School in the fall. I entered a room. It was pale and dark for a place of learning and not what I expected, or at least not what I was used to. There were about fifteen adult students in the classroom. The youngest among them must have been at least forty years old, but that didn't deter my enthusiasm. I took a seat while the instructor introduced himself. He was a man in his fifties with thick-rimmed glasses, a fringe of gray-white hair around his balding crown, a shuffling gait, and an almost inaudible voice. He looked old. He began the class by teaching us the basic colors of a transistor and what each meant. The lecture lasted three hours.

In the CETA program, every enrollee received a stipend after two weeks of attending class. Not only was I learning a new skill, I would be getting paid. They would soon give me a check. I thought about getting myself a new pair of shoes and a sweater and paying for bus and train fares.

After class, the administrator, who was an African American lady, approached me and asked me to follow her into her office. She opened the office door, waved her hand, and directed me to sit down. Before I regained my composure, with a grandmotherly instinct, she asked me a pointed question: "What are you doing here?"

I thought about her question. "What am I doing here?" I repeated. "Well, I am here to learn about electronics."

"But you know better," she said. "You don't belong here, child. You should be in school. This place is for folks who have passed their prime for schooling." She paused. "You are young, and you can get greater skills. Go back to a real school and apply yourself because you can do better." She was so articulate and blunt I recognized that she was right. I knew then that she was a prophet who had told me the truth.

"Thank you for the advice, and I will do as you say," I told her. I never returned to the CETA office. I couldn't wait to follow her guidance as I flung open her door. It was all I needed to hear. Good advice is worth more than its value in gold. If I wanted extra goading and a cogent argument, I sure found them in that CETA administrator. Now I was convinced my goal of going back to school in September was a noble one.

What had that saint seen in me that I hadn't noticed? She saw naïveté, ignorance, enthusiasm, eagerness, optimism, and a good dose of youth. If I stayed optimistic and was driven to make things happen, I was sure I would get somewhere better than I had first imagined.

The days of snow and ice and wind in Boston made me long for home. But when I began to see students my age with books and bags emblazoned with MIT, Harvard, BU, Simmons College, and Boston College logos, I knew I wanted to be one of them, or at least a high school student. As the snows of winter in Boston began to thaw and spring sprinted toward summer, I looked forward to the start of the new school year.

I had already found a full-time job at the Sheraton Hotel as a housekeeper. In those days, I kept little company not because I didn't like people but because I had little to do with them. I was too busy with an uncertain future and too preoccupied with things I had little control over. I only had time for work, from six in the morning until two thirty in the afternoon.

Underneath this aloofness, I harbored a host of fears, insecurities, and shortcomings. I soon started spending the rest of the day at Codman Square Public Library, staying until closing and reading books on various subjects. I worried constantly. I feared the Boston School District would not allow me to enter the twelfth grade at Dorchester High School, the school I liked. It was only two blocks from home. With that in mind and as fall neared, I began looking in earnest for a job that would accommodate my school schedule. The echoes of a former Lucifer, her cohorts, and countless others continued to ring in my head. "You won't amount to much."

Codman Square Library was a treasure trove! What freedom for fertile minds! Reading again became a distraction for me. I found a sort of spirituality within the written pages. Each month, Rock would bring home the French political magazine *Afrique Asie*. He also subscribed to *Scientific American*, *Popular Science*, and *AAAS*. Though neither of us could grasp much of what was inside their pages, particularly the mathematical equations, we kept reading. With our limited English, we devoured every copy. These magazines were written in jargon only scientists understood, but we didn't care that we had little grip on the mathematical equations or the latest discovery about relativity. Codman Square Library was my haven and sometimes my heaven.

Every weekday when I left work, my gnawing hunger for knowledge continued, yet, when I saw college students entering the Sheraton Hotel lobby with their wealthy parents in tow, I became discouraged. I still didn't know whether I could ever attend high school again. I'd left Haiti before I completed my studies. Why bother to dream about all the big shots stomping on Commonwealth or Massachusetts Avenues? I was a nobody without the money to pay for college. I started doubting myself even more. In May, the city became a parade of graduating students and their families. I dreamed of the time I could mimic these folks. I would become a peacock for everyone to see. I would trek along with professors with PhDs discussing subjects of great importance to the intelligentsia. On graduation day, I would wear a beautiful cap and gown. I would stand on the corner of Massachusetts and Huntington Avenues waving at passing cars. I would listen to the honking motorists until their horns deafened me. I would give the biggest smile for the world to see.

If I wanted to stuff my brain with books heavy enough to carry in a backpack, that would be my burden.

22
CHAPTER

Dorchester High

I'm not bitter, neither am I cruel
But ain't nobody paid for slavery yet
I may be crazy, but I ain't no fool.
About my forty acres and my mule.

—OSCAR BROWN JR.

I finally entered Dorchester High in September of 1980. My new full-time janitorial job at Orion Research began at three o'clock in the afternoon and went until eleven thirty at night. Between catching the red-line and the orange-line trains plus a bus, I arrived home at one o'clock in the morning, sometimes later. Meanwhile, the school guidance counselor, Mrs. Jacqueline Murray, badgered me the entire first two weeks of school. She felt it would better if I attended English High.

This woman did everything in her power to deny Rock and me entrance to Dorchester High. She came close to being our George Corley Wallace and Ross Barnett—two wicked men who did everything in their power to block black students from entering the doors of the University of Alabama and Ole Miss at the height of the civil rights era. Though they lived in different times than Mrs. Murray, they acted the same way. Perversely, this woman was a Haitian immigrant who wanted us to attend English High School for the wrong reason—because she wanted to fill the pews of English High in order to guarantee their English as a Second Language program would survive and some Haitian teachers would maintain their employment.

From my perspective, she was working at my now-defunct Dorchester High solely to scoop any new Haitian immigrant students for English High School. She wanted us to attend their ESL program. However, Dorchester High held the key to the America I had come for.

Mr. Cray, my chemistry and math teacher, was a congenial young man who wanted to see all his students succeed. His inspiration and encouragement led me to choose chemistry as my first major in college before I switched to pharmacy. The school was almost all-black with white teachers. These teachers made me feel at home. I am sure many of them could have chosen to teach at a whites-only school, but they decided to teach there instead.

Mr. Lievens, the school's English teacher, introduced us to Shakespeare, Ernest Hemingway, John Steinbeck, T.S. Elliot, and many others—though I wished he would have exposed us to Zora Neale Hurston, Langston Hughes, and many of the other great black writers as well. He would take us to new play matinees, such as *Satchmo*. But every time I spoke in his class, I became the subject of derision because of my English accent. At times, I was so embarrassed that I did not want to participate in class discussion.

Mr. Palmieri, our social studies teacher, ever the idealist for socialism, was dedicated to his craft. He denounced the dangers of Mussolini's fascism, Hitler's Nazism, and Stalin's totalitarianism. These were fun days. Dorchester High made learning possible.

The common thread among the teachers at Dorchester High was a genuine sense of purpose. They went out of their way in coaching, tutoring, and encouraging students to dream and by providing us the tools we needed to succeed. They were disinterested in the political expediency of the time. One day I was shocked to hear Mr. Lievens say that none of us could ever be president of the United States because of our skin color. Where did he learn that? In the US Constitution? I knew that as a non-native I couldn't be president, but the other students could hope to be at least. They had been born in America. Why rob them of a dream?

In addition to Rock and me, there were other emancipated young adults in that school with full-time after-school jobs. These students had no parents or guardians to return to at night. Rock and I were likely the oldest students in the school.

These were days I had no time for anything besides school, work, and making sure my mom was cared for in Haiti. Some of my old friends from the island who lived in Boston and Chelsea started to complain that Rock and I had become Jews. They felt that all Rock and I cared about was making money. We took that as a compliment. Why? Because we were busy and obsessed with school and work. I would rather spend an hour washing my dirty clothes at the Laundromat, brushing my teeth a bit longer in the school bathroom, or buying groceries at the twenty-four-hour store near my rented, furnished room than socializing on weekdays. These actions would get me further than ten minutes of mingling with people whose vision was so divergent from mine. I no longer had much to do with folks I had little in common with.

As mentioned, although the Boston School Committee had cleared mine and Rock's admissions, our school counselor Mrs. Murray was adamant in her refusal to let us attend Dorchester. She gave the lame excuse that we needed to be proficient in English to stay at Dorchester. But how could we become proficient if we didn't fully immerse ourselves in the language? That experience with my first school counselor in America created in me an aversion to dealing with school counselors. I told her I was not too fond of English High School because I felt I would be more proficient at Dorchester. Furthermore, I hadn't left Haiti to come to America to learn French.

It was an insult to Rock and me. We told Mrs. Murray we would prefer not to attend school at all if we had to go to English High. The name of the school was misleading. Students there barely spoke English. At that point, she had to acquiesce. She knew we saw her for what she was: a fraud. Whether Mrs. Murray was placed at Dorchester High to prey on school-aged Haitian immigrants for the English High bilingual program, I would never know.

I had noticed that the quality of the education the newly arrived Haitian students who attended English High received was inferior. The school wasn't preparing most of them for the academic rigors of college life. Ironically, English High had an abysmal English program with a bad reputation. Having experienced such a bias firsthand, I believe it's a disservice to teach students in their native non-English languages as they attend school in the United States.

In the summer of 1988, before I left Boston to attend Stanford University School of Medicine, my worst fear was confirmed when one of the bilingual Haitian teachers, a family member, told me not to make a case for abolishing bilingual education for these Haitian students. Some teachers would hate me. Their livelihood came at the expense of these new Haitian immigrants.

I still can't grasp why the American Teachers Association is against school reform, school vouchers, and charter schools, especially in exchange for failing schools. Don't they want to see students progress? Don't they believe in choices like those afforded the sons and daughters of the United States presidents? How can the rich and powerful have options while the poor have none? The ATA is the biggest detriment and the biggest reason many of the schools in America are failing. It's hard to reason with the ATA when everything boils down to job protection. America would do well to make the teaching profession a valuable, highly paid profession and as competitive as it is in Finland. In the words of my deceased half-sister, Bernadette Sylverain, "If America fails, the world will crumble."

And how can the ATA argue with schools like Kipp Academy Charter School in Brooklyn, New York? Kipp ranked seventeenth nationally, second in New York State, and fifth among charter high schools in America. It serves grades K–12, with 100 percent minority enrollment. Eighty-five percent of its students are economically disadvantaged. As of 2010, the school had about seventy-five teachers. How could school choice be bad for poor black and brown students in America?

When I heard a former Palo Alto Unified School District superintendent in 2009 state that minority students within their district couldn't succeed because of their socioeconomic backgrounds, I sat there, numb, thinking the superintendent parochial and lazy; he had failed to do his homework by not looking into the best way to address minority students' failure within his district. Perhaps he was a fraud too. He failed to offer a better vision because he had none. He ought to learn from successful school models across the country, like Kipp Academy.

Not surprisingly, a Stanford study by Francis A. Pearman and Joseph Gardella published by the American Educational Research Association in September 2019 shows a link between achievement gap and racial disparities in school discipline. The researchers found a 10 percentage point increase in the black-white discipline gap that is 17 percent larger than the average black-white achievement gap. "This suggests that the mechanisms connecting the achievement gap to the discipline gap, such as teacher biases and feeling isolated at school, may be more salient for black students,"[14] said Pearman. It seems that many of the brightest black folks in America are confined to jails and prisons.

Old habits die hard. That superintendent continued to see everything through the prism of black and white at a time we could ill afford to be doing that. He must have thought there were no consequences for the country for failing its black and brown children. The country needs every student to succeed to remain competitive on the world stage. As Victor Hugo [15] says, "School is a sanctuary as much as a Chapel."

As a young man from the country, I had very little knowledge of the streets of big cities such as Boston. Yet, when I drove a cab in Boston, I would find customers who asked me to take them into the "Combat Zone," as they called it. This zone was nestled near Tufts University School of Medicine, in the theater district. I picked up fares everywhere in the city. There were married old men returning home to face their lonely wives in the suburbs after a night of drinking and frolicking with young women. From Logan Airport, I once picked up a harried professor who'd given a lecture that morning. There was the nurse-aide who was running late for her private-duty night-shift job with the elderly.

One Sunday afternoon after driving a Checker cab all day, I returned to the taxi office and paid them for the gas and the car lease only to realize I'd made fifty cents for the twelve-hour shift. I used the two quarters for my bus fare home. I had worked from dawn to dusk but couldn't afford to buy myself a hamburger. I had to go to college to get a skill. I needed to contribute more to America.

Five hundred Haitians fought alongside the Americans against the British in the fall of 1779 during the siege of Savannah. They were skilled. "Our people have helped liberate South America. Our people have helped the Greeks from the jaws of the Ottoman Empire. Our people have brought a world empire, the French Empire, to its knees; this act not only freed Haiti but also prevented the French from invading mainland America. Our people gave a roadmap to the world to free humanity everywhere under the sun. The British have Robin Hood; the Irish have Cuchulain; the Greeks have Achilles; the French have their Dames Blanches; the Germans have their Nerthus. We, in Haiti, have Toussaint L'Ouverture with the singular distinction that he is real, while the others are myths. Our people have shown once and for all that there is great strength in unity," said Jocelyn Leveillé, another Temple Salem mentor, in a conversation.

23
CHAPTER

Pick up your
Corner

One day we'll stand up, put down our feet
As we did in Saint Domingue.
They'll know who the boat people are.

— FELIX-MORISSEAU LEROY

A fter Rock and I entered Dorchester High in the fall of 1980, he asked me to search for a furnished room. He was too busy with his night-shift security job. He also needed time to sleep and to complete his schoolwork. I obliged. I was tired of picking up discarded Styrofoam planks from my work to place on my side of the mattress I shared in Auntie's Princina apartment in September 1980. The bed was always cold, even though the boiler worked.

So Rock and I decided to rent a room. I followed his advice without thinking about the consequences. Every afternoon after school in October before work for three weeks, I would canvass the school neighborhoods. I trekked along Washington Street all the way to the Ashmont train station checking the realty rental offices. When I finally found a place, I picked up the few scraps collected over the last ten months in America. I thanked Tante Princina Romain for her three-bedroom apartment on Stockton Street. Without her help, when Yvette gave me Dad's divorce letter, I would have been homeless.

Before I found this place, a lady from Temple Salem told us she could rent us a room in her apartment. We paid her $200 for the month's rent. She promised we could move in the following month. Before long she learned that we drove taxis on weekends. Two weeks later, she met me in the Temple Salem church basement, took me aside, and demanded I see her after Sabbath about the room rental. So I dropped by her apartment before heading home in the evening.

"I learned that you and your brother drive a taxi," she said. "You know I don't allow anyone to enter my apartment after ten in the evening."

"Well, if that's the case, we won't be able to rent from you," I said. "Because when we drive a taxi, we expect to get home after midnight. Return our money, and that will do."

"Oh no, Brother Syverain," she said. "How can I return you the money? You have paid already. Besides, it is you who can't come earlier than ten into my apartment."

"But, sister, that curfew won't work for us. We drive all night sometimes to get the money to pay you."

"Well, as far I am concerned, there is no refund."

"How can you do that? You are a church member, Sister Lalande."

She stroked her lips and blinked her dead eyes at me, then added. "What do you mean your money?"

My face got hot. "Yes, the $200 deposit."

"I am done talking about this. Once you have made the deposit, there is no refund."

"You never told us that before, sister."

"Well, now you know. Please excuse me."

"If that's the case, I am going to call Boston Housing Authority on Monday to report you for renting space in a public housing project."

"Oh no, brother, you can't do that to me. We belong to the same church family. Why would you want me to get in trouble?" I stood in her living room with a Bible and a church hymnal clutched to my chest. She sat on her living room couch, wagging her finger at me. She finally stood up and said, "I don't give donkey dung about your whining and warning. They told me about your kind."

I walked toward the front door, grasped the knob, and turned my head to look at her. "You said you aren't going to return us the money. You leave me no choice but to report you." I propped up my eyeglasses.

"I don't care. Do whatever you want to do. Whatever you say will not ruffle my feathers. Besides, a 'just come' like you can't bluff me." She raised her head, checking the thermostat on the wall, and veered off.

"Okay. Come Monday, you will find out which tastes hotter: the cayenne seed or the stem."

"Who the hell are you, talking to me like that? That's what's wrong with boat people like you: once they land in America, they think they own the land." She stared at me as I moved away.

"I am no boat people. I came here aboard an Eastern Airlines flight. In any event, boat people made this nation, and I wouldn't be in such bad company."

Not long ago, a horde of Haitian and Cuban expats had come coasting into Miami from the Mariel boatlift. They'd made America their new home as all immigrants and their descendants before them. What had happened to the America of compassion?

I turned around again, bewildered that she had stolen my money. As I sprinted toward the staircase to escape her tirade, she ran at my heels and shouted, "Brother Syverain, could I talk to you for a minute?" Rock was waiting for me downstairs. I had asked him to let me talk to her about the refund. He rushed up the stairs, flung her front door wide open, and demanded she return the money at once.

"You don't need to do that. I will get you your money tomorrow morning!" she barked. I winked at her and said goodbye. Rock and I stalked away from her apartment like the comrades we were.

On Sunday morning, in desperation, I pulled out every magazine and local newspaper to look for room rentals. I looked at every real-estate office window in the Roxbury area along Warren Street. I also checked the real-estate offices in the Dorchester area where black folks lived. I finally found a crooked sign posted on an electric pole: Furnished Room, Call Davis at 456-3445. I placed the call. The owner must have been waiting, for he answered on the first ring.

A day later, after school, the landlord picked me up in front of the Codman Square Library. He drove a few blocks to a house tucked between Norfolk and Stanton Streets at 14 Dyer Street in Dorchester. From that first encounter, I felt we were on a collision course. But I was stuck with that landlord for better or worse.

I called the new apartment the Cowboy's Place because of the owner's attitude. He looked like he was in his forties and had a huge silver ring on his middle finger that could crack some teeth or even a skull if necessary. I feared I was fair game. Mr. Davis made it clear to me as he adjusted his trousers that he had a gun. When I got in his car to go look at the room, he blew a jet of white ganja smoke. He lifted his shirt so I could see the Colt .45 tucked in its holster. He saw me as a recalcitrant rube who looked at him with distrust and wanted to remind me who was in the driver's seat. I got the message.

Soon we got off the car. He ushered me to a decrepit one-level, chocolate-colored house with metal bars on both front windows. We climbed two flights of stairs to get inside. He pushed the first door on the left behind the entrance and shouted, "This is the room!" He offered a faint smile and asked me if I liked it. Before I could say yes, he said it would cost me fifty dollars a week.

The house was barren, except for a stove and a refrigerator as the only appliances. A bare, leftover mattress lay on the floor in my room. I walked toward the back and swung open the bathroom door; a dead cockroach gawked at me from near the toilet bowl. I quickly closed the door behind me. I looked for a table, a chair, or anything that would make this apartment look like a living space, but I couldn't find any. I saw no one near the other three rooms. What was I doing here? I opened the fridge but quickly shut it because of the vermin crawling inside. A broom or an ironing board would normally be found in the closet behind the fridge, but there was none. Nevertheless, Rock and I moved in so that we had a place to sleep after work and school.

Was the landlord trying to scare me, or was he scared of me? Was it the voice of youth that rattled him? I thought so. Did I look like a gangster or a troubled teenager? I was neither, nor was I a saint. I guessed it mattered little to him. He wanted to remind me that I had better pay him on time when I moved into his cage or else.

What worried me more than anything was the fact that the gas range was the only means of warming the apartment. So, at night, all four of the gas burners on the range stayed lit. The air inside the place was dryer than the Sahara Desert. It thickened my nasal passages, giving me a sinus infection. Still, I had to leave my door open for the heat to thaw my brother and me at night.

When I was asleep, I dreamed of people coming there with guns, knives, and other things. Sometimes I heard arguments in the next room, though I never saw anyone with dangerous objects inside the apartment.

What made this place so different from the other places I had lived in was the fact that the escape window on our room had those burglar bars. Plus, our room faced the street, and pedestrians often craned their necks to spy inside. If ever there was a fire, people would have seen us behind those grills being roasted like chickens. Every Friday afternoon, Cowboy showed up to pick up his rental money.

We moved there on October 28, 1980. By the end of January, Rock and I talked about leaving. It had become too risky to our health and our lives. There were cockroaches as giant as my thumbs inside the bathroom. Mice crawled near our milk cups on the floor when the door to our room stayed open.

In our carefree way, that week we failed to communicate with Cowboy about our intention to leave his ratty tenement. We stopped paying him, assuming he would use our security deposit for the rent. We were wrong.

One Friday night, I arrived home from work. I had trekked the block from the bus stop on that cold night of 1981 and entered the front door of the house. Soon, I found a lock on the door to our small room. What to do? I didn't want to stay outside for fear of frostbite or exposure. I was also scared of standing in the apartment lobby for fear of being looked upon as a suspicious vagrant by the other tenants. I doubted they knew me as a resident.

In Boston as in Haiti, I was never known as a pious or deeply religious young man. I never flaunted the scriptures at people. If anything, I resisted the urge to be fanatical about religious tenets. But I attended weekly church services, and I paid my tithes with the meager income I collected from my full-time work and taxi driving on weekends.

That night, I needed something different. I hungered for more faith. My fate hung in the balance at that very moment, and I took some time to think about my next move. I moved a few steps away from our door and thought about leaving the premises. But it was very cold outside and I had no place to go. Then I said loud enough for anyone to hear, "What do I have to lose?" I stepped back and did the unthinkable—I kung-fu kicked the door. To my great surprise, the lock tumbled down with one wimpy blow.

I entered the room, changed into my pajamas, and collapsed onto the mattress on the floor, falling into a deep slumber. Rock arrived at about six the next morning after driving taxi all night. "What are you doing there, bro?" he asked. "I came earlier last evening to eat some food and found our room locked and decided to go back to work." I opened my eyes and saw him standing before me.

"Well, if I were you, I would get my butt in here and get some sleep too before we go to church," I said. "Before Cowboy finds us."

At about ten that morning, we left the room. I put the lock back exactly the way I had found it the night before and went to church to pray. In the evening, we returned home and found everything undisturbed. As it was dark outside, Rock went to the taxi company to work the evening shift again. I sat on the mattress with my feet straddling the floor, completing some schoolwork. I sang some "Kumbaya, My Lord" and went to bed.

Early Sunday morning after the bus dropped me off on Huntington Avenue, I trudged toward the Checker Taxi Company on Gainsborough Street to lease a cab. Around six, I returned home and found Rock standing behind our door trying to keep it shut until I told him it was me. The landlord's behavior had flustered him. "The guy came in here and opened the door while I was asleep and demanded I pay him on the spot, so I paid him with the cash I made the last two days," he said. "I was afraid for my life." I became light-headed, so I crouched on the mattress.

"How much did you pay him?" I asked.

"I don't know. I gave the landlord everything in my pocket, and he took it all while laughing at me." That impish, unforgiving slumlord had taken more money than we owed him.

"You shouldn't have paid him since he has our deposit," I said. Then I thought about how, if I had been Rock, I would have paid the landlord for two more weeks to stay on his good side. After all, he had a pistol.

CHAPTER

24

Cummins Highway

We hang little thieves and take off our hats to great ones.

—GERMAN PROVERB

he next afternoon, I decided to look for a rental in another part of town. After traversing the Dorchester area on foot and in buses, no agent bothered to return my phone calls. I had failed to secure a permanent place to live three times within the last four months.

I went all the way to the Mattapan area, scouring the real-estate offices for postings. I turned right on Mattapan Square. Out of desperation, I turned right again at the junction of Cummins Highway and River Street.

I traversed the terrain, stopping, testing the area, and talking to a few gapers like myself, and then I took Cummins Highway. A block away, I stood still for a few seconds and scanned the street for apartments. Nearby was nestled either a Kentucky Fried Chicken or a Burger King; I can't recall which. Across the street sat two red brick apartment complexes where I was about to inquire. In front of the place, there was a large sign reading CUMMINS HIGHWAY APARTMENTS.

I started for the strange-looking place. It had a large tree in the middle and flowering plants circling the front doors on the ground level. I hesitated because the area looked too tranquil for this active part of town. A grocery store, a church, an ice cream parlor, and two banks all stood less than a block away.

I entered the building and began to look for the main office. As I crossed the yard of the complex, I found myself face-to-face with an old white man with snowy hair and laughing eyes. He asked if he could help me.

"Yes. I am looking for a place to rent," I said. "Do you have any one bedroom apartment available?" His eyes widened, and his cheeks reddened as if the question had caught him off guard.

"We do have a one bedroom available," he said. "My name is Elmer Lohan, the manager of the complex. I believe you can pick up a corner studio if you prefer."

"Well, how much are you asking for the rent?"

"The price is $390 every month."

"Could I take a look at the one bedroom instead?" I asked.

"Yes, you may. There is one problem," Elmer said. He instantly put me into a sour mood and made me feel like he didn't want to rent to me and wasn't going to. "You look very young," he said.

"It is true. I look very young. But I am a responsible person."

He looked at me, shook his head, and thought for a while. "We have a lot of old folks living here. You know how they are. You know what I mean."

"I wanted to tell him I didn't know what he meant. Old folks disliked noisy neighbors and many other things. All I needed was a place to live. Elmer had to find other reasons not to rent me the studio.

"Well, I am always working, and, besides, I am going to the University of Massachusetts soon. So I won't be spending much time at home."

"You know how much young people like to turn their radios so loud," he said.

"Sir, I don't have a radio." By now I understood he was talking about a boombox—a large portable radio/cassette player with two loudspeakers, a handle, and powered by batteries or live current. The boom box was quite popular in the late seventies and early eighties in America, and a backlash was happening. It had become associated with urban society, particularly among African American and Hispanic youth.

"You look young," Elmer said. "You know we don't want the elderly who live here to feel intimidated by the noise." I felt agitated by his continual talk about how young I was. I suspect he wanted to say that black youth scared the heck of old white folks. By now I must bear responsibility for every imaginable crime for my blackness. In truth, all I needed was a place to shelter me from the cold, the heat, and the rain and to get a quick shower and some sleep. It wasn't going to be, so I had to explain to myself who I was. Where were my roots? What did my old folks do for a living? How was I going to behave to make myself worthy of living in that enclave? Elmer was right to ask me those questions. He was working for someone, the property owner—someone much more powerful than he was, though invisible to me.

Why, more than any other group, did black folks suffer the brunt of dangerous diseases in America? The answer was everywhere for me to see. It wasn't what I'd learned through academia; I'd lived it. As a black youth in America, I saw injustice everywhere I turned. When I walked on the side-walk, I felt uneasy. I sensed I didn't belong. I felt like an intruder shaking up the order of things. The injustices done to every black man and woman in this land should have killed each one of them ten thousand times over, but they are still here.

After much deliberation, Elmer moved closer to me. Showing rare understanding, he whispered into my right ear that the studio would be cheaper. Maybe in his youth, he'd wandered a main street somewhere in America and understood that I, too, needed a break. I told him to wait while I headed to a grocery store nearby to buy a money order. Within fifteen minutes, I returned and handed him the check for the first and last months' rent and the security deposit. That was my entire fortune. Then he gave me the key to apartment G on the first floor. I had seen the one-bedroom, and it looked well kept, so I took him at his word before he could change his mind. As the apartment faced the street, it allowed me a glimpse from behind the curtains every so often when I heard a noise outside. The same day, Rock, Samuel Bauzile (nicknamed Ti Samuel, a smart youth from Temple Salem), and I moved into the studio.

By September 1981, we had moved out of the apartment on Cummins Highway. We had found a more affordable flat in the Mission Hill public-housing project on Ruggles Street in Roxbury. A whole new chapter was beginning for each of us. Our experiences would change us in ways unimaginable and shake our foundations to their core.

25
CHAPTER

Rock of Ages

*The degree of civilization in a society can
be judged by entering its prisons.*

—FYODOR DOSTOYEVSKY

In September 1981, Rock headed to the Wentworth Institute of Technology to study civil engineering, although eighteen months earlier, he had enrolled at ITT Technical Institute to study drafting. But he didn't stay. I entered the University of Massachusetts, majoring in chemistry. Ti Samuel continued to steer a cab in Boston.

Our Ruggles apartment was a bit bigger than my mother's rented room in La Fleur Duchene. The flat had a toilet and a kitchen, which made it larger. At $139 a month, we had no reason to complain. We were so busy we rarely saw each other. All Rock cared about besides driving a taxi some evenings and Sundays was going to classes. We needed to gain new knowledge that could one day open doors for us to earn a better living wage. That was our hope in getting a decent job after graduation. That motivation helped us to find our way to our two campuses every morning. We hoped we would one day walk away from the Ruggles Street public-housing complex.

The Mission Hill housing-project area was a place void of trees and communal life. The only time we spotted a bird there was when one flew inside our place two years later. Rock adopted it as a pet and landed himself in a nearby hospital with pneumonia due to a zoonotic infection called psittacosis he'd acquired from the bird. The housing project looked more like a Russian or Polish or Eastern European ghetto where they kept Jews in the previous century. Those ghettos came before the pogroms. The city of Boston had erected that apartment complex for folks like me. We lived among the destitute, the homeless veterans, and the undesirables of Boston. Mission Hill was an area I knew nothing about before. When I applied for public housing, I never imagined I would call the place home.

One quiet afternoon in 1982, Rock and I found ourselves alone in the apartment on Ruggles Street. It was a Friday, and we were chatting like we usually did most evenings when time warranted. Rock had quit the Wentworth Institute of Technology too. He couldn't provide the legal papers needed to get financial aid and thus couldn't borrow money for tuition to study in America.

My stepmother's brother Manny had told Rock in January 1980 that he needed to behave himself in the house. He must always obey and help Yvette. He should put the garbage in the trash compactor. He should bring the groceries upstairs from Manny's car. He was compelled to do the household's laundry. Otherwise, Manny would call the immigration authorities and have Rock deported to Haiti. Often, he would drive by the John Fitzgerald Kennedy building in downtown Boston with Rock to scare him about being undocumented. The federal immigration office was only five miles away from our Chelsea apartment. But Rock was the wiser. Before long, he slipped out of the house and went to live with Tante Princina.

It made perfect sense that Rock had left Chelsea right after Dad returned to Haiti. His situation had become precarious. He lived in a limbo only undocumented immigrants could appreciate. Though we can admit the history of humanity is the story of constant immigration and emigration and of people living in countries without being invited, it's no crime against nature. Jesus, Abraham, Mary, and Joseph all lived as undocumented refugees in Africa at one point; ergo, Jesus is known as the Rock of Ages.

Suddenly Rock stood between the kitchen and the small living room, watching the chicken thighs brewing with green peas, celery, garlic, tomatoes, onions, red peppers, and a few potatoes on the small four-burner stove, the strong odor of the seasonings pervading the inside of our apartment. When I tried to go back to check on the cooking, Rock was still there. He raised his right hand from his waist like a windstorm coming from the west, bringing it to his temple. He tapped his temple several times while standing still in his pensive mood.

Then he began pacing the apartment. He asked me about the meaning of life and our purpose here on earth as though I cared to know. I entered the kitchen and inspected my chicken gumbo. It spewed steam, its garlicky-prickly-cayenne-curry smell permeating the flat.

Rock asked two questions that caught me off-guard: "Who is the Messiah? When will he return?" Before I could answer, he said, "Comrade, do you know that I am the Messiah?" I stood there, shocked. I went to the pot and filled my plate with food. Then I sat down on a chair before the dinette table and began to clamp my teeth around a chicken thigh and tore off a large piece. I chewed it hard, my neck twisting as I tried to swallow it. My heart raced. This meat was tougher than an aging wild turkey. I took another bite and sat down as my heart quickened.

"You have met Christ today and you didn't even know it!" he said.

I cocked my head, listening as I looked into his dilated pupils.

"You know something, comrade? You and I are destined for great things according to Magrann's oracle." I adjusted my shirt collar, straightened my spine, and took one last bite, the sauce sprinkling my jagged beard and forming a ring of grease around my mouth as I sucked the flavors off my finger. *Go on.*

"The hour has arrived when we are going to do great things. We are princes of light. Other people know that already." Before I could wolf down the last chunk of potato, I had been transformed. I had become a believer and a disciple of Rock. I wished to hear more of grandma's prophecies.

The words resonated within my cerebral cortex. Everything I had heard as a young child was coming to fruition. Rock and I stood as the bearers of the Good News. What young man or woman wouldn't trade everything he or she had to be great? If you have any doubt, then open your Bible and find out why Simon or John or James followed Christ.

"Magrann said we are Igbo, a group of people with a great and noble responsibility. That we must walk into the light ever more diligently and carry the mantle of the history of our forebears to the four corners of the world. That, comrade we must take seriously." He tapped his head with his hand twice before continuing.

"Look at Palestine today. Their land is under Israeli occupation and military control. Their children are dumped into prisons without a day in court. Look at South Africa and Rhodesia under the guns of apartheid. The white invaders taunted the Africans, telling them they would extend their thousand-year reich right in their midst. It's a frightening reminder that one day you may be at peace in your land and the next you find yourself occupied by militaristic countries. They will terrorize your wife, your children, and your sucklings." He paused.

"The world doesn't give a hoot that Haiti helped to spread liberty throughout the globe. Our forebears fought alongside the Americans in the Battle of Savannah against the British Empire. Jean-Jacques Dessalines supplied Francisco de Miranda with rifles, munitions, and food to begin the wars of independence of South America. Alexandre Pétion armed Simón Bolívar to liberate South America. Jean-Pierre Boyer helped Greece and provided funding for them to fight the Ottoman Empire till they freed themselves. Yes, comrade. Our people were there. They helped the nations. They showed the world how to fight their way to freedom. All the newly liberated nations of the earth have learned it from us, comrade."

"I see that you have a point," I said. "I believe. But I am a man of little faith sometimes."

"I know that. I had the same issue before because every time I heard that voice in my head, I ignored it. Now I am certain the hour has arrived and you must believe. Moses ignored Yahweh's call the first time he heard Him. When he finally understood that Yahweh's highway was the only way, he acquiesced. He dared to tell Him that he was a stutterer and that he couldn't talk well—as if God didn't know." Rock's laughter trailed off as he pointed a finger toward the sky.

"Comrade, remember one thing and one thing alone—God can always give whatever you lack. If you need faith, ask Him. If you need money, go before Him and learn how to earn it. If you need a friend, He is that friend that will never quit you in times of trouble. If you need a zest for life, go and tell Him you need the fire in your bosom to get things done. If you lack patience, ask Him for it. If you need courage, He will make you brave as He did Sampson. If you are blind, ask Him to send you the balm of Gilead so that you see well. If you hate people, pray to Him to make you a Gandhi or a Martin Luther King in a world of wickedness and wretchedness.

"If you hate people to the point of self-destruction, however, your case is doomed like a brute beast, a creature of instinct acting out of fear. If you must walk a thousand miles alone in the desert, ask Him to be the oasis nearby. If you must fly like a bird, tell Him you want to be a good angel. If you must go without food often, thank Him for keeping you as lean as Christ. If people lie about you always, go and nod to them. Don't give evil for evil, otherwise you become the devil. If you have trouble hearing the spoken truth, confess to Him that you are now a believer. Even if your parents forsake you, He will always be with you.

"Now that you are embarking on your studies, you will have great difficulty going forward. But you must persevere and have confidence, and then you will get your reward. Life is made of more failures than successes. You must savor both to find the meaning of your journey. When parents make things too easy for their kids, they are only setting them a trap. Soon they both end up regretting that choice. There is much to learn in the grinding, the scraping, and the pains of this world—for only then can the gold be pure." He scratched his ear and squinted his eyes while I stood before him, motionless. "After all, our father in heaven is God, and He made us, those who are His are sons and daughters of the Most High." I was thrilled as he began the next soliloquy.

"The problem of our people isn't an issue of not knowing God. It's more a matter of meeting Him and not heeding His counsel. We instead sell our souls and say how much we love ourselves. Do you believe that, comrade?" he shouted. I said nothing. "But God calls you god in the Bible. That is why the Pharisees wanted to kill Jesus. He equated himself with God.

"As my spirit soars, and my soul glides, the parts that define who am I are no longer present. I want to be one with God, my Father in Heaven, and claim the universe as my playground. If people want nature to stop rumbling, flooding, shaking, dying, shattering, destroying, and the like, they need to stop hating, killing, lusting, angering, and the like. They ought to start living as though there are no borders and they have no names, no titles, no ranks. They must see themselves as children of God, living in spirit like Him. For the greatest challenge of our time is to become the spiritual beings our Creator intends us to be. We must experience silence as it lays still. For where there is love, there is no feeling of doom or loss or hopelessness. Where there is service, there is no time for self-pity. Where there is caring, there is a smile on every face."

That next day, I woke up with a new revelation. I began walking with a swagger that almost destroyed my fledgling friendship with my girlfriend Youla. I reminded her how lucky she was to trek along with a charming prince like me. After all, the kingdom was near.

As I lay down to sleep that evening, what Rock had said began to replay in my mind. He sounded like a prophet. Was he? I had found myself puzzled during our conversation the day before, failing to comprehend his prophecy completely. I thought about how he'd told me the hour of judgment had come and that we must bring the good news to the entire world and how we had a greater destiny. Suddenly, I began to worry about his health. When we lived at Tante Princina's apartment, an elderly man used to say, "Rock, you talk too much. I am worried for you." I hadn't lived long enough to understand he meant that Rock was having a mental breakdown. I hadn't seen him do drugs, but I was concerned about that when I remembered his drug experience in Haiti once.

A week later, Rock moved out and went to live with a new girlfriend, Gwen. By then our brother Wilfrid had come to the States to live with us.

Gwen was a very peculiar lady. Her weight was not the issue; instead, it was her callousness the day she called to say, "Come get your crazy brother out of my apartment." The rumors traveled a long way. Someone had told me there were unscrupulous women in Boston looking for gullible young male immigrants to live with. They would buy life-insurance policies for these men and put themselves as their beneficiaries. Without delay, if the men were drinkers, they would provide the men with an abundance of liquor. Or they would surfeit them with addictive drugs, get them high, and finish them off with a drug overdose.

Rock was acting strange. With his inflated crescendo of bragging daily discourses, he rambled to no end when he dropped by. Wilfrid and Ti Samuel and I began to question Rock's sanity. We had no idea what to do about it or what to think of it. Rock wasn't well. He suffered from something we didn't have a name for. Though the things he said still sounded plausible and the message was great, the messenger needed help and the sooner, the better.

Before he'd moved out of our flat, I worried about his sleepless nights. He would go on for days listening to music and dancing around the apartment. He would croon along with powerful and rhythmic reggae music. It was a soul-searching sound. The music was pleasant to listen to any other time, but those nights when I needed my sleep for another grueling day at school or work, it was brutal. The storm never went away, and I suspected Rock was high on drugs. I felt despondent as I watched him spiral into a vacuous nightmarish maze. He found himself in a position where many went but few got out alive to push through another day.

It was more than a struggle for him. He was in a full-blown war. Here was a sibling previously full of potential, dreams, and ambitions who now looked like someone I'd never met. I was losing him, and it hurt. I wondered what had gone wrong. What had happened to him? We were the first two siblings to come in America the same year, and we had overcome a lot of hardships together. I was losing my comrade. It became an unpleasant affair. According to Dr. Herbert D. Kleber of Yale University, an authority on addiction, "No one knows why some cocaine or crack users become addicted, how many suffering people stop on their own or with the aid of self-help groups, and what proportion of those who enter programs stay off the drug for good."[16]

I could see him collapsing with a cardiac arrest or in a car accident while under the influence. Worse, he could get shot during a drug bust at his dealer's place.

A week before he moved into Gwen's apartment, he bought a copy of either *Time* or *Newsweek* magazine. The front-page title read "Depression." It was an illness so alien to me. In the midst of my busy life, it didn't register. Though he and I were avid readers of weekly magazines, I hadn't bothered to read that latest edition.

Within three days, the phone rang. "Hi, this is Gwen, Pierre-Rock's girlfriend. I am calling to let you know your brother needs help. He is not well. He spends most of his time sleeping and sobbing, and I don't know what's wrong with him," she said. "Do you think he may have some Haitian voodoo tormenting him?"

I didn't know what to tell her. I knew about voodoo, but not about it harrowing anyone. There was a long silence.

"Well, I had noticed the other day that he was talking about many things I didn't understand," I said. "But some things he said made much sense to me."

"Well, he talks about more nonsense lately. Could you come get him out of my place?" She blurted, "Your brother freaked me out. I can no longer have him in my apartment."

I wanted to throw something or inject a few invectives into the conversation, but I restrained myself. After all, my brother was a single man. So why should she care for him? And, while in Haiti, he'd dabbled with the drugs Zagalo brought from the States.

How did we deal with Rock? What could we do about his problems? None of us knew. What did people in America do when their loved ones cried and slept all day? We had no roadmap. I had seen folks in Haiti taken to evangelistic crusades for prayers. I was not sure the same thing would work here. It wasn't because of skepticism of spiritual healing. None of us was sure whether prayers would be enough for such a grave problem. Some call cocaine the devil drug. And getting the devil out of him at this juncture required more than a legion of good angels.

Though Wilfrid was worn out after his regular night shift at New England Memorial Hospital, he and I drove to Gwen's house to pick up our corpse of a brother. When we entered the eighth-floor apartment on Tremont Street in Roxbury, we could see downtown Boston with its skyscrapers jutting into the sky. We also caught sight of a tiny balcony with a sliding door facing the bed where Rock lay. He looked frightened, like a bird nesting under a raging flood.

After we picked him up, he told us Gwen had drugged him or they had both gotten high on drugs. In any event, we helped him stand. His untrimmed long beard made him look like a survivor foraging the land after World War III. After all, he thought of himself as the Rock of Ages. He couldn't stay upright and had to lean on us to find his center when entering the building's elevator.

We brought him home, laid him on a cot, and did our best to feed him. He'd lost at least fifteen pounds while in the wilderness at Gwen's but had little appetite. We tried to make him laugh in the evenings when we got home from school or work. Slowly, he began to feel better, though his comparisons between himself and Jesus and Gandhi continued.

"Why do you think Joseph rejected Jesus?" he asked. "Because he thought He was crazy. Today we all revere him." Who could argue with that statement?

Mona Dorsinville, Wilfrid's girlfriend, was a physician. She devised a plan to help Rock when she heard that he went nights without sleep. She brought him some Ativan tablets for his agitation. The tablets did the trick for a few days, helped him calm down, and made him stay in bed during the day too.

Rock was an on/off switch. Some days he would talk incessantly, sleep a little, and other days he would stay quiet in bed.

One time, Mona came by our place to visit her patient. After Rock greeted her, he went into the bedroom, slammed the door behind him, and resumed listening to Bob Marley's music on his Walkman cassette player "I Shot the Sheriff." Mona suggested we take him to Massachusetts Mental Hospital located on Fenwood Road.

After she left, we talked Rock into coming on a joyride. Ti Samuel took the wheel of his brown 1969 Plymouth Dodge with another friend in the front seat, while Rock sat between Wilfrid and me in the back. Soon we pulled up to a building that, except for a tiny sign on the front lawn, was unmarked. We parked our car.

I went inside alone to meet the security guard in the lobby. One hour earlier, I had spoken with the hospital admissions service and arranged to bring Rock in for an evaluation. The guard came to our car and directed him toward the hospital lobby. Wilfrid and I walked behind them.

"What are you guys doing to me?" Rock demanded. "Are you selling me to this place? Remember, I am your brother, the Rock of Ages." He turned and gazed at us as he was escorted by the security guard. I felt like Judas Iscariot.

That evening, we met with Dr. Philip Sullivan, the chief psychiatrist. He wished to conduct a family interview since Rock was too incoherent to do a full medical interview. After the interview, Dr. Sullivan told us he was going to admit Rock for acute psychosis.

I went home feeling guilty but relieved at the same time. I didn't have to watch him constantly pacing the flat while listening to music on his Walkman.

The following evening, we all went to see him at the hospital. He was distant, sleepy, and withdrawn. Other patients near us smoked. To our delight, he was no longer pacing. But he did drool from the corners of his mouth as he sat with us in the visitors' room.

A month later, he came home with a diagnosis of manic depression, or bipolar disorder. He resumed his work driving a taxi at night. A few years later, he got a scholarship to attend Northeastern University but did very little work. He would experience cycles of manic depression.

One Sunday morning after a few weeks of quiet, he surprised me when he begged me for his money—the $200 he had asked me to save for him over the course of two months. Because he was psychotic, I reasoned that giving him the money was unwise. I feared he would buy drugs, which always preceded his moony hallucinations and cosmic voyages. I balked.

"If you don't give me my fu—ing money, I will destroy the taxi outside and rain fire in the street," he growled.

"You wouldn't do that."

"You wait to see what I can do. Wait and you will see."

The big bang outside took those of us in the apartment by surprise as the windshield of the Town Taxi was shattered to pieces. Broken glass lay on the front seat, the car floor, the back seats, and the street. He was a raging bull trashing the cab.

By then, someone had dialed 911. The person had asked for police help, explaining the situation to the emergency dispatcher. The culprit had a history of mental illness, and we needed help getting him back to the Massachusetts Mental Health Center.

When Rock heard the police sirens, he stepped back from the taxi and trotted along the sidewalk, stopping in front of the entrance to the apartment complex. "They should be content that they don't deal with a Toussaint L'Ouverture or a Jean-Jacques Dessalines in their midst today." He foamed as he shielded his eyes from the sun and squinted to catch a glimpse of the sky. "But there is still a Jesus waiting to rain fire on their tails."

I stood there, off the curb, flagging down the police car as it came to a screeching halt. Two black officers jumped out and strutted toward me. At the sight of the menacing officers, Rock became agitated and began hurling profanities at them.

My mind was suddenly taken back to when I was eighteen months in the country and hopping from my 1968 faded-white two-door Dodge sedan with its torn front seat. I'd parked near the Dudley train station. That Friday afternoon, I'd gone inside the First National Bank of Boston to cash my ninety-three-dollar weekly paycheck. When I came back out, I found a parking violation posted on my windshield. In disgust, I picked up the stub, shredded it, and threw it into the street, away from prying eyes. Or so I thought.

I unlocked the car door, but before I could get in, an officer shouted, "Excuse me, why did you shred the ticket?" I shrugged, then confessed I didn't know there was a law against destroying one's parking ticket. His eyes widened, his lips curled, and a frown formed. It was as if I had disrespected his mother. I kept my eyes off his, and he likely saw in them no sympathy or comprehension but disgust. I mumbled something again while trying to open the door. When I turned my head to look back at the officer, I noticed the pistol at his waist, like the cowboy landlord. I shuddered and became scared, for I hadn't experienced hostility from a police officer before.

He leapt in front of me and said, "You are under arrest." Then he handcuffed me, turned me around, and grabbed my arm. He led me toward his patrol car and shoved me inside. The police station sat across the street. He'd booked me for disrespecting a police officer. In spite of my juvenile protests that I wasn't doing anything wrong, his massive hands had fallen onto my 130-pound frame.

That afternoon, I felt the world close in on me. The only confined space I had previously stayed in was the Chelsea apartment. This place was worse than I could have imagined. The holding cell measured about six by eight feet and had brick walls and a metallic door that locked from the outside.

In one corner of the room was a squalid stainless-steel water closet that emitted a putrid odor. The smell made me dizzy. I wanted to vanish from the ignominious place. That afternoon, I felt like death was imminent as I stood in the ratty-looking dungeon that looked like something in a movie. It was crazy! I dreaded it.

Before the one-hour ordeal was over, I cried like a child. The inside of that ostensible torture chamber scared me. It felt as though I were in a Nazi death camp. Thankfully, one of the officers inside the police station allowed me to place a collect call from a payphone inside the jailhouse to a family member to post my bond. Otherwise I would have spent the weekend there. On Monday morning, I went before a judge at the Roxbury Courthouse, which was located behind the police station. He asked me what had gone wrong, and I explained. Within five minutes, the case was dismissed.

In Haiti, only criminals or political dissidents go to jail, whereas in America, even babies go to prison. In May 2018, the Trump administration instituted a zero-tolerance policy against refugees and other undocumented immigrants. They caged even infants and had planned a mass incarceration throughout the country for undocumented families. What did the Native Americans do when the Europeans came here uninvited in the 1600s?

Now, when I saw the same police officer who'd thrown me in jail coming in response to the call to help my brother, I froze. I had made a mistake in calling the cops. He must have sensed my uneasiness when he got out of his patrol car after I'd flagged it down. I couldn't tell whether he remembered me. I doubted it. He looked as menacing as he had when we first crossed paths. If that officer had dumped me inside a macabre urine-scented, decrepit, debased, state-sponsored place for tearing my parking ticket up, then nothing good could come from this unexpected second encounter.

In his book, *This Boy's Life*, Tobias Wolff writes, "I saw it years later in men I served with, and felt it myself when unarmed Vietnamese civilians talked back to us while we were herding them around. Power can be enjoyed only when it is recognized and feared. Fearlessness in those without power is maddening to those who have it."[17] Today, many police officers are scared, so they find it convenient to shoot black people without provocation. The problem is that many folks don't recognize or fear their power, and they therefore can't enjoy it.

This officer and many like him across the land pose a moral and physical threat to the people they're sworn to protect. There are many corrupt police officers in uniform patrolling our streets. The public may never discover them. They might be current gang, Ku Klux Klan members, or Nazi sympathizers. According to a 2008 FBI report, these criminals carry a police badge and masquerade as police officers.[18] They pose a grave danger for the country if they remain active in the police force. Who monitors these officers? Their continuous presence could create a volatile situation for the country in this age of terrorism. ISIS, Al Qaeda, and Boko Haram may well be looking for a cushiony haven in America. People like this police officer can't be good for America. They can only create resentment. If police abuse persists, it will force people to seek revenge. Some people may easily choose the option of Samson when nothing else matters. If one is going to die unfairly, who can prevent that person from becoming a suicide bomber?

The irony is that good police officers remain silent for fear of losing their jobs or promotions. How do these same people feel when doctors hide or bury their mistakes from one another? Do they think such behavior serves the public better?

As the Bible says in 1 John 2:15, "Do not love the world or anything in the world." In other words, as the New Hampshire state motto says, "Live free or die." Can Americans today truly experience freedom during their lifetimes? Can we reclaim what's lost while keeping the Union intact? Can it avoid the complacency that doomed most advanced democracies of the past?

"Put your hands up!" the other officer shouted. Rock ignored them both as if his auditory sense had stopped working. He told them to go to hell and that he was Jesus of Nazareth and would rain fire on them if they persisted.

"Stand back and let me take care of this skinny maggot!" shouted my nemesis, the sculpted pectorals and trapezius muscles beneath his uniform on display for all to see. He lurched forward and reached toward his waist, caressing his holster, then pulled his gun out and cocked it, ready to empty the magazine.

I never saw this nightmare coming. Without thinking, I shielded Rock, ignoring that there was an order in which to do things. I told the police I would calm him down.

The American standard of morality is packed with inconsistencies and covered in naked aggression displayed for the world to see. American society is intolerant of cockfighting and dogfighting unless it happens off the ground in military combat. The US military had no qualms about dropping ten-thousand-pound napalm bombs on innocent victims.

It will take a lifetime to undo the burdens of a civilization gone awry. I should understand that. America was created by violence, as were many countries. It is in the national DNA. But is it getting enlightened?

Well, somebody had to call the police. What did I expect when someone told the dispatcher we needed their help? They came to provide help the best way they knew in providing public safety. Were police officers clueless about how to deal with mentally disturbed individuals? Would it be more convenient to shoot the sucker and get it over with? Thankfully, they took Rock to Mass Mental, sparing him for another day. This wasn't a betrayal on my part. Calling the police was the only way I knew to get him help.

Rock's recurrent mental breakdowns made it hard for me to focus on my studies. Many a night, I would search for him in the alleyways, dumpster areas, and the areas strewn with discarded cardboard and trash cans near the housing project. I needed to desert him so that I could find time to complete my studies and go to graduate school.

My mother came to America sometime in the fall of 1984 or early 1985 for medical treatment. Her goiter was causing many problems. At one point, she had chronic migraines, fatigue, and trouble breathing. She was happy to be reunited with all her sons after many years apart, but she was sullen when she spoke about her nine-year-old Sherley, her last child and only daughter. Sherley's father had bowed out of their relationship and left Haiti seven years before. Mom had left Sherley in the care of a family member while she sought treatment abroad. Within two years, Sherley was reunited with Mom in Boston.

One night, my phone rang around one o'clock in the morning. I ignored it the first couple of times, thinking it was a wrong number. Who in the world would be calling me at such an hour? I had fallen asleep after completing some schoolwork that was due in the morning for my physics class at Northeastern. What could anyone want from me? How could I even help anyone? This was only the beginning. At the time, Youla and I had been living in Watertown, a small town about ten miles from Boston.

As her health improved, my mother began to gain her footing in her new land. However, a new, pressing set of concerns loomed on the horizon, competing for her attention. Rock's mental-health problems reminded her of my maternal great-grandfather's mental-health struggles, which Dad told me about a few years later. In less than three months from the time my mother arrived, her world had been turned upside down. Rock would disappear for long periods at a time, leaving Mom to wonder whether he was dead or alive, like Schrodinger's cat experiment in quantum mechanics.

One day, Mom called and asked me to come to her apartment. Every time Rock vanished for more than a day, my mother would call in the wee hours of the morning, pleading and begging for me to hasten and look for Rock. (It was a ritual that lasted until I left Boston for California to study medicine at Stanford University in the fall of 1988.) "We haven't seen him for more than three days, and I am scared he may be injured and lying somewhere unattended." She worried he might be dead given his numerous brushes with the Boston Police Department. At times, she thought he had overdosed on drugs. She became concerned that someone had shot him dead during an altercation when he was high on drugs. We knew he was injecting himself with drugs often and worried he could get AIDS.

I would leave my apartment, telling Youla I would be back soon. Many times, I drove on snowy nights amid frigid weather, taking Storrow Drive to Boston and heading straight to a police station to begin my inquiries.

On several occasions, my mother and I discovered that the police had taken Rock to Bridgewater State Hospital, a sort of prison for the mentally insane, and we would thank God for keeping him alive for one more day. We would have been grateful and elated if they could have kept him there for a year. Every time he stayed off the streets, he was safe. Every time Rock was released from Bridgewater Hospital, it was tantamount to a death sentence in the waiting. We were at the point where it was good news that my brother, my parents' third child, my comrade, was in jail or in the hands of the police.

One evening, the phone buzzed just after I had arrived home exhausted from an evening class at NU and was dozing on the living room sofa. The ringing startled me, and I wondered why Youla would be calling me so late from her work as a staff nurse at Boston City Hospital when her shift had just started.

Grumpily, I reached for the phone. It was Mom. "Ti Milliardaire, I need you. Could you come here now? Because I don't know what happened to Rock. He hasn't come home in two days. When he left, he said he was going to use his divine power to rain fire in Boston." My mother paused. I sighed.

Her voice, her anguish, and her worries were draining me, but the only way I knew to calm her down was for me to go to her apartment and devise a plan to look for Rock.

She stood behind the door, awaiting my arrival. I entered her flat and greeted her, then sat down and listened. My mother's eyes welled with tears as she spoke. Then she began wailing. "I don't know what I have done wrong to deserve this in life. Why me? Why me, Lord? Why don't you take my life and heal my child? He doesn't deserve such suffering in life." Whenever Rock failed to come home or was late, she assumed the worst. She assumed he was dead.

It was hard listening to Mom's pleadings. A mother is unlike anyone else. She can feel and speak about things only mothers understand. A mother will trade her life for her child's where others have misgivings. A mother will give it all if there is a chance that her child might have a new start. Of course, Dad would have none of it. Perhaps he didn't know how to handle his children's issues.

This was no ordinary night. There was a knock at the door. As I peered through the peephole: two wild, red eyes met mine. The phantom looked frail and ill and rambled about as he rapped at the door. I sensed his restlessness even before he bolted inside the apartment. A trail of dried blood zigzagged from the crease of his elbow all the way down to his wrist. His hair was tangled and bulged out in a knot. He was dressed in a gray, water-soaked T-shirt, mud-soiled blue jeans, and a pair of black sneakers without socks. He began searching everywhere. He lifted the mattress, opened the refrigerator, rifled through the cupboards, bent to search below the bed, then stood up and started foaming. He demanded money. My mother gasped and turned to me, then moved toward Rock. He looked shabby and thin, a ghost in human form, a cartoon skeleton with his soul elsewhere.

"Rock!" she shouted. "What are you do—" Before she could complete that sentence, she interrupted herself. "Rock. Oh, good God ..."

My comrade was possessed by whatever demon had taken over him that night. The deep creases under his eyes made him look old, a shadow of his former self. He used to enjoy wearing designer clothing when driving his white 1980 BMW. Now he didn't care. I stood motionless. I feared my brother, the child of my parents—this ghost I knew nothing about.

"What, Madoudou?" he snarled in his slurry staccato speech. "I am fine."

"Oh, Rock, my child, why are you hurting me like that? What did I do wrong to deserve such pain from you? Your father hurt me a lot when I carried you in my womb. I wanted the best for you. Why are you doing this to me? I don't deserve it." I learned that night how much my mother loved my brother.

"Mom, don't cry. I am trying to heal myself the best way I know. When I take drugs, I have no pain. When I take drugs, I am normal, like everyone else. When I take drugs, no one can hurt me."

"But, son, this is not you. When you are on drugs, I feel the pain of many trains rolling over me, squashing my legs, then my torso, until I feel the guillotine of the screeching metal on my neck. Why me, God? There is plenty of good in you, son. Why hate yourself like this? I plead with you to forget the deceptions, reject the devil's drugs, and save yourself for good. Drugs are our enemy, son, and so are the people who make and give them to you."

"Madoudou," he growled. "I am all right."

"Are you ok, son?" Mom shuddered.

"Do you have any money?" he asked.

Whatever my mother said fell on deaf ears. He searched the house again. He found a small bag inside the pocket of a jacket in the closet, placed it in the front right pocket of his jeans, and stalked out as he pulled his coat on.

"Rock, no!" Mom cried, trying to hold his arm, but he avoided her as he went downstairs. "You are killing yourself, my son! Let Junior take you to the hospital."

"I am fine, Mom. I am sorry."

"Rock, you are on drugs and you could die!"

He raised his head and with a look of terror in his eyes, stared at my mother, then vanished into the thick darkness of the night. My mother wept and told me she was afraid of losing him. She brought the back of her hand to her eyes and wiped the tears away as she trekked upstairs. Like a corpse inside a morgue's refrigerator, a massive shadow hung over me and left me feeling cold. I quieted and gazed at the linoleum floor, my head in my hands. I had failed to help Mom restrain my comrade when she needed me. Who could I have called for help? I stayed there with Mom, remaining alert throughout the night. I could hear her sobs until daybreak, when Wilfrid got home from work. Promising to visit her after class, I trudged away.

Sometime in 1987, my mother called me muttering something that sounded like Rock had been taken to Boston City Hospital with a gun-shot wound after an altercation with a Boston cop. Someone who had seen the story on the news had told her what happened. She believed he was dead. As the morning drew near, I got dressed and drove to Boston City Hospital, inquiring about whether my brother was alive. He had been in the medical-surgical unit after undergoing surgery and was now chained to a bed under the watchful eye of two Boston police officers. They looked angry when I approached him. Having these two guys inside Rock's hospital room made me nervous. They acted as if I were an accomplice in his plot to run over some police officers on the streets the previous evening. Rock lay in bed and was barely recognizable. His eyes and face were swollen, and his voice was faint. He had a surgical dressing above his left elbow.

Before long, rumors began to circulate among the Boston police brass that Rock was a lucky Haitian who had been helped by voodoo. Otherwise, he would have been dead. According to TV reports, he had been shot at thirty or more times by a platoon of officers who couldn't neutralize him. Any other time I would have laughed at their superstition, but not this time. They were serious. There was a different twist about that evening. It baffled the police. My mother's prayers and nightly interventions had likely made all the differ-ence in keeping my comrade alive, even though he failed to heed her pleadings.

Those nights brought my mother much anguish, sorrow, and despair. It may be true that suffering builds character, but it also takes a toll on people's brains. Looking back at the whole experience, I wished my mother had never gone through those empty, miserable, torturous nights. It was a challenging period in her life. The grief she experienced when Rock took all kinds of drugs likely caused her to develop post-traumatic stress syndrome. She was always being startled and rattled and was wracked with worry the minute her phone rang.

Often Rock darted into that deep corner not far from the project be-tween Ruggles Street and Tremont Street, then he would return and his mood and demeanor would have changed for the worst. He would stop joking and laughing. When he did drugs, he was horrible, and when he did them too much, he became a menace to those near him. He had the energy to move a mountain, but in these instances, the light was extinguished from his eyes. He would rush out of the apartment as if his craving for drugs was driving him crazy.

Rock got married but soon divorced. Today, he lives alone in California and has fewer relapses than he used to. Ti Samuel got married, divorced, and was expelled from America and sent back to Haiti for domestic violence against his wife. Wilfrid lives in Mattapan with his son, Wilmicko. My mother's journey with Alzheimer's robbed her of her joy but also of her pains and worries. Perhaps the multiple beatings she received at Dad's hands had brought her closer to the grave. Over the ten years they lived together, Dad had used the arm of a cot to beat her on several occasions. All these drubbings took their toll. She died at age eight-two on January 21, 2019, in Boston. Her mother, Grann Bébé, died at the age of ninety-two in Ti Mouillage in 2010.

26
CHAPTER

Struggles in
Ruggles

*I want to walk barefoot in cities without streets
where admiration is a deep silence.*

— MARIAHADESSA EKERE TALLIE

It was true that I had moved at least ten times within the greater Boston area during my first five years in America. Before I moved to Ruggles Street in Roxbury, I lived in Mattapan. Before Mattapan, I lived in Dorchester at three different locations, and before that, I lived in Chelsea in two different places. Some of the neighborhoods were more blighted than others, but nothing looked like the seventh apartment I lived in.

The Ruggles Street housing project reminded me of an abandoned military operation, and it scared me. Police cars continuously roamed the place, their sirens blaring in the deep of the night. The grim reality of living in America flickered before my face some eerie cartoon. It had been almost two years since I'd left Haiti and settled in Boston. Until now, my sheltered life had kept me from the stark realities of people struggling with all sorts of demons, such as homelessness, drug addiction, abject poverty, and mental illness. I had seen nothing of the sort in Haiti. Drug problems were almost unheard of in the country. People in those days had many issues, such as poverty, ignorance, and superstitions, but they were never hopeless. In Ruggles Street, I came to understand what chronic depression with guilt, worthlessness, and despair looked like.

Beer and vodka bottles littered the floor of the apartment complex. A few young men would gather along the stairs of the building day and night. Some would lean on the wall across from our door, overlooking the street below. I worried that one of them would come bursting into our apartment at any moment. The door chain always remained on when I was home.

One night, I was home alone and got so disturbed that my hands became clammy and cold. I craned my neck and scanned the front corridor through the peephole of our apartment door, spying on the young men. When one of them leaned against the door, blocking the view, my heart sped up in my chest. I had goose bumps and my stomach churned. I kept thinking they had seen me looking at them. I expected them to bolt in, even with the door locked and the chain fastened. My face flushed, my heart pounded, and I felt short of breath. I stayed quiet and hauled our small dinette table over to block the door.

Whenever it got cold outside, one or two of the men would pee right there on the concrete, and the stream of urine would run down onto the first floor. The graffiti on the walls grew almost daily even as maintenance tried to clear it up.

I never tried to strike up a friendly conversation with any of them. That lost opportunity made my education about America's underclass incomplete because I never fully understood these neighbors. What had gone wrong in their lives? How had they gotten to this point? Who were they? There was no danger in saying, "Hey, guys," yet I was afraid.

It was hard to ignore their words as I left for school or work: "These f—ing foreigners are here to take what's ours. I dunno why our government give dem everythin' and let us hangin' cold in our track to die." They would give each other high fives, flap their hands, and laugh as I scurried downstairs as though I were late for school.

"Yeah, suh, they come here with an attitude like niggas walking on gold." I froze in my tracks, not knowing which foot to put forward while dashing into the street. It hurt hearing these accusations hurled against my brothers, friends, and me. I had also heard those words at Dorchester High. All we ever wanted was to live in peace and mind our own business. Sadly, it wasn't enough.

"The other day I saw the short one, the one who smokes reefer outside sometimes. He had the nerve of lookin' at me with a sneer and tried to scare my wits here in our place. Our country sucks and has lost its priorities. I dunno for suh what's wrong with our politicians. Everywhere you go these days in town, you see these niggas all over our face. Before long we won't be campin' here no more. They will have the place for themselves."

The way this guy alluded to Rock made me want to shrink away. These words, reminiscent of the 1980s, sounded a lot like what a future US president said to feed the masses in the 2016 United States presidential election. The odd similarity reminded me of that universal adage: When the country is in trouble, look for a perceived enemy to blame for its woes. In Carrefour, I had Lucifer for my bogeyman.

"The whities suh know what they doin'. They bring all these lowlifes here to work for scraps. They don't want to pay us a far' wage hopin' that we all would die before their eyes. They can't get away with the fact that our families came here four hundred years ago and never got paid a cent for their hard labor." All they wanted from their country was to be taken seriously and to feel a sense of status, dignity, and connection with their community. Like a column of ghosts, a small fog rose around the housing project, marching and swallowing the glare from the light bulbs across Ruggles Street.

What he said struck a chord with me. I should always be indebted to black America and its sacrifice of blood and grit. Today, as I am living the life of a physician in the United States, I must thank the lions of the civil rights movement of the 1960s. I am standing on the shoulders of giants, of diligent folks who not only paid the ultimate price to make America great but better.

Was it fair for the pilgrims to roll up and take this land from the Native Americans? Was it just to forcefully import slaves to work the Southern fields? We must never forget that in this beloved country, a black person was once considered to be three-fifths human, according to the laws of the land.

The folks who lived in the projects who had drug, alcohol, and mental health problems weren't bad people. They were children of tragedy. Social scientists have told us that human beings aren't categorically evil. As Jean-Jacques Rousseau meant to say in the eighteenth century: "Mankind is born good, but society corrupts him." Most people can learn from their mistakes. They need redemption and deserve a second chance to right the wrongs they've committed.

The folks at Ruggles who struggled because of past abuses, neglect, rejection, humiliation, deceptions, traumas, and the like deserved no less. Some of these people had spent most of their lives in the prison system. Prison isn't a place that offers proper mental health treatment or rehabilitation or that teaches any skill. These people had no safety net before going back to the streets to grind themselves to a pulp. According to a Vera Institute of Justice study released in 2012, the annual average cost to incarcerate a prisoner in 2010 was $31,286. New York State was the most expensive, with an average price of $60,000 per inmate. In some states, prisons are a private industry. Where is the country's morality? Does it care about its children? On average, in 2015, America spent only $11,392 per year to educate a child.[19]

Some believe prison is the answer for stealing a hamburger. But we can't ignore what we know quite well: the laws were never made to benefit black and poor folks. White-collar crimes are costing America its future, yet how many Wall Street CEOs ever go to prison for robbing the country? This is no justice, America can do better. We can expect the cost to incarcerate a prisoner in America to explode in the next decade. Our taxes bankroll our prisons. America worries about foreign invasions that are unlikely to occur, but we are committing economic suicide every day. America is its own worst enemy.

First, consider this: in August 2021, the United States had a debt of $28.4 trillion. China has four times more people than the United States but incarcerates 118 prisoners per 100,000 people, while the United States incarcerates 698 per 100,000. These two factors constitute a grave danger to the country. What's the alternative? What's the cheapest bang for the buck? We need to oil the pistons to prevent engine failure.

Second, America is becoming a blacker and browner nation. What's the path to viability? America needs to strengthen its families and discard the old vestiges of white privilege if it wants to remain competitive.

Third, we know what we need to do. We must take bold steps to get the job done.

Parents of at-risk school-age children must see a family therapist at least once a month to discuss difficulties, progress or the lack thereof, and come up with strategies to address these issues. Schools can identify at-risk children very early. From K–12, school districts must provide regular counseling to their most vulnerable pupils; this could be done in groups or in the classroom to minimize disruption. A financial incentive, such as a tax write-off, could be given to encourage parental or guardian participation. The parents of these children need psychotherapy too. If America could send a man to the moon, certainly it can solve its social issues.

The reality of what was happening in America became clear to me one afternoon as I watched some of the tenants of the Ruggles Apartment complex. It was like a revelation. These people had stopped living all together, the brightness in their eyes gone. With no hope of a better tomorrow, why should they even bother trying? They found themselves in a cycle of poverty they'd inherited from past generations. This could be traced back to the plantations. The forty acres and a mule that were promised their parents never materialized. Thus they continued to struggle on Ruggles Street.

When slavery ended, the shackles were taken off, but the persecution against black folks was far from over. It continued in the hands of the Ku Klux Klan, the Posse, and the like. These groups grew like the tentacles of a truculent octopus, and they had one goal: to deny black people a fair share of the American economy—an economy their forefathers created with free labor. In St. Louis, Missouri, white mobs burned down black businesses and killed close to 250 blacks in the early summer of 1917, driving the black families and their dependents into poverty. The Wilmington, North Carolina massacre of 1898, not only decimated Black political and economic power, but also saw America's only successful coup d'état against a newly elected bi-racial local government. Black Wall Street in Tulsa, Oklahoma, was burned to the ground on May 31 and June 1, 1921, when mobs of white residents attacked black businesses and killed at least three hundred people.

Sadly, the police and firefighters stood by and did nothing. Among the black survivors, more than six thousand were interned in a concentration camp for days. After the Tulsa Race Massacre, 10,800 of the survivors became homeless, thrown onto the streets with no means of subsistence and a guarded freedom. The country asked why these people had failed. But who wouldn't fail in that situation? It took the Jewish diaspora more than two thousand years to regain its equilibrium after they were exiled in Babylon. They were the lucky ones. Other groups have vanished completely.

As a physician, entrepreneur, and social scientist, I only wish America well. I love America. We can do better; we *must* do better. We are far away from putting a colony on Mars. We only have Earth for now.

As the days and months passed, I felt more than sorry for the tenants of the Ruggles apartment complex. I became disillusioned with how the country I loved treated its citizens. If you want to understand the soul of a nation, look at how it treats its elderly and its children. The people on Ruggles Street were the most vulnerable souls I ever encountered. Each time I witnessed their whisky debauches, I became discouraged and felt defenseless. They ceased to care. That part pissed me off more than anything. Only the devil and a society that hated its children could have moved humanity toward such a precipice.

Rock, Ti Samuel, Wilfrid, and I grew tired of breathing the ammonia-scented urine and alcohol seeping beneath our front door. We needed to protest. There were days we were frightened to come home. But it was our refuge. The dwelling at 300 Ruggles Street was awful, but it was our shelter from the cold in winter, the rain in summer, and the sun now and then. There were around sixty apartments on each floor, but I never ventured past my corner apartment.

I remember seeing a lady with pale white skin occasionally on hot summer days. None of us knew what ailed her. Mrs. Crockett would stand there, her gaze elsewhere, avoiding eye contact. I wanted to say good afternoon to her, but she would look the other way. She wasn't crass or vulgar or angry, but she never spoke. It troubled me. She lived with her three children and shut everyone else out. What sort of bargain had they struck with life? Or how had their lives come to this denouement?

My relationship with Ruggles was one of profound love and deep hatred. I loved it because of its proximity to public transportation and downtown Boston. Most importantly, it was the only place I could live in for $209 a month. I would not say I liked this place for its filth, blood-smeared floors, gin bottles, beer cans, rivers of urine, and police sirens in the middle of the night. I was not too fond of it because there was tension in the air right in front of our door whenever we tried to enter our tiny one-bedroom apartment. Our backpacks full of notebooks and books were subject to the mockery of one or two hooligans looking to beat the crap out of us for having the audacity to go to college. That was one more struggle to deal with which none of us liked.

Quite often we felt we belonged elsewhere. But where could four young men share a studio in Boston on such a small budget? With our low wages from driving taxis or cleaning hospital floors and hotel rooms, we couldn't afford to pay rent anywhere else in the greater Boston area. Our apartment was also a place for our newly arrived friends from Haiti.

At four feet eight inches and maybe ninety pounds, Ti David was a small man. He had a raspy voice that made him sound like he had a chronic cold. He had a smooth face and never grew a beard or a mustache. He was thirty-one years old and told us he had a young daughter in Haiti. Whenever I talked to him, he would turn toward me. One day I said, "David, why do you have to turn your head when talking to us?"

He paused for a moment. "I used to work as a welder back home. I would use the torch without a protective mask or goggles. One day a piece of the metallic flash landed on my pupil and blinded me in that eye." He pointed at it. We never mentioned it again.

Sometime in the summer of 1983, the phone rang while I was in the kitchen cooking. The phone rang again. "Hello, who is this?" I asked. "I can't hear you. Are you asking for David?" Brigham and Women's Hospital was calling to inform us that David had been admitted and would need brain surgery in the morning.

"What?" I said.

When everyone got home that afternoon, we rushed to the hospital. We knew David was in good health and hadn't needed brain surgery when he'd left our apartment that morning.

"The doctors are trying to kill him," Rock said. "You can always borrow the West technological prowess, but you must reject their morals." Who could argue with Rock for his thinking?

"Let's find out," Wilfrid said. "Maybe there is something wrong with him." He was annoyed by Rock's resistance.

"Wilfrid, be careful! You need to read about the history of this country a little deeper, brother." Rock tapped his temple and groused, "They killed Martin Luther King. They killed Malcolm X. They almost killed Milliardaire, our Dad too. If he wasn't smart, he would be dead already. While we spend time arguing, machinations continue about how to decimate and emasculate our people like they did the Indians."

Rock turned toward me. "Comrade, you should study the life sciences. At least we would know about their plans and could prepare. We must have the tools to control our destiny. Do this work well, but don't let others claim the credit. Joseph Bologne, Le Chevalier de Saint Georges, born in Martinique from an African slave mother, the finest swordsman Europe had in 1765; was regarded as the most accomplished man of his generation, a violinist whose musical style Mozart copied, died without getting his proper recognition." He paused.

"What happened to me two weeks ago when the police car stopped my taxi and asked me to get out, was repugnant? 'Should we f---him up? F--- him up or let him go?' One of the two white officers shouted. The older one demurred. 'Easy man, easy. Let the kid go, man!'" Outside our apartment windows, a drizzling rain fell, the drops muting our voices.

"Okay, okay, Rock. I heard you," Wilfrid said. "What about if he truly needs the operation?"

"Wait! Remember the Tuskegee experiment? Hundreds of black men with syphilis were left untreated under the auspices of the government. They watched these men die year after year instead of curing them with penicillin, a treatment widely available at that time. The US Public Health Service began the experiment in the 1930s and ended it in 1972 only after a child of God blew the whistle against the injustice!" Rock howled. "It wasn't long ago they shot a black teenager in the Franklin Park area and the sonofabitch officer placed a knife in the boy's hand and reported to the media that the boy attempted to jump him. That is worse than Nazi Germany, man."

"Well, you have a point there," said Wilfrid.

"It's more than a point! We need to dig through the history books and learn fact from fiction," he cried. "Wait! There is more. The Harriman family founded the eugenics movement in America, which called for mass sterilization of the 'feeble-minded' and 'racially inferior.' That movement began in America in the early part of the twentieth century in the name of science. The Nazis copied this idea, which originated in America in the 1930s and '40s. I know you have heard about Auschwitz, Dachau, and Treblinka, where millions of Jews and their babies died in the gas chambers." He paused. "These Nazis could always come back."

"Does this remind you of something in your own history? Did you know that millions of Africans died during the slave trade crossing the Atlantic? Sure you do! Your great-uncles died, your great-aunts died, and many of your blood relatives are buried on the ocean floor. Among those who survived, the French buried many of them standing in their graves with their heads jutting out and their hair sodden with honey to let the ants finish them off." Rock rolled the sleeves of his sweater to his elbows and shook his head, then he ran his fingers over his scalp. His eyes were bright and intense.

"I know," said Wilfrid. The rain had stopped; the clouds continued to scoot across the sky.

"Well, if we as a people fail to learn from the past, our future will be bleaker than the darkest days of our forebears." Rock raised an eyebrow as he listened to the footsteps outside our door. "In late 1500, more than twenty million people lived in Mexico. By early 1600, fewer than two million remained. The Europeans killed them with strange diseases." He said it for our collective knowledge.

"I see," I said without much to add. "Rock, you've become an encyclopedia."

"Wait! There is more." Rock continued. "The history that tells us Pizarro and his cohorts of bandits, thieves, rapists, and murderers defeated the natives of America is a hoax. In the Americas lived more than one hundred million people, a population way larger than the one in Europe. But the diseases that traveled from the old continent to the new one decimated the Indians. In one incident in 1800, the US Army distributed smallpox-infected blankets to the Cherokee Indian chief. This ended up killing the entire tribe.

That was genetic warfare and population elimination." He slapped his forehead twice. "Where is God?"

David had been whisked to the hospital that morning after a back injury sustained at work. During his physical examination, the doctor noticed he was blind in his left eye.

Given Ti David's short stature, lack of virility, blindness, and baby face, the doctor ordered a brain CT scan. He was found to have a large tumor lodged in his pituitary gland, pressing on one of the optic nerves.

The doctors explained he needed surgery to avoid complications or even death. Ti David had already signed the consent form and agreed to go under the knife in the morning. He lived five years after the surgery and died from a brain infection likely related to his surgery, though people contract meningitis all the time without ever having brain surgery. We would never be the same without him, but we grew up as much as we could. Living on Ruggles Street next to Northeastern University had its struggles but also its rewards.

In 1984, Northeastern University became a legendary, exemplary private institution in the city of Boston. It created a full scholarship program in partnership with the Boston Housing Authority and offered full tuition to anyone who academically qualified and resided in the Mission Hill public housing tenements. Ruggles Street housing was part of the Mission Hill project. That charitable gesture was my lifeline. It not only got me out of poverty but also became a source of encouragement as I fulfilled my lifelong potential.

Many of the young men and women pursuing their education gave up hope for lack of educational opportunities and upward mobility. And many couldn't afford the tuition at the university because banks wouldn't loan them enough to pay for their education.

I bore witness to that reality. My first dream in Boston was to study pharmacy after I graduated from Dorchester High in June of 1981. Since I couldn't afford the tuition at the only two private pharmacy schools in Massachusetts, I entered the University of Massachusetts in Boston, majoring in chemistry. I preferred pharmacy because I needed to earn a living wage after graduation in case I didn't go to medical school. I dreaded that choice, but it was my only option.

My lifelong goal was to study medicine. I knew then that even with the best academic record, there was no guarantee of automatic admission to a medical school. I wanted to explore a subject that I not only liked but that also would allow me to find work right after graduation. I could ill-afford to drive a taxi for the rest of my life. I needed certainty and a guarantee of employment.

I am forever grateful that my first alma mater, Northeastern University, provided me with that safety net. Without that full scholarship, I couldn't have changed my major and pursued my enduring interest. I cannot fathom how different things would have been for me, my family, and my larger tribe. Without Northeastern University, there wouldn't have been the Stanford University School of Medicine for me.

27
CHAPTER

A Girl from Nowhere

*On the judgment day, Armstrong's trumpet will
be the interpreter of man's sufferings.*

—PAUL NIGER

The first time I saw Youla, she was waiting for the corner deaconess to signal her to come to the podium at Temple Salem. She wore a white turban corset dress that was as smooth as snow on that frosty fall morning in New England. Her shining black hair was wrapped in a bonnet. Once signaled, she glanced up, climbed the stairs, and headed toward the lectern as the crowd gazed upon her. A mob of squirming girls flopped down on the front row, gaping at her like she was some sort of strange creature. She made no eye contact. Her white teeth flashed as an elder called her full name: Yves-Renée Jeremie. She glanced toward the right and into space. Her eyes were bright, her face composed and cherubic. The pastor stood inside the baptismal pool and said that the young convert was tired of the world.

As she strolled barefoot onto the red carpet, her hips floated gracefully. Though it was a Sabbath Day, a holy day, there was in her visage a certain finesse I was instantly attracted to. I had never felt this way toward any other girl. Her manner was dignified and courteous. Whether it was my repressed carnality poking its head out from beneath my sainthood, I couldn't tell. She was remarkable—the prettiest girl in the assembly of saints.

Sitting in the pew like a prowling cat, I waited for her to pass me and say, *"Salut Milliardaire, d'où viens-tu?"* But she didn't know me. As she stood at the edge of the baptismal pool, she seemed at peace. Two deaconesses took her hands and brought her inside the water to meet the pastor. A girl sitting in my pew giggled.

The crowd stood, cheering and clapping as though Marie-Jeanne Lamartinière were making her entry in the battle of Crête-à-Pierrot to goad the Haitians soldiers against the French Army in March of 1802. I craned my head to see around the hundred curious souls that mid-Saturday morning at Temple Salem. Youla looked rattled for an instant by the thunderous applause of the assembly.

When I think of her on that day, a young girl at the helm of a boat in the middle of the Pacific Ocean who had been told to find her way home to a Caribbean island, my emotions threaten to overwhelm me.

Her bewildered amusement fascinated me. Never had I noticed anything distinct about a young woman before that experience. She had a powerful pull on me, a sort of hypnotic effect strong enough to make me want to kiss her without even knowing why. She beamed with confidence and faced the assembly with aplomb, much like the rising sun on a cloudless day.

Why had the pastor said she had turned her back to the world? At such an early age, how could she be tired of the world? What had she experienced to have given up on this world? The world was still a beautiful place. She could go to theaters. She could watch a good movie. She could vacation in Haiti. She could listen to sensuous or evocative music or a hymn. She could read a good book.

It couldn't be true. But I had heard it that morning: "She got tired of this world." The pastor must have been confused. She fascinated me, almost to the point of insanity. Was she the girl I had dreamt about a few years earlier when I was in Haiti? She had hooked me with her beauty and simplicity. She did not comingle with the other young people like KD., Maggie S. L., and others. Instead, she strode to the altar, receiving the water baptism.

What has she done wrong? I wondered. Much like my friends had questioned me that day as I'd returned home from the procession in Carrefour at the age of thirteen and I'd confessed to them that I hadn't done anything wrong in the sense of wrongdoing, no one had been quieted that day. It didn't matter that she had tuned out the assembly for a while and I had witnessed it. Too bad she had failed to see me in the crowd. She had no family in the church. At least I'd had Rock, my comrade in the assembly. She looked like a kid coming from nowhere doing the Julius Caesar thing: *veni, vidi, vici.* She came out of the water and headed to the back room to remove her wet clothes. Then she disappeared.

Months passed. The cute girl never came back to Temple Salem. I asked myself, *Whatever happened to that young lady who got baptized after being so tired of this world?* I suspected that the same day she was baptized, she turned her back on the Lord and returned to the world. The memory of her remained a mystery, for I knew nothing about her. And life continued. No one ever mentioned her in their missionary visits for the sick, the downtrodden, the apostates, or the like, at church gatherings. No one spoke of the girl from nowhere.

Turn the clock forward a year, and there she was, dressed in a long gray skirt and blue sweater, walking as if on eggshells in the middle of the large chemistry lecture hall at the University of Massachusetts. Was it her? It must have been. A few days later, she came and sat on the left side of the hall a few feet away under my watchful gaze. The two of us were there before anyone else came into the lecture hall. By habit, I arrived at least ten minutes before anyone else. Sadly, she didn't know who I was.

One morning, halfway through the semester, out of the corner of my eye I noticed my belle walking toward me. I feigned not seeing her as she trekked toward me, my heart jolting when she asked, "Excuse me. Do you happen to have the class notes from last week's lectures? I missed some, and I was wondering if I could borrow your notes before class starts?"

It was almost surreal. The cute girl had spoken to me. Me, the gawky young man who wore eyeglasses that looked like they were made for a donkey, their huge lenses courtesy of 1980s fashion eyewear. I was at once that young man who didn't know what to say to a young lady to keep her talking.

"Oh, sure. If you don't mind, we could stay after class to share these notes," I said, "since the lecture is about to start." It was an ambush, but I wanted to make sure I had her to myself for a while. "It would be much better later."

That was Wednesday, October 14, 1981, a day stamped in my memory. While I sat in the chemistry lecture hall that morning, I tried to memorize her face. She had big brown, brilliant eyes above her comely cheeks; her nose and her straight posture gave her the imposing look of Nefertiti. Her cheerful attitude was captivating, and I saw no need to be in a hurry.

Two days before Christmas, she asked me for a ride to the Greyhound station. She needed to visit a family member in New York. I had known her for two months but had interacted with her only during the chemistry lectures and a few other times after class in the library. On my way to pick her up from her home in Mattapan, I felt lonely. She was going to be away for almost a month until the next semester began. I consoled myself with the fact that a year ago, I'd known nothing of her. I even wrote her a tender poem and handed it to her that third week of December 1981.

> My whole soul seems to blast,
> As you quit as the sunset
> Quits the skyline to the last,
> Honey, any of your "that's it."

I knew I would miss her. She was only a friend to me, but I had never felt a more significant loss. She became closer to me than Rock or any other of my siblings or even my parents. A month to absorb the pain of her absence was too much for a soul like mine. I doubted she felt the same way.

Our friendship remained dormant for two months, until early March 1982. It was cold outside when I left the gates of the University of Massachusetts one day. I was tired and had a throbbing headache. I thought I was catching a cold because Youla and I had spent a large part of the previous Saturday afternoon begging for the SDA Church Giving for Humanity on the streets of Roslindale—much like the Salvation Army's annual collection. I noticed that neither the pastor nor his wife or any of their children had gathered on the snowy pavement to beg for donations. And I had walked the streets the previous Friday after school working as a hawker of religious books trumpeting Christ's return.

That day after class, I went straight home and fell asleep on the couch. I woke up two hours later feeling feverish. When I lifted my hand and rubbed my neck, I noticed a hard lump on the right side. *What is that? What could that be? What does it mean? Should I go to a hospital? Where?* I had never been inside a hospital in America before. I couldn't recall whether Wilfrid or Rock or Ti Samuel were home, but I knew it was time for me to go to one of the area hospitals. I knew about the Longwood area hospitals. At least five of them stood within a half-mile radius of my Ruggles apartment. I finally decided on the Boston City Hospital, two miles away, as it was the most familiar to me. As a cabbie, I had dropped off a lot of black folks at the emergency room.

I took the ten-minute drive to Boston City Hospital that afternoon. They sat me down in their ER. There was no talking, smiling, or joviality. Most of the folks there looked fearful or peeved.

A nurse called my name and asked me to follow her. She wore a white blouse with seams so tight they hardly showed a crease. She took me into a small room behind an old dark curtain and began to ask me a series of intimate questions after ushering me to a chair and said, "You may sit down." Then she took a seat behind her wooden desk. Beneath her sat a rusty trash can.

"Mr. Syverain, what brought you here tonight?"

"I have a fever, and I feel a lump in my neck."

"How long have you had that fever?" she asked.

"It started today."

"What about the lump? How long have you had it?

"I felt it only a few hours ago."

"How many sexual partners have you had in your life?"

"What?" I whispered, embarrassed.

"Have you slept with a man or woman?" My head jerked back. Now I was scared since I didn't know where the conversation was going.

"I never slept with anyone," I said. The nurse's piercing blue eyes glared at me, and then she leaned back and cackled. She dragged her chair closer and peered at me as though she had trouble hearing me.

"Are you single or married?" She clasped her hands and gazed at her writing pad as her jowls quivered a bit.

"Always single."

"Are you currently in a relationship?"

"No, I am not."

"But why do you have a fever?" She said. "And you are from Haiti?"

"Yes, I have a fever, and that's why I came here now."

"You said you noticed a bump on your neck three days ago."

"I noticed it when I rubbed my neck today, not three days ago."

"Do you live alone?"

"No. I live with two of my siblings and some friends."

"Is anyone sick at home?"

"Not that I know of." She must have sensed my uneasiness because she pivoted her line of questioning.

"Do you have an appetite?"

"Yes, I do," I said.

"What do you do for a living?"

"I drive a cab on weekends, but I am a full-time student at UMass."

"You are a full-time student? Where? You mean the university near the JFK library?"

"Yes, the University of Massachusetts."

"Have you ever had these symptoms before?"

"No."

"You can tell me the truth."

"Yes. I am telling you the truth, nurse."

"Where are you from again?"

"Haiti."

"How many partners do you have?"

"Partners? What do you mean?" I asked. "None." I wiggled in the chair and scratched my head.

"I am sorry. It is hospital procedure to ask the same question many times sometimes," she said.

"Oh, I see."

"How long you have that bump in your neck?"

"I only noticed it today."

The nurse wasn't trying to be difficult. She had to vet me well, making sure I answered all her questions consistently. Asking me the same questions many times seemed right. I remembered how many young men forgot to brush their teeth every morning or put deodorant on or tie their shoelaces. So making an inquiry about the bump on my neck and listening to my answers were the right things to do.

"I am going to check your vital signs."

"What do you mean?" I asked.

"I am going to check your BP."

"What do you mean?" I asked. I was thinking the worst and feeling squeamish about being in the hospital.

"Sir, I mean to check your blood pressure."

"Oh, I see."

"Could I have your right arm?"

"What do you need it for?" I asked.

"I am sorry you didn't understand me. We are not going to cut your arm. We only need to check something important in your body."

I held out my arm. She stood up and grabbed a clunky blood pressure cuff from a basket on the wall, then sat down and asked me to straighten my arm so she could wrap the cuff around it. She pulled out a gray stethoscope with PVC tubing and smacked its diaphragm between my sleeve and the greasy cuff, listening through the earpieces. She nodded with approval after squeezing the inflation bulb of the sphygmomanometer while she watched the dial of the pressure gauge. "Good." She said as she stood up, pulled an instrument from a cabinet above her, and reclaimed her seat.

"Open your mouth," she said. "Stick your tongue out. Whom should we call in case of an emergency?" She blinked as she folded her handwritten pad, stood, and got ready to walk away. "Could we contact any of your brothers?"

"Yes."

"Well, wait here. The doctor will be with you shortly." She pushed open the curtain and left the room.

I sat down for a while with the thought of escaping the hospital grounds before the doctor arrived. After the doctor examined me, an orderly came in and asked me to sit in a wheelchair; he told me he would take me to my admission room. I balked and told him I could walk. He told me that hospital policy required me to sit in the wheelchair.

It was dark and cold outside. Only a handful of people were in the emergency room. I obliged. I sat down thinking I must be seriously ill.

Oh no! Am I going to die? I am going to school tomorrow. How will I be able to catch up when I return if I miss a class? I was already struggling in my honors English class, and now I was going to miss the next day's round-table lecture. *What about my General Chemistry 2 class? Do I call my calculus class professor to explain? How can I miss my physics class for two days in a row? What can I do? I need to call Rock or Wilfrid or any of our friends living in our apartment and tell them what's going on.*

My mind went to a quiet place until I began to think about what the orderly had said in the elevator. It piqued my morbid curiosity that evening when he'd said, "I think you have cancer." He made it sound like a crowning achievement.

"Last week I took care of a man like you with something large in his neck. He didn't come out alive. He died two days ago."

I gasped as he gave me a weighty grin. "The man died, why?" I asked. I noticed a tiny, fresh smear of blood on the elevator wall.

"Well, he died."

"But what killed him?" I wanted to know as though I could have done something about it.

"He came here sick, like you." I slumped in the wheelchair like dead weight, afraid of asking any more questions. The elevator came to a stop with a loud thump, causing me to grip the arms of the wheelchair. The orderly wheeled me down the fourth-floor corridor and into my admission room. There, he asked the nurses to help me into bed. As he glanced at me, he looked somber and shook his head. My fate was sealed. I was as good as dead.

I couldn't sleep. In the middle of the night, I crawled out of my bed to call my brothers. It was too late for them to visit me. The only thing left to do was agonize over what the orderly had said. One of the nurses came in to ask me if I was well. When I told her I was fine, she turned off the light, but I struggled to fall asleep.

What do I know? The man works here and must have seen many people dying in the hospital corridors. He knows his stuff. Did someone tell him something about me when I was in the emergency room? Well, they must have told him somehow. Otherwise, how did he know about the gravity of my illness? I was going to die because this middle-aged man had told me I was. A man of experience like he was wouldn't lie to me. He was a black man like me. He was a brother, a comrade, and a new friend who understood me. He knew how I felt. He knew about our plight, us black folks. He knew many of us didn't leave this place alive. I'd brought myself here and had only myself to blame. No one had asked me to come here. I'd done it of my volition. My thoughts shifted.

I should ignore what he said. I think the man was lying to me. He isn't a doctor—one who knows everything about the human body no matter how frail the corpse. The man hates me and wishes I was dead instead of alive. I know this because he didn't ask me how I felt. I saw him frowning at me before he spoke to me. So I know he hates me. I suspected it when he first opened his mouth and let go his death diatribe. What kind of man is that? He dared to look me in the eye and say I was going to die. Perhaps he was a living corpse himself, a zombie, a ghost. Besides, no one told me he was coming to pick me up. The orderly must be joking. Who brought me here, then? How did I get here? Where am I? I know. It's a dream. Aha. I have nothing to fear. I am dreaming, and when I wake up, I will find myself at home in my warm bed. There is no nightmare or drama here.

Early the next morning, four physicians entered my room. One was an older man with grey hair at the temples. They approached my bed and introduced themselves. I couldn't remember any of the younger ones' faces or names. I recalled from our conversation that they would return to take me to the operating room.

"Why do I need to go into the operating room?" I asked.

"That is the only way to do a biopsy of that lump on your neck."

"You mean you are going to cut my neck?"

"Oh no, we are going to stick a needle in your neck to pull some liquid from this mass and possibly cut the mass out for complete analysis."

You are correct. It's a real mess indeed. Do we all agree? I thought. No one had asked for my opinion. I was a college student full of ambition and dreams and unabated optimism. This was not the way I wanted to go, but no one has a say in death.

I hated the imposed silence that fell around me as they left. It reminded me of those curfews I'd lived through in Haiti when there were rumors of an impending coup d'état. Those nights terrorized everyone.

Two days later, some friends and family members came by the hospital to learn that I was still alive. Among them was a vivacious young lady I had befriended at Dorchester High. The garrulous Myrtza François, her palpable presence was felt inside the room, had dropped in only a few minutes after Youla. She sat at the head of my bed and kept me in conversation as though no one else was there. She didn't care, for it was her right to talk to me like two good old friends would.

"Milliardddddaire, tell me how you feel," she asked. "Is there anything I could do to make you comfortable?"

"Sure, be here with me," I said as I looked at Youla, who shuffled closer to the bed. She stood quietly, the same way she had in Temple Salem on her baptismal day. I'd loaded my answer and lobbed it at her, not Myrtza. Back in November when we studied chemistry together, I confessed how much I loved her. But the more I begged her to be my girl, the more she withdrew her interest in me. I became teary each time she would zone out as I spoke of my love for her. At least I had hope when she said she couldn't imagine seeing me walking with another girl's hand in mine down the aisle of a church. That day, since I was dying, I wanted to be frank with Myrtza. I needed a friend.

On several occasions the previous semester in the school cafeteria and library, my advances toward Youla had fallen upon deaf ears. She had a boyfriend who lived in New York. Youla had never met Myrtza until my hospital admission, though Myrtza attended Temple Salem every Saturday and was my classmate at Dorchester High. The young sisters in the church were decent and beautiful.

How could *ma petite amie*, who had rejected my advances so many times before, know what ailed me more than anything? Youla was what ailed me. She was the one thing I wanted before I died. She'd ignored me time after time. She'd rejected each advance. *Even if I offered my body for immolation as Brother Antoine Thurel did for Haiti on the steps of the Boston Statehouse on September 1, 1987, with all the love inside me, she still wouldn't care*, I thought. All my attempts remained futile. But Magrann had said to me once, "Patience always wins, my son."

After classes, I tried bringing her with me to the local YMCA, where we played racquetball and squash; this failed. I took her to Boston Symphony

Hall for many a Sunday matinee, but this, too, failed. I spent countless hours in her company, making her laugh; this too became vanity.

Yet, that day in my hospital room, something changed—something magical I would cherish into eternity: It seemed Myrtza's presence had made Youla wonder whether I was falling in love with my High School former classmate. After God, I had her to thank.

"Your presence here meant a lot to me. I never imagined you would have heard about my admission to the hospital," I said to Myrtza. I turned my head to look at Youla. She lowered her head, staring up at me.

"Do you like grapes, Milliardddddaire? Myrtza asked as she dragged out every letter of my first name, caressing it with her rich, silky, melodious voice. "I have brought you some."

Poor Youla. Only an hour earlier, she had brought me some Lifesavers. We had shared the candies last semester on the school campus.

"Thank you, Myrtza, for bringing them," I said. "I love grapes."

Youla scanned Myrtza's face and then squeezed the bed rail. A few rays of bright sunshine passed through it from the window in the room. She sighed. We had been friends for the last five months, but she had seen me not as a suitor but as a colleague. I, however, loved her more with each passing moment and felt grateful for her presence in the room.

The days in the school cafeteria and library were behind me. My advances had gone the way of the blowing winds off Columbia Point, each one drowned in the waves of the churning water below. I had a lonely and empty existence as Youla kept her distance during January, part of February, and early March, when we'd traversed the city streets, begging for the church. Soon I entered the hospital grounds. She felt a little guilty.

That afternoon, as Myrtza left my room, I sensed a change in Youla. Perhaps she realized my fragile mortality. Her insouciance toward me and our friendship might be on the wane if Myrtza and I became best buddies. Youla tried to mend this imbroglio. As she left my bedside, there was élan in her voice, and I knew a new day had dawned for me. Yet how could I enjoy this change when I lay on a sickbed?

The biopsy revealed hyperplasia of the lymph node, and I was released from the hospital to pick up where I left off. I was relieved. Though I regretted staying away from my classes for so long and needed to play catch-up when I returned, my time spent at the hospital was worth something.

That hospital admission had done something else for me. It was like a jolt from a high-voltage electrical wire to a sleeping body. I realized that my time on earth was evanescent, my days finite. A surge of energy came over me, and I wanted to be useful to my loved ones, my friends, and the community at large. I started to volunteer more at my church. I visited the sick and elderly more often and worked with underprivileged youth. Youla had always enjoyed missionary visits more than I did.

Most importantly, she and I became inseparable. We resumed going to the YMCA near NU to play squash and racquetball on school evenings. We attended quite a few Boston Symphony Sunday matinees.

On Saturday, May 22, 1982, we stood before a justice of the peace in Dorchester at eleven o'clock that morning. We tied the knot with no witnesses, no money, and we told no one about our decision. We lived apart from each other as before because we didn't have the money to rent our own place, but we were married only seven months after she'd introduced herself to me. We asked no one for advice or guidance or direction. Cocky we weren't. We wanted to keep the whole thing private. We were two crazy kids doing what crazy kids didn't usually do: get married.

28
CHAPTER

Cloudy Sky

Omniscient and naïve conquerors

—AIMÉ CÉSAIRE

rofessor Carter staggered into the lecture hall of the University of Massachusetts like a drunk on the verge of a hostile divorce or a judge presiding over a cheating spouse, then slammed the door with a bang behind him. He bucked at the suggestion to leave it open. Whenever he was in the lecture hall, everyone had to be quiet. He was Dr. Robert Carter, PhD in chemistry. He must have seen himself as an avatar, a potentate, or a significant other we needed to reckon with. Whenever he stomped up to the podium to deliver his lecture, he was unshackled and full of self-importance.

It was early in January of my freshman year at UMass. One male class-mate spoke loudly enough for all the students in my row to hear. "How long is he going to continue babbling like this in class?" He sat behind me in the amphitheater. "I bet you he must be thinking he is in Professorville."

I giggled quietly, dropped my head, and pretended to write something in my notebook, though there wasn't much to put down on paper since Dr. Carter hadn't said much about his course, General Chemistry II.

"Whether he is in Cartersville or Charlestown, we must know by now that Dr. Carter is a joker," said another classmate amid the inaudible guf-faws. "He should go on with the lecture."

"No, it isn't that. I want to see that jaybird stop and go back to the lec-ture. This man is getting scarier by the minute. At least our first semester General Chemistry professor, Dr. Walter Weibrecht, was kind enough to answer our queries, not like this clown. Don't you agree? One good thing about Dr. Carter, though—he keeps us worried about our grades. It's always a one-sided affair, where he speaks and we students listen without permis-sion to ask any questions." I heaved a sigh and winced at the thought that we would have three-plus months in his classroom.

"I am beginning to dread him too," said the fellow to my right.

When he barged into the hall that morning, Professor Carter jerked his neck, sniggered, and glared at the students. His crinkly, bushy eyebrows rose above his cold, gleaming, deep-set green eyes—eyes the color of the old lizard I had seen many times in Carrefour. His navy-blue trousers were starched enough to cut a lip. His white shirt was buttoned to the neck, and a black bowtie perched at his throat like a butterfly. He marched toward the lectern, then watched us sneak into the lecture hall. He looked angry, his frown betraying his contempt for us. When he caught sight of us, his face flushed. Every so often, he adjusted the gold-rimmed reading glasses that hung around his neck. He was the master of that lecture hall, and we were at his mercy.

The words that sprang from his lips leapt at us as if they had a life of their own. They stung. Professor Carter leaned against the blackboard, uncrossing his feet as he straightened himself. He looked over his shoulder at us while cracking his knuckles and widening his stare, giving us a killer smile, his tightly bonded teeth sparkling. Then he embarked on the most strident speech I had ever heard as a student.

"I've heard rumors that many of you in here are premed students. Well, I have news for you. I don't think 99 percent of you will ever qualify to go to medical school." Who had asked for his opinion?

But as these invectives escaped his mouth, they hit me like a brick in the back of my spine. I wanted to run away from another dream killer. He was trying to sentence me to death or lock me inside a cage in the bowels of another ghetto. His words weighed on me like a caterpillar roving over a small ant. It's a reality many minority students were subjected to from kindergarten through college. We were a throng of youngsters born into inauspicious circumstances, most of us the descendants of former black slaves. A few of my colleagues had forebears who had likely built the White House a century earlier. If one lacked the family pedigree, which most of us did, it made it all the worse. Professor Carter's invective burst through my marrow like a sharp knife through the throat of a sacrificial goat or a ram in a bush.

Yet his words failed to have the impact he desired.

Instead of discouraging us, his words forced us to look inward and work harder. That afternoon when we came out of his classroom, as we met on the dry, cold grass outside the lecture hall, many of us vowed to never give up on our dreams. If anything, Professor Carter had reminded us why we needed to remain vigilant, confident, and resilient. Though we had no idea how we were going to stay the course. It was only a promise.

Professor Carter's words tormented me the same way Lucifer's had when she'd said, "You will never amount to much." Professor Carter must have been in his early thirties when he began teaching at the University of Massachusetts, the sole public university in the city. If it weren't for his impeccable dressing and lordliness, he might not have seemed that different from any of the white male students at the university. He was vibrant and clean-shaven and had a bright complexion, sharp nose, impish chin, and thick, brown hair trimmed close.

In the classroom, he was intimidating, had no natural warmth, and spent most of his time strutting like a peacock instead of keeping his eyes on the blackboard writing chemical

equations. How could he find us threatening when we were among the most peaceful and forgiving mortals on the planet? Perhaps he wondered why these greasy black faces looked like people afraid of being dragged to a public lynching. Who could blame them?

Not long ago, I heard and read stories about a white teenager gunning down a black boy who had climbed a tree to watch a football game in East Boston. The white boy claimed he had seen a blackbird perched in the tree. What kind of bird was that? The black boy's body was riddled with bullets. His corpse lay as though ready for crucifixion. Dad also told me of the killing inside Boston City Hospital of an unarmed black man, Franklin Lynch, and its cover-up in the hands of the Boston Police Department. My Dad had been punched in the eye without provocation by an unemployed white bandit. He had to have surgery to close the wound.

Was my General Chemistry II professor bitter because he had been rejected by the medical schools he'd applied to? I don't know whether he'd ever wanted to go to medical school. But where was that hostility, jealousy, envy, and contempt for a few teenagers who dared to dream of becoming medical doctors coming from? Racism against black people in America is real.

I felt terrible for Professor Carter. He lacked one of the essential things in life: perspective. I had no resentment toward him. Professor Carter may have forgotten one great thing about this life that we share, as illustrated in Ecclesiastes 1:14: "I have seen all the things that are done under the sun; all of them are meaningless, a chasing of the wind." If he is alive today, he could take comfort in 1 Corinthians 13:13: "And now these three remain: faith, hope and love. But the greatest of these is love."

When I returned to the chemistry class after a week of my hospital admission, my whole demeanor had changed. Whether it had to do with my brush with death or my previous experience with Professor Carter or both, I couldn't tell. Though I struggled to catch up in that class, I had a mental block and no further recollection of him after that lecture. By the end of the semester, I had given up and almost ceased to care.

However, I had a harder time relating to another chemistry faculty member, Dr. Glabrous Head, a moniker I have given him since I can't recall his real name. At first I thought I had an ally in him. I was wrong.

In the fall of 1982, I came upon an organic chemistry professor, a Haitian expat like me, who had immigrated to the States in the early 1960s. He had a plaque on his office wall beside his PhD diploma that reminded all visitors, "Bald is beautiful." He told me that a street in Haiti carried his family's famous name.

Every time I went to his office for some clarification or the latest developments in his field or an explanation of the Grignard Reaction, he would be sitting there, smoking his cigar with his eyes shut like a transcendental guru. He would probably have been oblivious to an intruder entering his space. That strange, exotic bird even told me, "Over there," meaning in Haiti, "I wouldn't be sitting next to people like you." He would have had second thoughts about sitting next to Rosa Parks, I guess. This professor meant to tell me he could pass for a white person because of his lighter complexion.

I wanted to ask him a question but I dared not, for he was the professor of organic chemistry. First, I wanted to say, "Who told you people like me would want your company? Second, what country are you talking about, Professor? Haiti?" If he was talking about the island he had left and never returned to, that country had died when Papa Doc (Francois Duvalier) had taken the helm and given folks like me a chance. Third, I wanted to remind him that the likes of my esteemed professor had gone into exile once Papa Doc became Haiti's president in 1957.

I had the professor for two semesters of Organic Chemistry I and II but failed to remember his name. He must have been that toxic and full of deception. Although he wasn't a white man like Professor Carter or a dark-skinned man like me, he looked like a tragic mulatto. He must have been a lonely and confused Griffe, Marabou, Sacatra, or Quadroon. Whatever he was, he likely felt he belonged nowhere, not even in his smoky office under a cloudy sky.

29

CHAPTER

Cabbie Goes
to Stanford

*There can't be a history about the age of
revolution without the history of Haiti.*

—MILLIARDAIRE JOSEPH SYVERAIN

"If you want something badly and are willing to put the effort without worrying about how many times you may have to pick yourself up to repeat the same tasks, you will get it," Dad had said. I see how that aphorism became true for me when I look back at my earliest school failures, deceptions, rejections, and mockeries.

One misty Saturday morning on May 7, 1988, Youla and I found ourselves on the streets of Palo Alto after an evening flight from Boston to San Francisco. We left the Stanford Arms Hotel in Menlo Park and walked toward El Camino Real to attend a meeting for the incoming minority medical students. It was our first time in California. Deep within Campus Drive, the trees were as green as the leaves of Franklin Park Zoo in Boston. As we tromped toward Louis Pasteur Avenue and Fairfield Auditorium, it became a bit tricky. There was a heavy downpour that splashed rain into our eyes and kept us from seeing where we were headed. Eventually, we made it to the medical school building, and I managed to get inside the Fairfield Auditorium in time for the welcoming presentation. Youla went to the school library to wait for me.

"Good morning, everyone. It's such a pleasure to have you all matriculating in the fall at Stanford University School of Medicine," said the soft-spoken Dr. Patricia Cross to a group of fifteen black, Latino, and Native American students. We were part of the first-year medical students, class of 1993. After her brief introduction and welcome, she handed the microphone to C. David Rios, a second-year medical student.

"I know some of you may have misgivings about coming to Stanford and leaving the familiar and families and friends behind. In my case, it was one of the best decisions I've made in my life. I have no regrets and nostalgia or disappointment yet, and I am sure it will be the same for you," said David. "But first you must matriculate."

Thursday, September 15, 1988, marked the beginning of a new life for me. Gone were the hot summer days of the East Coast. I was to experience the cool evenings and chilly nights of Silicon Valley. Only a few months earlier, I had spoken to Youla about forgoing medical school altogether that year, resigned to the fact that I wouldn't be well enough after my Northeastern University graduation. I had requested a deferment and got one from Columbia University School of Medicine for one year.

The winter of 1987 and spring of 1988 were enervating for me. When nobody was watching, I would squat down while walking, hoping that the dizziness would go away. I would crouch like a fearful cub with beads of sweat rolling down my cheeks and falling on the curbside, spraying my nose. I was tired most of the time. Week after week, I got weaker in my knees. I continued visiting my physician at Harvard Community Health Plan but never received a definitive diagnosis. Soon I gave up on the idea of a recovery that would allow me to attend medical school in the fall.

After finding a few atypical lymphocytes in a blood test, my physician continued to reassure me that I probably had infectious mononucleosis, or "kissing disease." He'd given me a diagnosis and I had a name for my condition, but it was incorrect and raised more hell in my head than he realized. I had been married for five years. Youla worked as a staff nurse but had never been sick, let alone with a kissing bug. Whatever I suffered from ailed me to no end.

When I began doing rounds as a pharmacy intern with the doctors at Saint Elizabeth Hospital, I worried I wouldn't have the energy to stand and follow them and the medical students around the hospital all day. My knees would wobble, buckle, and sway during those morning conferences. My eyes would grow red, and I would see floaters. I would lean on the hospital wall or a patient's bed during rounds. Before each patient's presentation ended, I would worry about what a fool I'd look like if I fell and passed out. The whole experience baffled me. Youla would see me at home and say, "If we could crawl to California, things would be different." She thought a change of climate might bring salutary benefits. She was my tower of strength in a time of trouble.

We had visited the Stanford University campus last May out of curiosity. We wanted to see the Pacific Ocean and California rather than trying to make up our minds about moving there without seeing it. We knew we must leave Boston to avoid dealing with Rock's recurrent breakdowns and the draining effect they were having on me.

It was delusional to think we were going to a tropical place like Haiti when we left Boston that day. We hadn't brought any warm clothing to cover ourselves that Friday evening. Though California has more sunny days than most states in the union, it is cold most nights in Silicon Valley.

The airport minivan hurried to drop us off at the housing office before closing time so we could get our dormitory key. The driver took us to Palm

Drive, then turned right on Campus Drive, and we finally arrived at Galvez Mall at the housing office. The place looked desolate, dark, and foreboding, with not a soul in sight. I was nervous but told no one until I got out of the van. A small breeze whisked through the trees, stirring the leaves of a nearby eucalyptus. I shuddered. My heart jumped. My knees gave out the same way they had over the previous ten months. I shook a little in the cool of the night, and I felt like there was no blood in my body. If Youla could see in the dark, she would have noticed how my face had grown pale with worry.

The campus looked spooky enough to remind me of the hundreds of starry nights I had experienced as a child on the beach of Ti Mouillage. Civilization was distant when the sky looked closer to me than my neighbor's next door.

Thankfully, the front door of the office opened. Within fifteen minutes, we had our keys and the address of our apartment. When we came back and took our seats behind the driver, we found him cracking his knuckles while looking at the small clock near the speedometer. The van lurched forward with the middle-aged man behind the steering wheel, his black-and-white Los Angeles Raiders cap low over his face and almost blocking his view. He rolled down the window and let a gust of cold air fill the cab as he put his head out and spat on the concrete road. He looked straight ahead while the van rattled over the curb and banged down onto Sierra Drive, taking us to Escondido Village.

"Easy," Youla said quietly.

The housing office had assigned us to the eighth floor of the twelve-story Quillen building, a dormitory for married graduate students. It was one of two of the tallest student residences on campus. The other was Blackwelder.

The moment we got to Quillen, I began planning my escape route in case the "Big One," the next huge earthquake, hit California. I slept badly that first night. The next day, I woke up around five in the morning and began to look through the Yellow Pages. I found a Sears in Mountain View near El Camino Real and San Antonio Avenue. I thought about buying myself a long rope, but I lacked training in mountain climbing. How would I use it to escape from the eighth floor? Where would I tie the rope? I had no idea.

After a few days, I gave up on the idea. My hope was that the Big One would occur during the day. I grew more and more anxious living there and knew I would have to leave sooner or later. I needed to bring a doctor's note to the housing department to explain my rationale for requesting a low-rise apartment.

Here I was on the Stanford Campus in the fall of 1988. A few months prior, I had taken only buses and trains to my medical school interviews. I didn't even have to fly to Stanford University for my medical-school interview. The school conducted its regional admission interviews in Boston, likely having realized the plight of students like me who couldn't afford an airline ticket or who were fearful of flying. I fell into both categories.

I had never heard of Stanford before the spring of 1986 but discovered its allure during a biomedical conference I attended in Maryland. The premed committee at Northeastern University chose two students to attend the conference, which was to be held at the National Institutes of Health. The goal of the conference was to encourage minority students to pursue careers in medicine and medical research.

I got a ride early Wednesday morning to the Amtrak station located near downtown Boston and boarded a train to Baltimore. Ten hours later, a taxi took me from Baltimore to the 4-H Youth Conference Center in Chevy Chase. That suburban city of Maryland was unlike any of the towns I had lived in before in America. Flowering trees lined its hushed streets. Every home on these streets had a well-tended lawn. It looked like only white people lived within the affluent enclave of historical homes.

My affable Italian–Puerto Rican roommate, E.P. had a square jaw. His tanned skin made him look like a young George Clooney on vacation. We'd both come for the April 3, 4 biomedical conference at NIH. As we visited, he told me that the best way to prepare for medical school admission was to take a review class for the Medical College Admission Test. That advice would serve me well twenty months later when I took the MCAT. On our way to the conference, he told me that Harvard and several other medical schools had offered him admission. He preferred Stanford but hadn't received a letter of acceptance yet.

"Edgar, you said you want to go to Stanford. Where is Stanford?" I asked.

"How do you pronounce your name again?"

"Milliardaire."

"I like to go to school in California," he said. I asked no further questions about Stanford since I didn't know much about it.

"What does a student do when work at the NIH?" I said.

"A classmate told me that at the University of Chicago, there are times they need student volunteers. Working there is part of it too. They need them to become guinea pigs for their experimental vaccines."

"Do you think we could become subjects of an AIDS vaccine?" I said.

"I don't know. Do you think NIH will tell us?"

"Knowing what I don't know, how can I trust the scientists there?" he said.

"How could I forget about the Tuskegee experiment? The government knowingly allowed syphilis to spread among the hundreds of black families in its care. A cure was widely available. It's the stuff of the Nazis, man! Sorry if I am paranoid about the people running this country. They don't always work in the best interests of the poor and minorities in their midst. Sometimes they think there are too many of them, and they would rather kill them off. Trust me, they are still at work and won't be content until they kill every single one of them," I said.

"Man, this is deep stuff we are talking about." E.P. touched his nose.

"Recall our history in the so-called Columbian Exchange. Be careful of so-called civilized men like Captain William Trent. He made it his duty to decimate Native Americans with smallpox-infected blankets, handkerchiefs, and other trinkets in 1763 at Fort Pitt. His goal was to steal their land."

E.P. turned his head and squinted at me. He smiled and pulled his lower lip, exposing his teeth. He finally turned away with sadness in his eyes.

"Remember the former congressman. What's his name again? Our vice president and former CIA director—George Bush. He thought there were too many of us. He sat with Henry Kissinger devising a solution and may have found one. They forgot that Europe is the smallest of the continents, not counting Australia. My dad often told me to be watchful of these macabre plots against us."

Many young fellows didn't give a squish about what's going on around them, but E.P. was different. He was a couth, thoughtful, remarkable young man who knew and learned well from history. That day, I began to understand a shameful part of America's history I knew nothing about. "The heart is deceitful above all things, and desperately wicked: who can know it" (Jeremiah 17:9).

E.P. wanted to forgo Harvard for Stanford. I felt he was insane. My bias about Harvard was natural and regional. When my turn came to apply to medical schools, I sent out a total of eleven applications. One question that bothered me for years was why Harvard Medical School hadn't offered me an interview. Was it because I had written in the lengthy application that I was a cabbie? I had driven a taxi for a living and picked up a fair amount of Harvard faculty and students, taking them from Logan Airport to Longwood Road or Harvard Square from the fall of 1980 until the summer of 1988.

Even though I knew I had made the right decision in moving to California, I had misgivings. My siblings and parents lived in Boston. How were they going to handle Rock? It was likely a selfish decision to leave my comrade behind. How could anyone complain instead of singing daily for me for having left town to find my spirit in another part of the country? My grandfather Dufrène would have understood my decision.

Two years earlier, an African American Harvard medical student had come to Northeastern to give us premed students a pep talk, reminding us that the sky was the limit. In my case, the sky over Longwood Road was more than a limit; it was a dead end.

In college, I dreamed about attending medical school, though I had my share of doubts to overcome. I avoided pessimists and negative individuals and their advice. They seemed to lurk on every street corner, laundromat, barbershop, church hall, classroom, and office corridor officiously giving advice. I feared they would crush my mind and my spirit by exposing my anxieties, my doubts, and drive. I wanted to go on a journey not yet traveled by any of my folks in America. The farther away I moved, the closer I could get to my goal of becoming a physician. I wanted to go to a place where nobody knew my name. That was one of the reasons I chose to move west.

My second day in medical school was something to dread. I wanted to care for people, but nobody prepared me for what was coming. I gazed at the long black plastic bag lying on the table, a corpse wrapped inside. What did it look like? I wondered. Was the body cold or warm? I unzipped it, starting at the toes, and thought I saw them wiggle. But I couldn't hide or run from it. My peers looked at me, and I glanced at them while poking the cadaver's left foot with my gloved finger. The gross smell of formaldehyde was overwhelming in that anatomy laboratory. Perhaps if one cadaver was assigned per student, I could have easily slipped away and dropped out of medical school. But having three students per corpse made me stand straight and hide my fears. At least that was how I felt. I had originally come from a country where people had an aversion to creepy things, dead bodies, and ghosts. These corpses made me uncomfortable.

When I got to the lab that afternoon, I had no idea how I would feel. The day before, Dr. Lawrence Mathers, our anatomy instructor, had made a few critical remarks about the bodies the class was about to dissect. They were gifts to the medical school, and we were to treat them with care, respect, and a reverence reserved for the saints. When the door of the anatomy lab opened that afternoon, I first heard a series of "oohs and ahs" as the eerie scene lay before us. Two minutes into the lab, once all the sixty-five students had clattered into the room, it became as quiet as Saint Peter's Basilica in the Vatican. The students stood still. With eyes wide and teeth chattering, some became as nervous as if they had entered a morgue. I thought for a minute that the university was playing a joke on us. Why bring us to see the corpses on the second day of class? That afternoon as I rode my bicycle home, I wondered, *Is it worth it? Is becoming a physician worth it?*

The next day, reality began to sink in, for within ten weeks, the class would be over. I began in earnest to cut, dissect, disembowel, prod, and examine with the utmost respect for this person I had never known. I was grateful for the privilege.

The school trimester went too fast for me to find time for small talk. For some students, everything came easy. Many were second- and third-generation medical students. But for a Haitian cabbie going to Stanford, it was confusing. The only anatomy training I'd had prior to entering medical school was when I'd performed an autopsy on a dead frog in a pharmacology class at Northeastern University. I had seen an amphibian menace as I looked at its carcass.

There was no need to remind anyone of where I had come from. Dead humans should be considered sacred. There was nothing natural about death for a superstitious Haitian. Both my grandmothers passed away in their nineties in their homes. Some folks believed they died of unnatural causes. No one dies of natural causes in Haiti—zombies included. Mention the word "zombie" during an encounter in any village in the countryside at dusk, and most people huddle in their homes. Talking about the dead in Haiti makes people freak out. It's an irrational fear.

Many a night, I lay wide awake in my eighth-floor dormitory in the

Quillen building, thinking of corpses during an earthquake. By March of 1989, I had had enough of my anxious, sleepless nights. I obtained a physician's note from the student health center telling the housing office I had a phobia of heights, which was true. The housing office wouldn't have budged without that note.

A few weeks later, Youla and I moved to one of the low-rise apartments in Escondido Village, where we stayed in 15 E until the spring of 1993. It proved to be a great relief for me. When the Loma Prieta earthquake occurred on October 17, 1989, I was relieved to be on the ground level of Meyer Library.

My time as a medical student was fun. I could learn for the sake of learning, not to get a decent grade to be admitted to medical school. My most difficult subjects were neuroanatomy and cellular biology. Neuroanatomy was, as many of my peers admitted, a strange subject most of us had trouble making sense of until the eighth week of the ten-week quarter. As difficult a class as it was, everybody passed.

J.O. was a mystery. During the first three quarters, she shuttled between Khartoum, London, and Dubai visiting her fiancé. She would return a week before finals to review the lectures on VHS tapes. When she took the final exams, she aced them all. She told me that in college, she'd studied psychology and graduated with a grade point average of less than 3.0. Stanford had accepted her after another applicant had declined admission during the summer. She was always among the top scorers of our class of sixty-five students. So much for GPA!

During the first quarter, I was called more than four times by the student office to provide Mom's and Dad's income-tax returns. Each time, I told them I didn't have such things, and they refused to believe me. It was annoying. I had been responsible for myself since I had come to America in December of 1979. What the heck were they talking about? They were relentless in their pursuit, constantly reminding me that all medical students must provide copies of their parents' income-tax returns. Finally, I made up my mind to lie and tell them my parents were dead so they would leave me alone.

My first quarter at school was a tough one for me physically. I was always tired. It took me considerable effort to bicycle to class every weekday morning. While my classmates were bursting with energy and engaging in animated conversations and expansive speeches, I had to almost crawl into a corner like a mollusk under its shell to save the little energy I had. As soon as class was dismissed, I'd disappear into the maddening crowd and head home to study before the deep night fell. I dodged any interactions with my classmates. I was as ill as when I'd left Boston, and I didn't know what ailed me.

It was hard to figure out what was going on. I had good circulation in my legs, and they looked fine. My problem had baffled the old doctor in Boston as well as the many other physicians I saw after him. He prescribed me some stockings. After wearing them for a few weeks, I put them away. They didn't work.

I remained in a state of continual exhaustion. I had been ill for more than eleven months. The first time I had an apoplexy-like attack was around December of 1987. Youla called the paramedics after I became short of breath, and they rushed me to the Carney Hospital emergency room. They released me within two hours with a prescription for an asthma inhaler.

By the time I arrived at Stanford, I wasn't sure whether I could continue my studies. I got winded with the least amount of effort and avoided most campus activities, nonacademic events, and meeting people. Even though I slept, my eyes were always bloodshot. Though my classmates treated me with respect, I wondered if some of them thought I was taking drugs or drinking alcohol.

What rattled me more than anything was the fact that I didn't know what was wrong with me. I made no effort to see another doctor after my Boston visits. The first quarter I dragged myself to class. The second quarter I hauled myself to the lecture halls. The third quarter I stopped bicycling to class altogether and slouched after taking the campus bus to the medical school.

Then one day I saw the light while listening to a lecture given by Stanford endocrinology professor Dr. Carlos A. Camargo, Sr. He described a condition, a hormonal imbalance, where the people affected lacked *joie de vivre.* I loved life, but I had no life in me. I knew he was talking just to me as I sat slumped in the front row of the Fairfield Auditorium. He had given me hope. I'd had finally found the information I had been seeking from heaven and on earth for the last two years.

Before that lecture, I thought there was no treatment for my undiagnosed condition. Now I had a language to share with any physician who was willing to listen to me. The adage "Knowledge that is used is power" is true. My colleagues may have found endocrinology boring. For me, it was a matter of life and death. Only people who've experienced my condition or similar conditions can grasp what I am talking about.

It was the spring of 1990. The day after the endocrinology lecture, I made an appointment at the Cowell Student Health Center on campus. There, I met an old caring family physician who sensed my uneasiness about the situation. I told him my health was the wastebasket. He didn't scoff at me. He smiled and shook his head. Instead, he told me I was a student with a health problem and that his job was to help as best he could. That statement was like soothing water from an oasis in a scorched desert. I felt good. Before I left, he gave me a referral to see Dr. Randolph Linde, an endocrinologist at the Palo Alto Medical Foundation, located a few blocks from the Stanford campus.

The next Thursday afternoon after class, I took my two-door Ford Ranger truck and drove to PAMF. In the lobby, I gave the receptionist my name and told her I was there to see Dr. Linde. He arrived within five minutes. An affable man of good manners, he was soft-spoken, slender, and of medium height. He invited me to follow him, then asked me to fill out a questionnaire. During our conversation, I told him about the lack of *joie de vivre* I had been experiencing the past two years. He did a thorough physical examination, leaving no stone unturned. Before I left, the phlebotomist came and drew some blood.

Dr. Linde's diagnostic acumen was as accurate as a sharpshooter in a foxhole against a formidable foe. The day I went back to see him, I realized why I hadn't gotten an interview at Harvard Medical School. I laughed, knowing that my healing was to come from the West and not the East. "And we know that in all things God works for the good of those who love him," as Romans 8:28 said. Had Harvard accepted me, I would have stayed in Boston and likely wouldn't have found someone who could diagnose me so quickly.

During my next appointment, Dr. Linde discussed the test results and gave me a prescription. Within two weeks, I was a different person. Once I started the treatment for my hormone imbalance, I wanted to live forever.

What I had learned as a patient is to be persistent when something is wrong. One must gain as much knowledge as possible because most of the time the patient will lead the medical provider to the diagnosis.

The advent of the personal computer and the internet makes this more possible. Though technology can't replace humans with their caring touch, it can give people the tools and language they need to learn something about themselves. To know is to apply knowledge.

And in that application of knowledge, there is something magical about the soothing voice of a gentle caretaker. Physicians who neglect these things do so at their own peril. It is no wonder people are feeling sicker than ever in spite of the billions of dollars being spent on healthcare in America. Machines can never replace human touch, a pat on the shoulder, a simple hug, or a little reassurance. We need to remember that, most of the time, the soul needs healing more than the body does. Humans should be cared for by other humans, not machines. Machines should be an extension of a caretaker. Those who have been caretakers to me have served me well by giving me back my life, my *joie de vivre*.

I had written to Columbia University College of Physicians and Surgeons in April of 1988 to postpone my acceptance to their medical school for another year. I didn't know whether I would live long enough to find a treatment for my condition or whether I would be well enough to attend medical school. When I did rounds with doctors as a pharmacy student intern every morning in the spring of 1988 at Saint Elizabeth Hospital, I shook like a leaf, my knees rattling and buckling, and I felt ready to give up. I pretended I was exhausted from overwork. If I had explained my situation to someone there, perhaps I could have found a solution to my health problem much earlier. Who knows?

In the fall of 1987, my pathology college professor at NU, a physician, reminded me to live life in a jovial sort of way when I told her I must have an acoustic neuroma because of the constant buzzing I heard in my ears. She had given a lecture on the subject and reassured me I didn't have a brain tumor. I remain unconvinced, so I went and saw a specialist at Mass Eye and Ear Hospital. They told me the brain CT scan was negative, and the buzzing stopped the same night.

This professor had told me to live life and learn to relax. She sensed my anxiety, my fear of failure, my fear of flying, and a myriad of other worries masquerading as health problems. After that, I tried to live life, except I didn't know how to live it when my knees kept giving out. I was falling apart.

When Haitian immigrants went to the doctor in the 1980s, the assumption was they either had AIDS or carried the human immunodeficiency virus.

That stigma came from the Centers for Disease Control and Prevention's banning of 4-H groups, which included hemophiliacs, Haitians, heroin addicts, and homosexuals, from giving blood.

As a college student, nothing infuriated me more than Haitians being parked in 4-H groups. This was personal for me. I'd followed my people's travesty from the very first time I set foot inside the National Institutes of Health. One day in the spring of 1986, I sat watching the names of Haitians being mercilessly lampooned. An editorial in the *Stanford Daily* in the early 1990s predicted that within ten years, there would be no more Haitians. They would all be dead by then. I doubted Dr. Antony Fauci, director of the NIH, and many like him truly understood. They had become the new disciples of junk science masquerading as scientific gospel. Fauci's attitude echoed the CDC's mantra: Haitians, hemophiliacs, homosexuals, and heroin addicts.

I'd gasped when I heard this pronouncement against Haitians and Haiti. I sat numbly in the throes of a conference at NIH that April of 1986. I felt the sting of false doctrine. It felt like many wished for the destruction of my people. Some were predicting it. The oracles of Magrann were accurate: "Our people will suffer at the hands of strangers and haters at home and abroad. Their persecution will continue until the day a rescuer will rise to unite them from the four corners of the globe henceforth. Haitians have become the modern-day Hebrews as told in the Bible. I see a world gone askew in quest of a boogeyman."

Most of my black colleagues who knew my plight understood. They had heard and read about the denigration of the people dear to me. They were sympathetic and offered no further argument about my needing to meet and speak to Dr. Louis W. Sullivan.

However, one of them, a brilliant fellow named E.K., pleaded with me to contemplate the insignificance of the issue in the broader context. "Milliard, don't worry about it! Is it necessary for you to see Dr. Sullivan for that?" Rightly, Merlene Robergeau, Paul Christian Namphy, and I founded Stanford Haitian American Students Association (SHASA) in 1990 with the goals of addressing and teaching the Stanford Campus about Haitian issues.

"Eric, you miss the point. Not only is it important to me, it's sacred to the well-being of the people and nation that gave me life and succored me at its breast."

In 1989, Sullivan became the first African American secretary of Health and Human Services. He came to Fairchild Auditorium on October 23, 1990, to deliver a lecture titled, "Health Care Strategies to Improve Access to Care and Better Meet the Health Care Needs of American Citizens." His presence at the Stanford University School of Medicine was a watershed moment and a turning point for many of those who attended. After his presentation, he asked to have a moment with the minority students.

All this happened around the time Dr. Benjamin Carson (the most famous neurosurgeon of the era who happened to be a black man) performed a groundbreaking surgery to separate Siamese twins conjoined at the head. That surgery took place at Johns Hopkins Hospital on Labor Day of 1987 and was reported on all major television networks. At age thirty-three, African American Ben Carson had become the most famous and youngest chief of pediatric neurosurgery in America. He was the world's best and most popular pediatric neurosurgeon.

Dr. Louis W. Sullivan stood tall and exuded confidence and authority. I was determined to speak to him. Whether the question I had for him had a broader perspective or any merit to the students there, I couldn't tell. But for me and the people I represented, it meant a lot.

Back then, many with Haitian ancestry, when questioned about their country of origin, would claim they came from places they could barely spell. Sadly, some of the countries they claimed to be from had higher rates of HIV than Haiti. Who could blame them for following the Russian maxim of Stalin Soviet Union: *"Ugadat, ugodit, utselet"* (Sniff out, suck up, survive)? That made perfect sense. They were discriminated against in the workplace, at school, and in public meetings. We all felt trapped.

Haiti's tourism sector and economy were crushed either intentionally or ignorantly when the Centers for Disease Control and Prevention stated in March of 1983: "Persons who may be considered at increased risk of AIDS include those with symptoms and signs suggestive of AIDS; sexual partners of AIDS patients; sexually active homosexual or bisexual men with multiple partners; *Haitian entrants to the United States*; present or past abusers of IV drugs; patients with hemophilia; and sexual partners of individuals at increased risk for AIDS."[20]

The same report also said, "Each group contains many persons who probably have little risk of acquiring AIDS … Very little is known about risk factors for Haitians with AIDS." Few bothered to read this fine print.

The CDC had selectively specified Haitians. I wondered why. Even though this statement was junk science at its best, it did a great deal of damage to a people, a country, a community, and a nation. For Haiti's tourism industry, it was the coup de grâce that placed the country's economy on life support for at least a century. Soon people were formally talking about a 4-H Club for those at risk for AIDS: homosexuals, hemophiliacs, heroin addicts—and Haitians. Every other group mentioned spoke of individuals; only the last group represented a nationality.

I understood what my old biology teacher in Haiti once said: "Thank goodness for this new world. You all could learn the rudiments of science. Go overseas and perfect your knowledge and your skills to make the antidote for the next plague looming on the horizon. You are going to live in a world where humanity will need to create a vaccine every week. In the absence of that, a scourge could wipe out the world, especially your kind."

After Dr. Sullivan gave a short speech to our group, I raised my hand and asked the first question, the mouths of my fellow students dropping open. I asked why the Bush administration continued to support a policy scientific evidence differed from? Why place Haitians in a category as risk factors for HIV transmission when the CDC claimed little was known about risk factors for Haitians with AIDS?

"I knew little about the CDC approach to this issue. When I return to Washington, there will be a more thorough review about such policy," he said. Sullivan kept his promise when he wrote me a letter in January of 1991. The new policy had removed Haitians as a group by rejecting the discriminatory practice and began to look at individual risk factors instead. My conscience had become my guide.

Beginning in the early tenth century and continuing through the twentieth century, Europeans relentlessly discriminated against, harassed, and pestered the Jewish communities. During the Great Plague, they accused the Jews of harboring the plague and being responsible for it because of their dirty ways and wretched existence. When the European economies collapsed, the Jews were blamed for being greedy and for bringing poverty to Europe. When wars ended, they were arrested for treason and condemned for their sinister agendas and for fomenting trouble. The Jews were accused of causing Europeans to fight among themselves. Notwithstanding these accusations, criticisms, and hatred against them, they continued to contribute their knowledge to Europe. Fritz Haber, a Jewish scientist, discovered how to use ammonia as fertilizer. Among other things, he also pioneered nerve gas, which gave Germany, his country, a leg up in World War I. Sadly, Hitler used nerve agents to kill six million of Haber's people.

As shocking as Hitler's gas chambers were, he didn't do it alone. It didn't start at Treblinka. The Jews' death march began years before in the kitchens of Berlin, the church pews of Cologne, the classrooms of Saxony, and on the streets of Bavaria. It all happened with the quiet consent of most European countries. It was merely finalized in the corpses of babies and the elderly inside the gas chambers. The history of this world is one of travesty for less-militaristic nations and people. Is today any different?

The first modern-day genocide occurred in Europe when the Turks massacred a million and half Armenians, Greeks, and Assyrians because of their religion. To make matters worse, history has called that tragedy "deportation." During the Namibia Genocide from 1904 to 1908, German soldiers slaughtered seventy thousand Herero and Narma peoples. In the process, many others died and had their land seized, with new borders drawn for them. Worse, many remained homeless, much like the Palestinians of today. A young army corporal in 1916, Hitler learned human depravity from the Turks.

History repeats itself. The past told us of Germany's campaign to ostracize the Jews in the 1920s, which eventually led to Hitler's final solution at Auschwitz. Haitians could expect to suffer from stigmatization as the world turned and churned and chose its stops.

When it isn't death at the hands of humans, it is cruelty and violence in the fist of nature that pummels and kills Haitians. Then on January 12, 2010, a 7.0 earthquake came rumbling beneath their feet, leveling everything in its path. No one foresaw it. Just after 4:53p.m., another nightmare hit the island of Haiti. The ground slid. The mountains tumbled. Trees moved to and fro before people's eyes. Bricks and shabby tenements weaved and bobbed up and down, bending and twisting before falling to pieces.

From inside homes, schools, offices, and stores, people heard cups, pens, glasses, plates, fans, chairs, forks, knives, and beds rattle from their secure locations. Bricks, concrete roofs, twisted iron poles, and glass windows came crashing down on them. Out of this mayhem came the saddest sounds of "Ammwwey!" and the screams of babies, children, mothers, students, the old, the infirm, and the strong caught in the crossfire of the massive quake that trapped them under piles and piles of debris. With legs sticking out, skulls cracking, and eyes gawking in their sockets, the people cried for help from the mounds of rubble. The scene was too awful for an innocent people to bear. In the midst of it all, roofs collapsed and walls swayed before finally caving in. It was as if ten million people were wailing at once. "Ammwwey!"— the Haitian cry of agony.

A week after the quake, someone's dog was found licking its master's eyelids. A slender elderly lady was found alive on a corner inside the Cathedral of Port-au-Prince twenty-nine days later. She survived with no water and food—an enigma for many, but not to us, a robust, intelligent, resilient, and beautifully dignified people.

A woman with a blue apron covering her green skirt clutched her baby between her legs and bent over her, trying to spare her from the falling debris. Panic-stricken faces were stained white with concrete dust. Bodies were left behind, limp and languishing, their frightened eyes staring into emptiness, surely having seen or felt something sinister before they died. It was a scene of eternal doom, gloom, and destruction. Still, my people rose.

Though there were many aftershocks the first week after the *Goudou Goudou*, or tremor, as they called it, dogs continued to crawl over the rubble looking for their masters. Whatever humanity had built, nature conspired against. Everything had come down crumbling and clattering like knives inside a bag. A plume of smoke and a cloud of dust arose and could be seen within a twenty-mile radius of the Capital City.

More than three hundred thousand innocent Haitian souls perished in the aftermath of the quake. Millions of others were permanently injured, both physically and emotionally. The country was left in ruins.

As if nature were conspiring to foment more problems for Haiti, nine months later, an outbreak of cholera hit the island for the first time in its history. The disease came to the country from distant places and metropolises. This time it was under the guise of the United Nations presence in Haiti. That act would likely set in motion the decimation of a people for years to come. Like the scourge of AIDS, HIV was given to Haitians as a gift from larger nations. All this occurred in a country born to endure, dream, and rise from the ashes like a phoenix. Haiti will rise.

Haiti lurches from tragedy to tragedy. On July 7, 2021, a group of

Colombian mercenaries along with some corrupt Haitian police officers and politicians went to President Jovenel Moise's residence and assassinated him. On August 14, 2021, a 7.2 earthquake struck the southwest of the country killing thousands of people and seriously injuring many more.

Many Haitians had to flee their homeland to stay alive. They needed to tell the world their story, if it cares to listen. The people sought aid from its diaspora and others to safeguard themselves against cholera, Covid-19, hurricanes, terrible earthquakes and new scourges soon to come. Bredaism (a neologism, a word that has to do with the birthplace (Breda) of Toussaint L'Ouverture of Haiti, which transcends every act that's right, noble, and laudatory) teaches that.

Life is full of contradictions. As John Steinbeck says in the *Grapes of Wrath*, "I'm learnin' one thing good," she said. "Learnin' it all a time, ever' day. If you're in trouble or hurt or need—go to poor people. They're the only ones that'll help—the only ones."[21]

One Saturday in late December 1990, I returned to Temple Salem and reclaimed my former seat. Sister M.J., with her son in tow, sat behind me asking my mother, loud enough for the saints to hear, where I had been these last two years. She could have asked me but chose to annoy my mother instead.

"He is in medical school in California at Stanford University!" my mother shouted. "He is leaving tomorrow."

She laughed at the idea. "You mean Milliardaire, a Haitian cabbie, goes to Stanford?"

"*Bay kou bliyé, poté mak sonjé.*" Mother quoted to her that old Haitian adage while smiling. "The giver of the blow forgets, but the bearer of the scar remembers."

So I thought while sitting there, *Why did she have to doubt my ability as a cabbie to become a physician? I drove a taxi. That was correct. I looked for fares, but I also attended college. Wasn't that true too?*

Monsieur Dumond Guerrier, an old sage in Carrefour, once said to a group of us teenagers, "Your ancestors have gained this land by grappling it with grit and gusto to unshackle themselves from the clutch of Napoleon Bonaparte and the grip of the great French empire, the world superpower then; unequivocally, all generations from here thereon are destined for larger struggles and greater things to clinch. And thus, Haiti and its children have a rendezvous with destiny."

30

Long Journey

*To be ignorant of what occurred before you were
born is to remain always a child.*

—MARCUS TULLIUS CICERO

The phone rang three times in the middle of the night late in May. I struggled to clear my eyes with the backs of my shaking hands, then fumbled through the bedroom until I made it downstairs to the first floor of the apartment to pick up the phone. *Is it Mom calling me from Boston? Could it be Dad, who never seemed to know the time difference between Massachusetts and California?* It was three o'clock in the morning Pacific time. The ringing reminded me of a distant past when I used to leave my bed to search for Rock on the streets of Boston. Each time he failed to come home at night, the family feared the worst.

Any phone call past midnight meant trouble. No one that I knew would call me at such a moment just for small talk. I lifted the receiver as I peeked through the curtains at the apartments of Escondido Village. I would soon complete medical school and move to Miami. I peered up at the night sky while clearing my throat before I spoke. Who in the world was calling me before dawn? Blood rushed to my head and my heart pounded as I heard the commotion and a female voice on the other end of the line.

A star sparkled in the deep blue sky, its light rising and receding like a Cheshire cat. "Hi Junior, this is Tante Jocelyne calling. Youla has gone into labor. I am here at the hospital with Samuel. I will call you back as soon as I can when I have more information."

I was breathless as I learned that my father-in-law and Youla's aunt had to bring her to the hospital. I tried to ask her a question in a hushed voice for fear of waking my neighbors through the thin walls. "How is she doing?" I asked, but she had hung up.

Only two weeks earlier, Youla had flown to Florida ahead of me, in her seventh month of pregnancy. It wouldn't have been safe for her to fly in an airplane later.

Kwame was born on May 22 on a Saturday morning. Youla and I had prepared for everything humanly possible. We tried to time the pregnancy and delivery to coincide with the beginning of my internship. But we got it wrong. As much as we think we have some power over them, many things in our lives are beyond our control. Life in general unravels and falls hard on our laps when we muse that we are in charge or ought to be.

I stuffed my backpack with an extra pair of pants and other items. The air was crisp and cold, with a tinge of bright sun peeking at the horizon as I trudged toward San Francisco International Airport to board a flight to

Miami. I could see the foggy mountains with their peaks and valleys lying dormant off Highway 280 North. I watched the trees change color. I sat and zoned out, staring into space during the six-hour flight, my body draining of energy as though a vampire was sucking all the blood from my marrow. Upon landing, I bolted from the airplane with my bag, went outside and flagged a cab to take me straight to Jackson Memorial Hospital, the hospital where my dad was admitted to in 1982 after being gunned down while driving a taxi in the streets of Miami.

I found myself walking the hospital corridors again, this time to meet my son for the first time. He lay in a crib, fighting for his life in the neonatal intensive care unit, just like his grandpa had done in the surgical intensive care unit ten years before.

Even with two months of training in pediatrics, I knew little about caring for small babies, especially premature ones. My heart constricted knowing that my son could die at any moment. He had been born with an Apgar (appearance, pulse, grimace, activity, and respiration) score of nine out of ten, but shortly after birth, that rating dropped to a five.

When most parents think about having children, they dream about a healthy baby boy or girl. They hope for a child who will always fit in, a physically perfect child—a child who is healthy, loveable, and pleasant. It doesn't occur to most of them that their child might be unattractive, sickly, or moody. Many parents with healthy children may not be aware that the children their kids are standing next to may have serious health challenges and that the parents of those children might be having trouble keeping their heads above water. Parents of children with emotional, physical, and learning differences need compassion, not pity. It is difficult for them to take criticism from those who have never experienced their difficult journey. For many Americans, there is a perception that all negative behaviors stem from moral failure. How sad! We live in the twenty-first century.

Youla walked often and watched what she ate during pregnancy. She took care of her body. She wouldn't drink sodas for fear of the fetus being exposed to caffeine. No one smoked or even used foul language around her. On many occasions, I sang hymnals and played classical music while I cupped my hands over her domed belly. I did all this in our campus apartment with one goal in mind: to give our baby an edge, an advantage, and even a surplus of good omens. If I had known what I know now, I would have played hip-hop or reggae or jazz, which likely would have served him well!

In the past, I had met children and parents with special needs, and I had always moved on and made the least effort to inquire about what life was like for them. I had never *seen* them before. They didn't exist because I was always too busy to pay any attention to them.

That Saturday evening, my presence at the NICU brought with it a new reality. My son was dying, and I needed to call on my God for divine intervention. I had prayed for many years without a true purpose. That evening, however, I had a need that required a quick response. As I approached the door of NICU, I grappled with the fact that my faith must become my courage and my hope.

Gritting my teeth, I flung the door wide open. I heard several machines creaking. Ventilators jiggled, and wires dangled over cribs. I passed the first set of cribs, and my baby wasn't there.

"Can I help you?" asked a nearby nurse.

"Yes, please," I said. She smiled, her gapped teeth showing. "I am looking for my son. His name is Baby Syverain. He was born earlier this morning."

"Oh! Are you the father who lives in California?" she asked.

"Yes, I am. I just flew in today and came directly from the airport."

"Well, follow me." She whirled around, her face radiant, then glanced back at me. "Are you squeamish?" she asked.

"I am." My heart fluttered within my chest, and I felt the thumping getting harder with every step I took.

"Sorry for talking nonsense. You are a doctor, and this wouldn't be your first time at a NICU unit," she said.

"It isn't." My voice cracked. I wanted to admit that she was right but kept my mouth shut. Twelve months earlier, I had done a rotation at the pediatric intensive care unit at the Santa Clara Valley Medical Center in California. What had brought my surgical team there that day was the opportunity to observe an eight-year-old child with third-degree burns. Her mother had abused and neglected her. One morning, she'd seized the child and thrown her into a bathtub of boiling water. She'd kept her there until the child was scalded and passed out, with burns across her buttocks, thighs, legs, and feet. The mother thought that demons possessed the girl. Where had she come up with that? She felt it was her duty to get them out of that innocent child by immersing her in a cauldron. I almost fainted when I saw her skin. The odiousness of what this mother had done to her child unnerved me. The girl spoke not a word and had likely regressed in her behavior. Would she ever trust anyone again?

The PICU unit at SCVMC was smaller than the large floor I traversed as I followed the nurse. The rumbling, banging, and flickering monitors in this NICU startled me. I had never cared for neonates before. Yes, I was squeamish. My lips were as dry and as cracked as sunbaked mud.

"You know what?" the nurse exclaimed. "Why don't you stay outside for a while till you regain your cool or feel better?" She waved me goodbye. I nodded as the double doors swung closed behind her. Her question flooded my brain. I stood there as though looking up from the bottom of a deep well. I gazed through the glass window, feeling like a pale ghost or lost animal. The hair on the back of my neck stood up. I had come to see my baby and Youla. I needed to muster the courage to stand next to my child's lonely incubator. What did this nurse know about my child? Why had he been born seven weeks prematurely? He'd ended up in a hard place. One lifetime wouldn't be enough to answer those questions. But I would gain some humility.

My breathing grew fast. My feet felt heavy. Five minutes later, after waiting in the hallway, staring, I sighed and pushed open the door. A receptionist sent me to wash my hands before I entered the room full of small incubators that looked more like the chicken cages I had seen in Haiti. My hands throbbed. My palms sweated. My son was receiving light therapy because he had jaundice from an excess of bilirubin in his blood. I stood at his bedside and offered a prayer that God would grant him a full recovery.

It is one thing to care for people you have no personal relationship. It's quite another to watch your child with tubes exiting and entering his bodily orifices. That would unsettle any caring parent. I was stunned by the sight of such an onslaught, but I tried to remain hopeful. I whispered into my baby's ears that he was going to be okay and that he had nothing to fear. God had made the promise He would keep, as written in Psalm 23: 4, "Even though I walk through the valley of the shadow of death, I will fear no evil, for you are with me; your rod and your staff, they comfort me." That day, I called on both science and God to bring our baby, who seemed on the verge of dying, back to us. Three days later, he began to improve.

A week after being with Youla and our newborn in the NICU, I returned to California to vacate our campus apartment and prepare for my medical-school graduation. I had to pick up our kitchenware, clothes, books, and albums from the dormitory. "Take good care of yourself and Kwame until I join you both on June 15," I reassured her. "The time will go fast." Kwame had a brush with death several times while in the hospital. He had hypoglycemia, pneumonia, necrotizing enterocolitis, and sepsis, but he went home two weeks later.

31
CHAPTER

Ahead of Time

*I am sanguine ... O Haiti dear! I believe in
you and you are my unique idol!*

—LOUIS JOSEPH JANVIER

A fter a year of living in Florida, we moved back to California. Many a night, our son had trouble falling asleep, so we would drive him around in a borrowed 1980 silver hatchback Subaru with a missing headlight. After long, meandering rides down the streets of Palo Alto, he would become drowsy. We would carry him inside our six-hundred-square-foot apartment without disturbance. Inside, we would place him in his bed, only for him to wake up a few minutes later when he realized that he was in his bed alone.

Colicky from birth, Kwame often suffered nightly abdominal discomfort. We used to feed him a soy formula and, years later, learned he was allergic to all dairy and soy products. He'd had several ear infections by the time he was five years old. Some nights, when I wasn't on call at the hospital, I could see his eyes wide open as he lay in the dark. He had gone to that place in his mind where none of us was privileged to wander.

That period taught us something we had little knowledge about. It's hard bringing a child into the world. It's even harder to raise a child without extended family, friends, or the support of loved ones.

When we came back to California in the summer of 1994, I was desperate to get relief for Kwame's bouts with colic and insomnia. The baby was wearing Youla down after a year of caring for him almost twenty-four hours a day. She needed help. She went back to work for a respite. Now it was my turn to care for Kwame. I had no one to guide me. The nights were the hardest. Providently, I found a book written by a Dr. Richard Ferber titled *Solve Your Child's Sleep Problems*. He was the director of the Sleep Disorders Center at the Children's Hospital in Boston. The essence of my child's sleep problems was night feedings. Solving the problem was quick but elaborate. I decreased each night feeding by one ounce over seven days. Voilà! By the fourth day, he stopped waking up at night.

It was Tuesday, October 4, 1994. I stood inside our apartment with Kwame in my arms. He had nasal congestion, dark circles under his eyes, and sneezed every five minutes. I heard about fifteen "thump, thumps" coming from the second-floor apartment above us at 3833 Park Boulevard. *Who is doing this? And why?* I wondered. The next day, the same noise returned around ten in the morning.

Outside, the sun shone. As I gazed through the French door overlooking our small patio, two doves landed on the azalea bush and cooed while picking at the dirt floor. A few minutes later, there were three hard knocks on my door, as if someone was about to burst in. If I had been in Compton, I would have thought the police were coming to smash the toilet, as they did to innocent poor black folks, in search of drugs, as reported in the news in the 1990s. But in Palo Alto, most of the time police officers showed restraint toward people, poor and rich alike.

"Who is here?" I asked loudly. With trepidation, I approached the front door, stooped my head down, and scanned the peephole. Two police officers stood a foot away.

I turned the doorknob with my right hand while holding Kwame with my left. The two male officers lurched into the apartment, inspecting the baby. They told me they had come because someone had heard a baby crying and called 911. They said goodbye and walked away. The next day, a lady from Santa Clara Children Services showed up to gawk at our place. She inquired about how the baby was faring.

"He is doing fine," I told her. "I am afraid that if you linger much longer, you will scare him like the ex-scoutmaster who lives upstairs and doesn't seem to like children."

On Monday, February 10, 1997, Wesline Jean-Michel, a family member, came along with me to drop Kwame at the Stanford Rainbow School for the first time. She stayed with him at the school for an hour while I went to work. Youla was very nervous about the change in routine, but it was a boon for Kwame. He made a friend named Yasin the first day he attended. They bonded quickly. As soon he arrived at school on Wednesday morning, he called, "Where is Yasin?"

On Wednesday, something went wrong at the preschool. It created great confusion at home as well. Kwame's regular school schedule was Monday, Wednesday, and Friday from 8:30 to 11:30 a.m. Wesline would pick him up. That morning, she called my receptionist and said she needed to speak to me; it was an emergency. The receptionist was still on the phone with Wesline when I happened to drop by to request that she make an appointment with a specialist for one of that day's patients. She handed me the phone and moved away.

"What's wrong, Liline?" I asked. There was an ominous silence for about five seconds. "Please speak. Did something happen?"

"Well, today when I went to pick up Kwame, they reported to me that Ms. Mickie, a teacher, had slapped him for not following her commands."

My throat went dry and I became numb after I hung up the phone. I was crushed. Ms. Mickie, a lady in her fifties, had submitted her resignation by the time I walked into the school.

The school had a crisis. They hadn't had enough teachers before the incident. The parents who saw the incident became upset, confused, and rattled by the teacher's behavior. They couldn't comprehend how an experienced teacher could lose her cool with a toddler. The staff got scared. They expected Santa Clara Children Services to drop in. They were anxious about what my family's reaction would be.

When I got home that afternoon, I called Ms. Mickie and asked her to reconsider her decision for the sake of the other children. But it was too late. The school had likely told her that her position had been terminated and they no longer needed her services. Or maybe she was too embarrassed to face the other teachers, administrators, parents, and children. The school expected the worst: forced closure, lawsuits, and an SCCS visits. They got none.

Friday morning, Youla and I met with the school administrator. We demanded the staff get psychological counseling with anger-management training. We wanted the school to avoid dealing with a similar fate in the future. We thanked the staff for the privilege our son had had to interact with other toddlers for those two days, then walked away from Stanford Rainbow. Kwame never got to say goodbye to Yasin.

On the first day of kindergarten in August 1999, Youla and I introduced ourselves to Kwame's teacher, Janice Small Brethauer. Before we left that morning, we handed her an article about atypical children. This was before we knew he had Asperger's.

A few weeks before bringing him to Juana Briones Elementary, I had tried to enroll him at Barron Park Elementary: "Good morning, I was at the school district earlier, and they told me you are still accepting students," I said. "By the way, he is already six and should be in school."

"Who told you that?" the principal thundered. "Yesterday was the last day for admission here. We can't help you." She looked at me as though I were a trespasser. If the principal at Ohlone Elementary where I enrolled him a year earlier for only two days before taking him out was indifferent about children with differences, this one at Barron Park Elementary was more than rude. She was creepy. Perhaps she thought we lived in East Palo Alto, a poorer city nearby that bused some of its students to Palo Alto.

Even if she had called me the next day to offer admission, I would have declined. I loved my child too much to entrust him to someone so hostile. The principal at Barron Park epitomized everything wrong with certain elements of American society. The place was sick! Even given our politeness, she wouldn't crack a smile.

Thankfully, Juana Briones Elementary and Janice Small Brethauer restored my hope in America. Her kindness reminded me that better days lay ahead. Janice was a godsend.

"Mr. Syverain, I am grateful you gave me that article this morning." I scratched my throat. "Everything that is on that paper describes your child exactly." I didn't know whether I should be relieved or concerned. When I dropped my son off earlier that morning, I felt strange standing outside on his third attempt at an elementary school. Youla and I were impatient to know how his half-day kindergarten class would go.

Youla looked nervous as Kwame stormed out of the class to meet us. We were both afraid that the new school would ask us to train him more before he could be enrolled. We had a gnawing feeling he would be rejected again, and we had run out of options. "How was your day?" Youla asked.

"Fine," Kwame answered.

He looked tense, and we wondered if they might not keep him in that school either. Even at his young age, he knew what rejection felt like. He slung his backpack over his shoulder, lowered his arms through the straps, and turned and walked away with sad eyes. He said, "Let's go, Mom." He left us talking to his teacher as he stood near the school playground. Perhaps he couldn't bear to listen to the grown-ups' conversation.

We wanted him to be in a safe setting where he could socialize with other children. Yet we had our doubts that he was ready. Mrs. Brethauer was glad we had given her that article. She had been teaching kindergarten for more than twenty years and had the experience and the willingness to learn with each child in her care. She accepted our child into her ranks as though he was her own.

It still hurts when I remember what the Palo Alto School District principal Susan Charles at Ohlone said about my son: "Even a dog can be trained. I don't see why you parents can't train your child." That morning, when the school called me to pick up my son at Ohlone Elementary, her words stung and made my blood freeze. I couldn't believe that a principal, a Caribbean immigrant like me, my color, would say such a thing about a black child.

So I felt the best thing I could do for my child and everyone else was to pull him out. That was a year earlier and his first attempt at kindergarten.

Schools deal with all types of children. Some children have many idiosyncrasies. My child couldn't have been much different than many of the kids with varying styles of learning. As a young man in Boston, I had always asked myself the same questions: Do all teachers care about their pupils? Like many other parents, I know the answer. Some teachers are angels. Others are destructive to a child's psyche. Simply put, it is like criminal cops in the ranks of a police department who remain undetected for years.

My son had listed the abuses he'd suffered at the hands of unscrupulous supervising adults, such as when he was on the school playground as a six-year-old and another child pushed him against the monkey bars. That day, November 16, 1999, he'd sustained a concussion (an X-ray taken fifteen years later revealed a depression in his skull). Two days later he was still complaining of memory loss. The aide in attendance made no effort to check on him or report the incident to us. Or when he was eleven and went to a theater club in Palo Alto. A staff member told him they no longer had scholarships for kids from East Palo Alto. The most liberal counties in America are the most politically intolerant ones in the country. I live in one of those counties in California. In fact, the city of Palo Alto where my family and I live is the emblem of what's wrong with neoliberalism in America.

Kwame's first year at Juana Briones Elementary renewed in him a sense of hope. The school accepted him like any other student. Thus, when Milliardaire Yves Rashid Kwame Syverain III's name was called during his graduation for his bachelor's degree at San Jose State University cum laude in 2018, Youla and I beamed with joy and knew we ought to posthumously thank his kindergarten teacher.

As I sat in my home office reading an email from Northeastern University thanking Youla and me for the recent scholarship fund we created for students in financial need, it occurred to me that Dad's wish for me to become a billionaire as my name translates hadn't come to fruition. I take consolation in being a physician entrepreneur in Silicon Valley. But with or without wealth, I am the same person who bears witness to the absurdities of life while living in Carrefour, Lafleur Duchene, and Avenue Muller. I can't unsee what I saw as a child: poverty, pride, and a resilient Quisqueyan people with dreams but also nightmares. When Youla and I established the nonprofit organization "Friends and Children of Haiti Foundation," we knew it would only be a drop of water in a sea of need, but if that small gesture could serve as a template to remind many Haitians in the diaspora that not much has changed since they left the island and that the people remaining behind are counting on them, so much the better. A childhood friend, Jean-Claude Yves Colin, once remarked: "A people that like to lead, but not to follow, need to go overseas in order to come to the rescue of those who stay behind."

On that dreary afternoon of March 18, 2021, Kwame was reading a magazine article about the current COVID-19 viral pandemic shutting down the US and the global economies and killing millions of people. I moved away from the computer desk, fascinated by his page turning and reflected on what the future held for him.

Before he entered kindergarten, he learned how to read with images velcroed to a board. I knew he wasn't going to be a hare but a turtle in getting his schoolwork done. I would goad him, saying, "If you only use 10 percent of your mental capacity, the work will get done." But mental fatigue would occur before physical exhaustion. Many times, beginning in first grade and throughout his college years, he would complete his homework late in the evening. For many school-aged kids, learning seemed to be a breeze; for others, like Kwame, the work was laborious and onerous. The trait that helped him on this journey was perseverance. He was hard on himself and would sometimes say to teachers that his parents would be displeased with him if he didn't succeed. I don't know where he got that idea.

Suddenly, Kwame stood up, turned toward the sliding glass door, and looked at a bird skittering in the orange tree in the backyard. He turned to me and said, "Wow! This is a great country, Dad." As a 5-year-old boy he had two finches and one parakeet when we lived in an apartment in Palo Alto.

"Yes, indeed," I said. "I love America." *But wouldn't America be a better country if it could cull its caste system, get rid of Jim Crow, and reassert what it stands for?*

Then I remembered what I had written in his baby album on May 28, 1993: "Even while in the crib, he displayed all the qualities of a fighter, a believer, a man of character, and, above all, a true son. He was ahead of his time."

Perhaps one day, from distant lands to closer shores, we will make a pilgrimage to Quisqueya and the heritage we left behind. At least we will get some sunshine.

ACKNOWLEDGMENTS

The old African proverb says that it takes a village to raise a child; I will go one step further and say that it takes a people to raise a child. I can never fully convey the love and gratitude I have for all those who gave me succor and direction as a child in Haiti and as a teenager in the United States.

My immense gratitude to my parents, Milliadaire Joseph Syverain and Marie Madeleine Thibaud; my stepmom, Yvette Castor Syverain; and her mother, Rosa Celenie Esteve Castor; to my grandparents and great-grandparents, Bernadette Boncoeur Syverain, Manassé Syverain, Dufrène Syverain, Demoncier Alphonse, Ervita Roi, Exina Syverin, Durocher Dextra, Josaphat Thibaud, Espèno Boncoeur, Abélide Alphonse Jeudy; to my brothers and sisters, Marie Fernande Syverain, Dr. Jean Etienne Thibaud, Gertha Sanon Syverain, Jean Wilfrid Thibaud, Pierre Rock Thibaud, Dufresne Syverain, Bernadette Sylverain, Rose-Marie (Magalie) Chery, Sherley Thibaud Reese, Taryn Jude Castor Syverain, Tracy Jude Castor Syverain, Kasseem Jude Castor Syverain, and Dr. Fabrice Pascal.

I also want to thank my uncles and aunts and cousins and nephews and nieces: Nereta Syverin, Anna-Févrina Théodore, Ilfrène Syverin, Orica Syverain Constantin, Josseline Constantin Baltazar, Eddy Baltazar, Princina Syverain Romain, Pierreline Janvier Romain, Ramsès Jeudy, Sermonfils Dextra, Duvielat Constantin, Liza Jeudi, Berince Constantin, Kerby Constantin, Eusebe Constantin, Bertin Constantin, Kelly Constantin, Cheristin Syverain, Vital Syverain, Aliese Syverain, Rodrigue Syverain, Nella Syverain, Kanny Syverain, Madame Milio Chassedin, Erita Pierre Dextra, Ramil Jeudy, Marie Iveline Jeudy, Ralph Jeudy, Cheriph Jeudy, Marie Junette Payen, Peterly Jeudy, Ramses Jeudy II, Bastien Jeudy, Rhita

Jeudy, Yvette Syverain Lafleur, Charitable Syverain, Songélia Syverain, Homène Syverain, Roseau Syverin, Frantz (Fanfan) Edvard Romain, Joseph Hervé Romain, Clerveau Romain, Alberte Syverin, Marsolyn Mahotiere, Rose-Laure Romain, Thierie Romain Mathieu, Joshua Mathieu, Jonathan Mathieu, Jean-Marc Mathieu, Kendra Tarah Romain, Anne Romain, Denise Saint-Pierre, Marc Endy Stephen Lauraque, Keshan Theodore, Sankara Theodore, Gallardeo Theodore, Lynda Henri Romain Cesar, Juldany Cesar, Kettie Romain Louis, Daniel Louis, Ginelle Louis, Darnell P Louis, Marie Carmel Syverin Jean, Luc Domond, Élise Domond, Pierre Emmanuel Domond, Madeleine Domond, Iveline Syverin Bustros, Valérie Syverin Bustros, D'Esparbès Syverin, Gregory Ilfrène Syverin, Ruth Daika Syverin, Paulverel Syverin, Allen Marvel Syverin, Taina Paula B Syverin, Naurlaica Paula Syverin, Jo Syverain, Marie Françoise Syverin, Emmie Leila Désire, Randal Désire, Patrick Romain, Alexandra Romain, Quethia Melissa K Romain, Ginadelle Romain, Daphnee Romain, Marie Denise Marcelin, Dimitry Romain, Nikholas Romain, Henrick Romain, Michelet Jeudy, Francso Jean Orel, Guérin Syverin, Marie Josée Syverain, Fritz Gérald Syverin, Debrha Syverin, Sanaa Isabelle Syverin, Samarha Syverin, Marckenley Syverin, Pierre André Syverain, Jovan Carter Syverain, Kervin Dave Syverain, Viviane Dextra Francois, Xavier Francois, Eddy Chassedin, Kathelene Francois, Marie Alcina Dextra, Michel Ange Brunache, Pierre E Cothias, Maria Cothias, Edmond Brunache,Vesta Destra Pierre-Louis, Valery Pierre Louis,, Veronique Dextra Pierre, Herbert Leon Pierre, Vasthi Pierre, Vladimir Pierre, Renaldi Marcelin, Jimmy Pierre, Michelet Pierre, Nagda Theodore Chassedin, Ghislaine Destra Marcelin, Reno Marcelin, Wendy Ridore, Anite Cothias, Annie Thibaud, Marie Renée, Laeticia Grace Pascal, Mathieu Syverain, Marc Syverain, Jacob Anderson Syverain, Sasha Syverain, Marie Maude Constantin Élysée Bouquet, Gracia Barthelemy, Maude Syverin, Modjossorica C Elysee, Fabie C Elysee, Jacqueline C. Elysee, Yvon Elisee, Emmanuel Bouquet, Renes Jude Syverain, Marlène Syverain, Lael Syverain, Emmanuel Syverain, Ulrick Syverain, Berenice Linda Sylverain, London Reese, Sophie Mercilienne Boncoeur, Oscar Boncoeur, Jean-Dykenson René, Wesline Jean-Michel, Christian Dauphin, Colson Roy, Valbrun Jeudy, Cassandra Jeudy Poluscar, Kermy Jeudy Poluscar, Saintide Sandra Poluscar Carillo, Jeffrey Carrillo, Sherley Carrillo, Blondine Constantin, Clarajyne Thibaud, Emlynn Beauzil, Jean

Etienne Thibaud Junior, Josue Abel Thibaud, Joseph Geffrard Barthelemy, Nathalie Barthelemy, Wilmicko Thibaud, Johanna Joseph, Lana Ulerio, Danae Syverain, Keisha Syverain, Marsha Syverain, Fedler Beaubrun, David Stanley Bruno, Vierge André Pierre, Darlene Bruno, Lujamesley Bruno, Robenson Bruno, and to all the Boncoeur, Valequite, Lafleur, Thibaud, Thibault, Syverain, Syverin, Romain, Alphonse, Jeudy, Dextra, Louis, Elysee, Pascal, René, Pierre, other family members, the readers of the book, and all exiles and refugees across the globe and countless immigrants like me.

I am grateful to many of my professors, amongst them Miss Léone and Maitre Dubé at Lycée Toussaint L'Ouverture, Maitre Fortuné at Lycée Alexandre Pétion, Dr. Patricia Cross at Stanford University School of Medicine, and Dr. Robert A. Shepard at Northeastern University. They gave me the confidence to forge ahead in finding my own measure.

I am indebted to a cadre of friends and colleagues: Jocelyn Leveillé, Maguy Leveillé, Debra Ambrose, Lessie James, Marie Genthyann Gilles Verna, Kathy Desrosiers, Sauveur Pierre Etienne, Jocelyn Nau, Yvane Macean, Sebastian Landeros, Hans Semelfort, Eleya Igwe Kalu, Mohamed Conteh, Iye Conteh, Jacynthe Lauture, Debra Watkins, Neville Reid, Arielle Reid, Lasoria Reid, Mario Reid, Walid Taylor, Annette Barnes, Adriana Benavides, Maria Vasquez, Maguy Frazier, Maria Chavez, May Gomez, Rafael Gomez, Rosa Ruiz, Maria Vazquez, Esmeralda Reyes, Mary Azah, Esther Tsinyo, Emma Acevedo, Veronica Sanchez, Amber Marie Morgan Sarwary, Nancy Padilla, Kinnari Shah, Jojo Adamos, Carina Wong, Leticia Benitez, Cinthya Ponce, Arlene Hernandez, Gina Tambanillo, Molly Bechauf, George Mattos, Debra Rousseau, Fab Rousseau, Kissinger Antoine, Calendy K Olouve Laurent, Gerard Semelfort, Harry Guerrier, Edith Semelfort, Gladys Semelfort, Maryse Cemelfort Joseph, Antoine Cemelfort, Orgason Sagaille, Chimene Daguerre, Orga Sagaille, Carol Derolus Laroche, Nadia Cemelfort, Dumond Guerrier, Denise Guerrier, Suze Guerrier, Gardy Constant, Slim Michel Bellegarde, Gabriel Augustin, Robin Casias, Jean-Claude Yves Collin, Judith Collin, Jean Claude Yves Colin junior, Jason Colin, Paul C. Namphy, Merlene Robergeau, Dominique Belfleur, Gerty Juste, Myrtza Francois, Othniel Francois, Faubert Smith, Rosemond Jolissaint, Frantz Joseph, Gary Jean Baptiste, Frantz Ovide Sainté, Micheline Laraque, Magalie Frontal, Madame Mombrun Nelson, Charles Nelson, Cootchill

Nelson, Clifford Nelson, Reynald Nelson, Jude Nelson, Wilner Nelson, Yolette Nelson Castor, Hervé Jacques, Évelt Jacques, Jean-Robert Cénat, Harry Cénat, Jacques Eusèbe, Lodinel Vertilus, Alex Louis, Alix Nau, Aygiana Jean-Pierre, Maurice Meroné, Madeleine Meroné, Frantz Meroné, Adèle Saint–Surin, Claudy Saint-Surin, Claury Adlah Darley Saint-Surin, Maureen Clo-Hadlie Saint-Surin, Adley J Claudy Saint-Surin, Myrlene Jasmin, Alexandre Jasmin, Kiara Jasmin, Tami Areus Lemke, Nick Lemke, Myriam Auguste, Clarence Auguste, Sarah Merone Damaryam, Vilandre Volcimus, Christine Volcimus, Louissaint Gerlain, Nick Charlesca, Danielle Alphonse, Hughes Lafond, Sultana Lafond, and Lessie James. Pastor Edner Eloi, Ketlie Eloi, Pastor Jose Brutus, Pastor Yves Piere, Dr. Joelle Osias, Ronald Lamarre, Guite Lamarre, Raoul Simon, Pastor Rene Urquia, Pastor Madsen Celestin, Pierre Simon Napoleon, Rachelle Napoleon, Odlarry Napoleon, Mayvan Napoleon, Rachelle Napoleon, Samuel Bauzile, Yonie St Hilaire, Nathan Cherizol, Lael Cherizol, Pastor Jean Cherizol, Pastor Lucson Souverain, Fenise Souverain, Lee Sonchard Bill Souverain, Pastor Moise Angervil, and countless others.

I am very lucky to have in-laws like Pastor Samuel Jeremie, Marie-Anne Vesta Paul Jeremie, Adeline Point-du-Jour Jeremie, Dr. Tatiana Jean Francois Pascal, Quincy Reese, Clarèle Alcide Thibaud, Liliane Alcide, Yolene Rochambeau, Sambois René, Shenessa Dontfraid Thibaud, Patrick Dauphin, Jeanne Simon, Jerome Simon, Jerome Simon Junior, Jeanane Enchie Simon Pierre-Louis, Jean Meres Pierre-Louis, Marcus Pierre-Louis, Julissa Astride Piere-Louis, Dieuveuil Jeremie, Ronald Jeremie, Thamar Jeremie, Jean Kiston Jeremie, Jerome Jeremie, Dieumenie Jeremie, Jocelyne Jeremie Beverly, Berthelot Jeremie, Barnabé Jeremie, Régine Delonnay Eugene, Elie Jeremie, Soeurette Jeremie Delonnay, Brunel Delonnay, Marie Dieuménie Jeremie Marseille, Dutroy Jeremie, Emeline Yves Jeremie, Remy Jeremie, Gihanne Jeremie Brinks, Nate Brinks, Joachim Jeremie, Emmanuel Jeremie, Christel Handal Abraham, Paul Samuel Jeremie, Marie Danielle Jeremie Jones, Marie Edwine Jeremie Constantin, Marie-Rose Jeremie, Paul Rémy Jeremie, Jessica Jeremie, Jerry Jeremie, Jodel Jeremie, Rémy Royce Jeremie, Clotilde Paul, Medjyne Jeremie, Gaetri Jeremie, Nyamke Jeremie, Noah Constantin, Ricot Constantin, Williams Andris Jeremie, Syhbil Jeremie, Jonathan Jeremie, Kara Green Ihedigbo, Christian Jeremie, Ilona Jeremie, Christopher Jeremie, Magareth Aubourg Jeremie, Frantz Castor,

Judith Castor, Emmanuel Castor, Ruben Castor, Renes Castor, and the larger family.

Finally, I would like to thank my editor, Michele Preisendorf, and the team at Archway Publishing for their valuable assistance and insightful advice in helping bring this book to life.

About the Author

Milliardaire Syverain earned his BS at Northeastern University in Boston, and his MD at Stanford University School of Medicine in California.

He was born in Haiti and immigrated to the United States as a teenager. The near-constant run-ins with his stepmother's mother and her abuse of him marred his experience in his home country. When he moved to Boston to live with his father and his wife, he experienced intense culture shock within the inescapable caste system of his adopted country. Eventually, he made his way through a combination of so-called menial jobs, though usually a city's or town's lifeblood and schooling and a good dose of optimism of the life he created for himself and his family. *Out of Quisqueya* is uniquely both his own story and a universal immigrant story.

Dr. Syverain is a recipient of the American Collegiate Poets awards, a published poet for *The Stanford Journal of Black Expression*. He taught SWOPSI (Student Workshops on Political and Social Issues) at Stanford University. He wrote for the *Northeastern News* and *The Stanford Daily* and attended workshops in creative writing at Stanford Continuing Studies.

Dr. Syverain is a social entrepreneur, philanthropist, poet, and writer who enjoys hiking, fishing, and camping. He lives in Palo Alto with his wife and works as a physician in Silicon Valley. They volunteer with the Horeb Seventh Day Adventist Church of Novato and the Haitian American Community Church of Silicon Valley and work with the Haitian refugees of Northern California. In 2018, they created a financial scholarship for first-generation students in the health sciences at Northeastern University. They also founded the nonprofit organization Friends and Children of Haiti Foundation. Most summers, they and their son go to Haiti providing free healthcare and scholarships for needy students and teaching English as a second language. They believe learning and health go hand in hand.

NOTES

1   A. Przeworski, et al, "What Makes Democracies Endure,"

2   Dambisa Moyo

3   *World Class How to Build a 21ˢᵗ-Century School System*, 109.

4   *Palo Alto Weekly*

5   Colin Powell

6   Ben Carson

7   Ta-Nehesi Coates, *Between the World and Me*

8   James Baldwin, *The Fire Next Time*

9   Lyndon Baines Johnson, *Washington Post*

10   Charles Abrams

11   Timothy Dwight

12   Eric J. Hobsbawm

13   Michael Eric Dyson, *What Truth Sounds Like*

14   Francis A. Pearman and Joseph Gardella, American Educational Research Association, September 2019.

15   Victor Hugo,

16   Herbert D. Kleber

17   Tobias Wolff, *This Boy's Life*,

18   FBI Report, 2008

19   Vera Institute of Justice, 2012

20   Centers for Disease Control and Prevention, March 1983

21   John Steinbeck, *The Grapes of Wrath*

CPSIA information can be obtained
at www.ICGtesting.com
Printed in the USA
BVHW071452240522
637934BV00005B/120